Race, Whiteness, and Education

In the color-blind era of post-Civil Rights America, race is often wrongly thought to be irrelevant or, at best, a problem of racist individuals rather than a systemic condition to be confronted. *Race, Whiteness, and Education* interrupts this dangerous assumption by reaffirming a critical appreciation of the central role that race and racism still play in schools and society. Author Zeus Leonardo's conceptual engagement of race and whiteness asks questions about its origins, its maintenance, and envisages its future. This book does not simply rehearse exhausted ideas on the relationship among race, class, and education, but instead offers new ways of understanding how multiple social relations interact with one another and of their impact in thinking about a more genuine sense of multiculturalism. By asking fundamental questions about whiteness in schools and society, *Race, Whiteness, and Education* goes to the heart of race relations and the common sense understandings that sustain it, thus painting a clearer picture of the changing face of racism.

Zeus Leonardo is Associate Professor of Social and Cultural Studies in Education, at the Graduate School of Education, University of California, Berkeley.

The Critical Social Thought Series
Edited by Michael W. Apple,
University of Wisconsin–Madison

Race, Whiteness, and Education

Zeus Leonardo

Routledge
Taylor & Francis Group

NEW YORK AND LONDON

First published 2009
by Routledge
270 Madison Ave, New York, NY 10016

Simultaneously published in the UK
by Routledge
2 Park Square, Milton Park, Abingdon, Oxon OX14 4RN

Routledge is an imprint of the Taylor & Francis Group, an informa business

© 2009 Taylor & Francis

Typeset in Minion by
RefineCatch Limited, Bungay, Suffolk
Printed and bound in the United States of America on acid-free paper by
Walsworth Publishing Company, Marceline, Mo.

Library of Congress Cataloging-in-Publication Data
Leonardo, Zeus, 1968–
Race, whiteness, and education / Zeus Leonardo.
    p. cm.—(Critical social thought)
    1. Racism in education—United States. 2. Critical theory. 3. United States—Race relations. I.
LC212.2.L46 2009
    371.82900973—dc22
    2008046100

ISBN 10: 0–415–99316–4 (hbk)
ISBN 10: 0–415–99317–2 (pbk)
ISBN 10: 0–203–88037–4 (ebk)

ISBN 13: 978–0–415–99316–6 (hbk)
ISBN 13: 978–0–415–99317–3 (pbk)
ISBN 13: 978–0–203–88037–1 (ebk)

Contents

Series Editor Introduction

In his influential book, *The Racial Contract*, Charles Mills grounds his arguments in the following statement:

> [We need to recognize] that racism (or as I will argue, global white supremacy) is *itself* a political system, a particular power structure of formal and informal rule, socioeconomic privilege, and norms for the differential distribution of material wealth and opportunities, benefits and burdens, rights and duties. (Mills, 1997, p. 3.)

Mills calls this a system for a particular reason. For him and for many others who have been so important to our understanding of the nature of race and racisms, these dynamics are not simply add-ons to the ways life is lived in our societies. Rather, they are truly *constitutive*; they form fundamental building blocks for the very structures of society, for the construction of our commonsense, and for the formation of our daily lives. He calls this a system of global white supremacy because the way it works out inexorably privileges specific groups and contains a logic and a set of "unconscious" rules and assumptions that disenfranchise people of color in nearly every sphere of social life.

More specifically in education, similar arguments have been powerfully made. The influence, for example, of Critical Race Theory is increasingly visible within critical educational studies, with powerful interventions being made by Gloria Ladson-Billings (2009), William Tate (1997), David Gillborn (2008), and the author of the book you are about to read, Zeus Leonardo (2005).

With all of its visibility in public discussions, in daily life, and in institutions such as education, health care, and so many others, however, "race" is extremely complicated. It is not a biological entity, but a social one. What "it" means, how it functions, its complex connections to other dynamics of differential power—all of this requires not simply slogans but disciplined and careful historical, empirical, and conceptual analysis. Obviously, it also requires constant political action by social movements that contest its power (Anyon 2005). The task is to connect the critical analysis to these movements so that there is a dialectical relationship between committed action in education and elsewhere and the reflexive understanding of the complexities surrounding race and racisms—and then a re-immersion in the personal and political activity that challenges the relations of domination that so clearly characterize our societies (Apple, Au, and Gandin 2009).

Zeus Leonardo is one of the very best in engaging with the kinds of reflexive analysis that are so necessary at this time. In this book, he gives us a sophisticated reading of what race and white supremacy actually mean in education and in the larger society, how we can more fully understand it, and why many of the theories and policies that have arisen to counter it may be flawed. In the process, he demonstrates that some of the usual ways critical scholars have tried to understand race and whiteness (by, say, reducing them to the workings of our economy and class relations or seeing racism in schools, the legal system, or the economy as largely the product of prejudice) are much too simplistic. Drawing on some of the most thoughtful literature in Critical Race Theory, philosophy, history, and critical education, Leonardo provides us with essential tools and insights that both challenge and enlighten.

Why is such a more detailed and nuanced understanding so important for those of us in education? The data on school achievement consistently point to the intersections of class and race—and to the immense and continuing power of race as a defining marker of differentiation in the institutions of this society (Ladson-Billings 2006; Ladson-Billings 2009; Gillborn 2008). This is clearly ratified in the empirical research that has been done on the discriminatory effects of our seemingly never-ending fascination with reductive high stakes testing in state after state throughout this country and others (see, e.g., Au 2009, Lipman 2004; Valenzuela 2005; McNeil 2000; Gillborn and Youdell 2000). Indeed, as I too have demonstrated in *Educating the "Right" Way*, a very large portion of the dominant models of school reform nationally and internationally have their roots in the ways race is thought about and constructed, in the fear of the "Other" and a clear sense of pollution and danger surrounding their culture and very bodies (Apple 2006).

This is very much an international phenomenon. As Stuart Hall showed in his critical analyses of the rise of conservative policies in England, for example, issues of "law and order" and the repressive forms of authoritarian populism that they spawned and that were spawned by them had much of their grounding in racial worries and assumptions. Economic anxieties were *dialectically* connected to an entire history of racializing discourses and practices. They weren't the automatic workings of economic dynamics, although they were clearly connected to these dynamics. They were both produced by and themselves produced a creative ideological process of political disarticulation and rearticulation, a process that required hard political and ideological work on the part of rightist movements. This is exactly what we are seeing in the United States as well with the growing influence of neoliberal and neoconservative policies in education and so much else (see, e.g., Apple 2006; Buras 2008; Pedroni 2007).

Leonardo fully understands this; and he fully understands what is at stake in our struggles to understand and challenge the ways in which race and especially whiteness function. His critical reading of such "reforms" as No Child Left Behind Here, for instance, is but one example of the kinds of insights this book can provide. While I have argued that it is impossible to fully understand reforms of this type without placing race as one of the key nodal points, he goes further. His critique gives even more power to the points that I, Gloria Ladson-Billings, David Gillborn, and others have made about the dominant tendencies in educational reform in all too many nations (Apple 2006; Ladson-Billings 2006; Gillborn 2008). He also builds on and then goes beyond earlier books in this series, such as the rightly well-known volume by Michael Omi and Howard Winant, *Racial Formation in the United States* (Omi and Winant 1994).

Leonardo is one of those rare individuals who can combine personal accounts of some of his own experiences with compelling critical interrogations of our conceptual and political assumptions. He has produced a book that is "unsettling." I mean this in two ways. First, it unpacks some of the all too easily accepted assumptions that so many of us—including critical educators—have about race and in the process challenges us to think more deeply about some of the most critical issues besetting us. And second, it makes it much less easy for democratically and critically committed educators to serve up easy answers that don't either involve taking risks or taking our politics as seriously they deserve. In so doing, Zeus Leonardo gives us what we need—a powerful set of analytic and political tools that are unsettling in the best sense of that word.

Michael W. Apple
*John Bascom Professor of Curriculum and Instruction
and Educational Policy Studies
University of Wisconsin–Madison*

References

Anyon, J. (2005). *Radical possibilities: Public policy, urban education, and a new social movement.* New York: Routledge.

Apple, M. W. (2006). *Educating the "right" way: Markets, standards, God, and inequality* (2nd ed). New York: Routledge.

Apple, M. W. and Buras, K. L. (Eds.), (2006). *The subaltern speak: Curriculum, power, and educational struggles.* New York: Routledge.

Apple, M. W., Au, W., and Gandin, L. A. (Eds.), (2009). *Routledge international handbook of critical education.* New York: Routledge.

Au, W. (2009). *Unequal by design: High-stakes testing and the standardization of inequality.* New York: Routledge.

Buras, K. L. (2008). *Rightist multiculturalism: Core lessons on neoconservative school reform.* New York: Routledge.

Gillborn, D. (2008). *Racism and education: Coincidence or conspiracy.* New York: Routledge.

Gillborn, D. and Youdell, D. (2000). *Rationing education: Policy, practice, reform, and equity.* Philadelphia: Open University Press.

Hall, S. (1978). *Policing the crisis: Mugging, the state, and law and order.* New York: Holmes and Meier.

Ladson-Billings, G. (2006). From the achievement gap to the education debt: Understanding achievement in U. S. schools. *Educational Researcher 35*, pp. 3–12.

Ladson-Billings, G. (2009). In Apple, M. W., Au, W., and Gandin, L. A. (Eds.), *Routledge international handbook of critical education.* New York: Routledge.

Leonardo, Z. (Ed.), (2005). *Critical pedagogy and race.* Oxford: Blackwell.

Lipman, P. (2004). *High stakes education: Inequality, globalization, and urban school reform.* New York: RoutledgeFalmer.

McNeil, L. (2000). *Contradictions of school reform: Educational costs of standardized testing*. New York: Routledge.

Mills, C. (1997). *The racial contract*. Ithaca: Cornell University Press.

Omi, M. and Winant, H. (1994). *Racial formation in the United States: From the 1960s to the 1990s* (2nd ed.). New York: Routledge.

Pedroni, T. (2007). *Market movements: African American involvement in school voucher reform*. New York: Routledge.

Tate, W. (1997). Critical race theory and education: History, theory, and implications. In Apple, M. W. (Ed.), *Review of research in education 22*, pp. 195–247. Washington, DC: American Educational Research Association.

Valenzuela, A. (Ed.), (2005). *Leaving children behind: How "Texas-style" accountability fails Latino youth*. Albany: State University of New York Press.

Acknowledgements

Some time ago, I pursued graduate studies in order to delve into race and explain it to myself, if not also to others. Instead, I received a solid background in Marxist studies from Peter McLaren. For this, I am thankful to Peter, who showed me the indispensability of class analysis in education. That said, I had unfinished business and worked my way back to race, but no longer as something I took for granted. My understanding of race developed into a complex relationship with class, sometimes harmoniously, sometimes at loggerheads. Charles Mills and David Roediger's work helped me appreciate this productive tension, enabling me to push the limits of both frameworks. Their thoughts on race and class are the clearest in extant. They also confirm the importance of writing with courage.

Along the way, for over a dozen years Ricky Lee Allen has provided an intellectual friendship that keeps me sharp and searching, able to fight the good fight. Since my brief career at University of St. Thomas, no one else has been my provocateuse like my close friend, Seehwa Cho. She is as brilliant a thinker as they come and I remember her as much for the good conversations we shared as I do her enthusiasm for intellectual life. My transatlantic best friend, Dave Gillborn, reminds me that warm relationships are as important as our commitment to the project of emancipation. It is nice to find a colleague who brings both.

A career is not made alone. We get some help along the way from people who believe in our work. Special thanks go to Henry Giroux, who published my first book on ideology in his series with Praeger. This current book is not disconnected from that project and Henry's support since then has not gone unnoticed. Michael Peters occupies a special place in my career. He has kept me busy by including me in his intellectual projects and providing outlets for my ideas. Michael is a true colleague and an ally who has done a lot for me. Michele Foster also deserves my appreciation for the collaborations over the years. Few people are more committed than Michele to the advancement of people of color. Michael Apple has been an important influence on my work and it is a distinct pleasure to have this book appear in his series. He has done so much for the critical Left in education. I, for one, cannot mention one without the other. Thanks Michael. Last, much appreciation goes to my editor at Routledge, Catherine Bernard, and her staff for shepherding this book from proposal to print.

During my year in Seattle, at the University of Washington, my only regret is that in Jim Banks' stead, I was physically away from him and could not interact face to face on a regular basis. We made up for this through frequent communications and subsequent meals together. Jim, many thanks for welcoming me into the family of the Center for Multicultural Education. My colleagues at UW and the Educators for Social Justice (you all know who you are) welcomed me into Miller Hall without hesitation. Thanks for your camaraderie and hospitality. To my Seattle brother, Jonathan Warren, it gives me pleasure to watch our kids grow up together. I relished the many dinners at your house with Michelle and the children, talking race politics and then putting away the toys. It has become our ritual to which I look forward.

I mention Seattle not only because it was important for me professionally but personally as well. In a span of six months during 2005–2006, my father, Jesus Leonardo, and brother-in-law, Brian Fitzhugh, passed away, and my second child, Zoë, was born. Sadness and joy were mixed together as I tried to make sense of these events' larger meaning. It confirmed that a complete life was full of both. This book is dedicated to all three people, particularly my daughter, Zoë, in whom the resolve of her Lolo and her uncle's mischievous innocence live on.

To many scholars, being productive is a mysterious concept. We get things done despite all the busyness and are not quite sure about the magic formula. Some say it is about having extended focused time, others say it is about weeding out distractions. Whatever the case may be, I know that I am most productive when I am happy despite the feeling of being overcommitted, producing at my best even at my busiest. Along with my daughter, my wife, Maggie Hunter, and son, Maxwell, confirm for me that a good professional life is an extension of a happy personal life. I am lucky to have both.

Permissions

Leonardo, Z. (2002). The souls of white folk: Critical pedagogy, whiteness studies, and globalization discourse. *Race Ethnicity & Education, 5*(1), 29–50.

Leonardo, Z. (2004). Critical social theory and transformative knowledge: The functions of criticism in quality education. *Theme Issue*: Disciplinary Knowledge and Quality Education. *Educational Researcher, 33*(6), 11–18.

Leonardo, Z. (2004). The color of supremacy: Beyond the discourse of "White privilege." *Educational Philosophy and Theory, 36*(2), 137–152.

Leonardo, Z. (2005). The unhappy marriage between Marxism and race critique: Political economy and the production of racialized knowledge. *Policy Futures in Education, 2*(3&4), 483–493.

Leonardo, Z. (2006). Through the multicultural glass: Althusser, ideology, and race relations in post-Civil Rights America. *Policy Futures in Education, 3*(4), 400–412.

Leonardo, Z. (2007). The war on schools: NCLB, nation creation, and the educational construction of whiteness. *Race Ethnicity & Education, 10*(3), 261–278. Special issue on *No Child Left Behind and Race*.

Leonardo, Z. and Hunter, M. (2007). Imagining the urban: The politics of race, class, and schooling. In William Pink and George Noblit (Eds.) [Michel Foster, Ed. of North American section], *International Handbook of Urban Education* (pp. 779–802). Dordrecht, The Netherlands: Springer.

Leonardo, Z. (2008). Reading whiteness: Anti-racist pedagogy against White racial knowledge. In William Ayers, Therese Quinn, and David Stovall (Eds.), *Handbook of Social Justice in Education*. New York: Routledge.

Leonardo, Z. (2009). Pale/ontology: The status of whiteness in education. In Michael Apple, Wayne Au, and Luis Gandin (Eds.), *Routledge International Handbook of Critical Education*. New York: Routledge.

Introduction

Recently, I attended a family gathering and became reacquainted with cousins whom I have not seen since the late 1970s. Thirty years have passed and like me, these "innocent boys" have grown into men with their own families, careers, and immigrant stories of the United States. During the luncheon, where I gorged myself on *lumpia, adobo*, and *pancit*, one male cousin recalled how he and I fought with other boys. I laughed uncomfortably, struggling to recall the scenes from my childhood without clear referents. My cousin assumed that I knew exactly to what he was referring. However, I did not recall engaging in too many fights, let alone with my cousin in tow. But it was a reunion and I went along with his "fond" remembrance; I wanted to connect. As he continued his story, he filled it in with details, in particular an altercation with Mexican boys in a Southern California park. It was at this moment that I remembered with precision the scene from my childhood, and the flood of memories came from the fight that should have been insignificant. He considered it a bonding moment, something he and I shared as young boys, a masculine story no doubt. Of the several memories he could have relived with me, he considered this one worth remembering three decades later. I was amazed that he recalled a memory that I had also thought about for over thirty years, one of my clearest introductions to race relations in a U.S. context. It was obviously meaningful to both of us, but perhaps for different reasons. My cousin did not know that I had been trying to make sense of that moment for some time now and it was not the appropriate occasion to seize the opportunity and analyze its racial significance. But this is precisely what I had been doing these many years, sometimes with my students, spouse, or friends, although this is the first time I have written about it. After this brief return to my earliest memories of the USA, my relatives and I continued with the reunion and enjoyed the rest of the afternoon under overcast skies in the Bay Area.

Let me retell the story as an adult remembers a significant childhood memory. On that typical summer day in Harbor City, Los Angeles, my two male cousins and I walked up the slight hill of a busy main street to the public park, dribbling our basketball on the sidewalk. The neighborhood was mixed in both race and class, with many immigrant Latinos and Asians as well as established whites and blacks attending the same schools. Those were the days of the Iran hostage crisis, the spike in oil prices and gas rations, the rise of the Carter administration. But these world affairs mattered less to a young boy than the end of disco, the arrival of Michael Jackson's "Off the Wall" album, and Kareem's legendary hookshot. When we arrived at the park, we reached the basketball court and began playing like the boisterous boys we were. I was a recent immigrant from the Philippines, green to the U.S. color line. There were no other kids on the court. A few minutes later, a couple Latino children whom we assumed to be Mexicans approached us. One of the boys took the basketball from my hands and hit me in the chest, warning "No Chinese allowed." He threw the ball on the grass and stared at me. My cousins were incensed and ready to fight. For one reason or another, including the fact that we were outnumbered, we chose to walk away dribbling the ball on the sidewalk on our way back home. We were partly dejected but enjoyed the rest of the afternoon playing other games. We did not debrief much about it, apparently unconcerned with a rather mundane interaction. However, the event made a definite impression on me.

I clearly remember being more puzzled by the fact that he called me Chinese than being concerned about the pain that pulsed from my diaphragm where the boy hit me. The event did not frighten me from ever visiting the same park again as I returned there many times. I walked away from the incident asking myself, "Why did he think I was Chinese?" As a Filipino, I considered my ethnic group clearly distinct from Chinese. It stuck with me for years, so much so that years later I consider the event one of my clearest introductions to race relations in the USA. As a Filipino American, I learned then and from subsequent racial events in my life that a new identity was in the making for me—a racial one—particularly the burden of being "yellow." In addition, I was already learning the ideal types of racial classifications as I assumed that my adversaries were Mexican rather than only Latino. In fact, as a new immigrant the category Latino was quite new to me despite the fact that I was aware of blacks and whites. There were representations of blacks and whites in the Philippines, usually through the armed forces and movies but not much of Latinos, and certainly not Asians as a pan-ethnic descriptor. I was not Asian before I stepped on U.S. soil. Ultimately, I learned that race was a source of conflict and brotherhood at the same time. The conflict between yellow and brown was punched into me at the same time that Chinese and Filipino proximity became a forced reality. I became a brown Yellow.

In the years since, the ironies of race have also set in as many Latinos and other racialized peoples (mis)recognize me as Latino, some of whom speak to me in Spanish before English based on changes in my physical appearance since childhood. I often take these moments as an embracing, rather than a hostile, move unlike my childhood example. I fluctuate between struggling to follow Spanish and informing the person that I do not speak the language. When I inform my interlocutors that I am Filipino, they fluctuate between being apologetic and assuming wrongly that Filipinos understand Spanish as a result of Spain's colonization of the islands.[1] As an adult, I sometimes also hear directed to me in subtle ways, "No Mexicans allowed here." Being racially ambiguous is a burden in a color-centered nation but it is also a gift, perhaps in Du Bois' sense, insofar as it exposes racial ambiguity and provides insight. I occasionally wonder about that kid who affected me in ways he never intended. I am tempted to assume that he never gave the event a second thought after it happened. Perhaps he has.

Many children learn these lessons as they traverse their daily school life. These events inform educators less about this or that kid, this or that inter-action, but more about the racial formation that is a reliable source of information at the same time that it is contradictory, a sense of both belonging and alienation, a process of our understanding as well as estrangement from one another. It strikes me now that at its best race theory is the move to remember our racialization, to reclaim the racial meanings of our lives not in order further to divide people from each other but to educate one another for mutual benefit. Ultimately, this is where I find the liberatory purpose of a critical study of race, which undergirds the otherwise abstract theories we have about our complicated racial formation. This is what this book is about: to use critical social theory in order to illuminate race as an everyday and educative process, to understand what we have made of race and what it has made of us, some of which we may no longer want to be.

In social theory, the critical tradition has enjoyed a long history, arguably traced to Kant's (2000) philosophical critiques of reason, the sublime, and beauty. Kant's interventions were so significant, it has been suggested that Western philosophy first became critical with Kant. Western epistemology and philosophy arose from the particularities of European culture and understanding. They are insightful, at times critical, but always partial like other ways of thinking. They are partial for two reasons. First, they are partial in the sense that Western thought represents a slice of understanding, not its whole. Second, they are partial because they articulate a preferred way of comprehending the world, that is, a politics. When it is constructed as the universal standard for rational thought and derogate worldviews of color in the process, European thought takes on a racial dimension. It becomes *articulated* with race and we witness its cultural particularity transform into a racial project. From Hegel to Kant to Marx, the procession of a white racialized worldview develops into a formidable phenomenon (Bernasconi and Lott, 2000; see also Churchill, 2005).

In education, the signifier "critical" is so central that no self-respecting educator or scholar would call himself "uncritical." It would be, as Eagleton (1991) has suggested elsewhere, akin to calling oneself "Fatso." An uncritical educator would quickly be labeled ideological, which is worse than being branded an idiot (Parker, 2005). No legitimate educator answers to the hail, "Hey stupid!"

To be uncritical is not to be an educator at all, at least not in any accredited sense, for only the most reactionary teacher education program would dare question the label of "critical." There is also something about the critical project that is inherently leftist. It seems to speak for the oppressed, those at the receiving end of disparities from wealth to health. For example, in the USA it is considered an irony to call a republican politico critical although in these fickle times being a democrat does not make one a lifetime card-carrying member of the critical club. That said, Dinesh D'Souza is not considered critical but his critic Vijay Prashad is; Allan Bloom may be grouped with the first and Alex Callinicos with the second. Of course, criticality is always relative to a spectrum of political commitments and scholars may find the line of separation shifting, where one's utopianism is, for another, nothing more than an ideology.

For the progressive left, being critical has become the norm. In a word: hegemonic. This is a good trend, if not a tradition, but as I will show criticality needs also to be delineated in specific terms lest it be stripped of its edgy and meaningful deployment, particularly for the study of race. Otherwise, the well-intended use of "critical" in education becomes meaningless . . . uncritical. If, in studying race matters, all treatises wave the flag of critical, then critical loses its differential status as something set off from commonsensical thinking. Critical thinking, critical education, and critical change are some forms of criticality that get taken up to suggest that schooling ought to distinguish between the epiphenomenal and essence of learning. As critical descends into common sense, it is in danger of becoming nonsense. Educators would do well to guard against this development.

In research on race and education, criticality enjoys some currency. With Ladson-Billings and Tate's breakthrough 1995 essay, "Towards a Critical Race Theory of Education," we might say that race theory in education becomes critical for the first time. I will not summarize the major tenets of a critical race theory in education here, which is largely a U.S.-based innovation, because there are many publications in extant that accomplish this task (Gillborn, 2008; Yosso, 2006; Dixson and Rousseau, 2005; Parker and Stovall, 2005; Ladson-Billings, 2004; Taylor, 1998; Tate, 1997). For my purposes, it suffices to say that race and racism are endemic to U.S. society.[2] This does not suggest that racism is pandemic or out of control and cannot be ameliorated. CRT in education is precisely that intervention that aims to halt racism by highlighting its pedagogical dimensions and affirming an equally pedagogical solution rooted in anti-racism. That said, CRT in education is a paradigmatic study of race to the extent that the problem of the color line is made to speak within a particular discourse, community, and postulates. For instance, the appropriation of Bell's (1992) well-known, defiant injunction regarding the "permanence of racism" is understood within the particular context and constraints (in the Foucauldian sense) of a CRT understanding of education. CRT focuses its attention on conceptual and practical strategies to end racism, less on ending race as an organizing principle.³ There are, as is usually the case, other competing paradigms for the study of race.

In addition to CRT, a Critical Theory of Race makes legitimate claims to a "critical" study of race, usually tracing its tradition to the Frankfurt School programme of emancipatory critique (Outlaw, 1990). Often, but not always, informed by a Marxist, critical interpretation of the Enlightenment, CTR is not typically U.S.-based and finds its inspiration in European philosophy. Some Marxist critical theorists of racism offer fundamental challenges to race thought, arguing that "race" is unavoidably caught in a reification of what is at heart an ideological concept (Cole and Maisuria, 2007; McLaren and Scatamburlo-D'Annibale, 2005; Darder and Torres, 2004; Miles, 2000; San Juan, Jr., 1992; Fields, 1990). In short, a critical study of race is not a study of race at all, but an analysis of class antagonism within capitalism, which gives rise to the reality of racial division that is not caused by racial structures *per se*. A Marxist-inspired version of CTR is not a racial analysis of race but a class analysis of racialization. In Fields' (1990) case, the concept of race is antiquated, which had its usefulness in explaining 18th century U.S. society and has since outlived its utility for understanding the current formation. Darder and Torres (2004) consider critical race theory a veritable oxymoron, arguing that no theory oriented to the study of an ideological concept passes the litmus test of "critical." In fact, a Marxist theory of race does not dodge the problems of reification if it focuses on an ideological concept like race, which leads Miles (2000) to argue that

> In so far as Marxism asserts that all social relationships are socially constructed and reproduced in specific historical circumstances, and that those relationships are therefore in principle alterable by human agency, then it should not have space for an ideological notion that implies, and often explicitly asserts, the opposite. The task is therefore not to create a Marxist theory of "race," but to deconstruct "race," and to detach it from the concept of racism (p. 140).

In education, this means that race has to be bracketed as a dependent concept and does not explain a primary relation, a status which belongs to class analysis. In writing and conversation, race is set off in quotation marks (what some call square quotes) to designate its ideological status. Racism, on the other hand, merits critical study because, as Miles notes, it is rooted in political economy as an "ideological relation of production" (p. 141).

Yet still, Essed and Goldberg's (2002) Race Critical Theory framework suggests that race is a discursive formation, which places the arguement within the assumptions of a cultural studies or post-foundational critique of race. This school of thought promotes being theoretically critical of race and being race-critical of theory while still employing race categories, unlike a Marxist theorist of race who does not lend much credence to them. Dissatisfied with a critical theory that does not tackle race and race theory that is not critical, Essed and Goldberg describe their project as "[C]ritical theory necessarily requires a focus, among others, on race: and racial theory cannot help but be, in a normative sense, critical. Race, critique, and theory, we want to insist, are constitutive of the possibilities of thinking each other in any satisfactory way" (p. 4). Goldberg (1990, 1993) maintains a continuity with "race men and women" who center race analysis (i.e., a racial analysis of race rather than a class analysis of race), while decentering and destabilizing essentialist renditions of it as biologistic, pigment-oriented, or deterministic. RCT treats race as culture—or better, a cultural formation—not in the sense of ethnic theories, but part of the overall turn to studies of subject formation in social theory (see Cho, 2008).

Gilroy's (2000) new position "against race" follows along the same lines to suggest that race, as a mode of analysis and organization, has reached its limits as a viable alternative in a world that disturbs racial lines of association through diasporic and crosscultural-cutting relations that require new modes of understanding. No amount of resignifying race can escape its problems in a world that approaches the limits of race understanding, a condition of "post-race" (see also, Nayak, 2006). Gilroy (2000) warns that race "cannot be readily signified or de-signified, and to imagine that its dangerous meanings can be easily rearticulated into benign, democratic forms would be to exaggerate the power of critical and oppositional interests . . . [D]estroying raciology and transcending 'race' are more than warranted" (p. 12). Sharing some commitments with Ignatiev, Garvey, and Roediger, who support the abolition of whiteness, Gilroy seeks the abolition of race. Inherently a problematic relation, race may be supplanted by the conviviality of planetary humanism and Gilroy reminds us that dismantling race is not something to be feared but posed as a possibility.

In education, this means that race analysis proceeds with "no guarantees." This suggests the necessity to analyze race in order to undo the relation itself, just as "we must be conscious of black and white in order to transcend black and white" (Wu, 2002, p. 27). The "post" in post-race signals the possibility of a social formation without race but this would be its most obvious reading. A more nuanced reading suggests that the post-movement opens new possibilities for critique, new questions to be posed about race in a way that was not possible heretofore. If race is to continue in the USA, it will be a nonessentialist relation or the risks become predictable (Omi and Winant, 1994). If race is to be dissolved, there is good reason for ending a relation that has, from day one, transformed education into enlightenment for whites and a burden for people of color. Post-race analysis suggests that an opportunity presents itself to critical social theory.

With these three schools of thought as the backdrop for this book, I will attempt to delineate the criteria for a critical study of race in education. In particular, I will pose the central problem of whiteness in education within a general critical study of race. In doing this, the following chapters do not engage race paradigmatically. It is an affirmation of criticality that does not locate it in any particular school of thought and subject to its assumptions but instead recruits multiple positions on the matter of race, which I will call a *critical social theory of race and education*. It is guided by the spirit and claim that race in education is a complex issue that requires a critical framework that testifies to this very complexity. If this sounds a bit eclectic and trendy, this is not my intent. Rather, I would like to build a project around race criticality that is less possessive and more dialogic.

The book deals with current themes in critical social analysis of race and education. It represents my publications on race, critical social theory, and education from a span of six years, between 2002–2008. The first chapter provides the framework for the collection with an introduction to critical social theory and education, signaling the importance of discourse analysis and studies of ideology. Discourse analysis is defined in Foucault's sense of the deployment of power and language practices in order to achieve certain political ends. Ideology is defined in the reconstructed Marxist sense of favoring (without valorizing) the cultural field, of affirming cultural politics without divorcing it from the material organization of society, in the sense that Stuart Hall (1996a) and Terry Eagleton (1991) have used it. However, the book does not center the study of ideology on class relations but appropriates its usefulness for the fundamental study of race, without conveniently forgetting its Marxist roots and systematic analysis of ideology.

Chapter 1 introduces critical social theory as a multidisciplinary knowledge base with the implicit goal of advancing the emancipatory function of know-ledge. It approaches this goal by promoting the role of criticism in the search for quality education. Through critical social theory in education, quality is proportional to the depth of analysis that students or subjects have at their disposal. As a critical form of classroom discourse, critical social theory culti-vates our ability to critique institutional as well as conceptual dilemmas, par-ticularly those that lead to racial domination or oppression. It also promotes a language of transcendence that complements a language of critique in order to forge alternative and less oppressive social arrangements. A critical social theory-based movement in education highlights the relationship between social systems and people, how they produce each other, and ultimately how critical social theory can contribute to the emancipation of both.

Chapter 2 is a general theory of racial ideology applied to contemporary U.S. society, what many social science scholars have placed within the "color-blind era." The color-blind era has been used as a generative description of post-Civil Rights in the USA, such as Bonilla-Silva's excellent book, *Racism without Racists*. In short, Chapter 2 sets the stage for the centrality of race and racism in contemporary U.S. society where race is assumed to be almost irrele-vant and racism on the wane despite the findings of most critical race scholars.

This chapter accomplishes insights on race by going through the concept of ideology as theorized by Althusser. In order to analyze the relevance of Althusser's theory of ideology for the study of race and multiculturalism (something which did not appear in Althusser's work), I appropriate his insights *sans* his problematic of historical materialism. Althusser's theory of ideology is useful for a study of race, which is an ideological, as much as a material, problem. Furthermore, Althusser's *discourse* on ideology enriches debates about race to the extent that his *general* insights on ideology are appropriate for such an analysis. First, I present a brief introduction to the multiple levels of Althusser's theory of ideology. Then, I appropriate his general insights and relevance, determining the most pertinent moments in his theory for the study of race and multiculturalism. Last, I pose the problem of color-blind discourses on race.

Chapters 3 and 4 continue the theoretical framework that will guide some of the syntheses I attempt in the book. Chapter 3 marries race with class analysis, a problematic to which I return in the chapters on whiteness. In educational theory orthodox Marxism is known for its commitment to objectivism (often bracketing subjectivity, according to Huebner), or the science of history. On the other hand, race analysis is well developed in its ability to explain the subjective dimension of racial oppression. The two theories are often at odds with each other, thus the "unhappy marriage" (a phrase from Hartmann). This chapter is an attempt to create an integrated theory between Marxist objectivism and race theory's focus on subjectivity, in a manner that strengthens both frameworks. An integrated race–class analysis means that one only understands political economy insofar as it happens within the context of racialization and that race, as Stuart Hall (1996b) once claimed, is a mode in which class is lived. A racio-economic analysis argues that racial hierarchies and class exploitation occur in a symbiotic relationship and that changes in one produce changes in the other. Transforming one means transforming the other.

Chapter 4 foregrounds the importance of language practice, or discourse, in our understanding of race and racism. In particular, it delves into the recent advancements in race theory that prognosticate about the future of race discourses. In this chapter, I engage three treatises on the viability of race both as a structuring principle and a conceptual form of understanding. First, in Marxist theory, race retains its ideological status and a racial cosmology inevitably subverts a clearer understanding of social life and the educational apparatus where race is learned as social practice. This does not mean that Marxism outright rejects race struggle, but it questions its scientific status and praxiological implications for change. Second, post-race discourses provide an opportunity to ask new questions about race that have been made possible by innovations in cultural studies and the politics of representation. According to Gilroy, it is an opportunity rather than something to be feared insofar as race understanding may be advanced in order that it may disappear. Post-race is a race politics that proceeds with no guarantees. Third, white abolition asks a different task of race theory to the extent that it prioritizes targeting whiteness. Race is dependent on what Lipsitz earlier called the "possessive investment in whiteness" so any utopia without race must confront the strongest form of racial worldmaking that is whiteness. Race sits strategically at a crossroad that demands scholarship which is attentive not only to its declining or rising significance but also to its very future.

The following cluster of chapters focuses on the problem of whiteness and white supremacy within the color-blind era. They engage a fairly recent innovation in race scholarship known as whiteness studies and reaffirm David Roediger's contention that race studies that do not sufficiently address whiteness are at best disingenuous and at worst ineffective. It asserts, with Noel Ignatiev, that the greatest challenge in civil society in terms of race is confronting the contours of whiteness. That said, these essays engage, rather than accept at face value, the findings of whiteness scholars. For example, Chapter 5 problematizes the popular but taken for granted notion of "white privilege," a rather passive description of racial domination without agents. The study of white privilege has reached currency in the educational and social science literature. Concerned with the circuits and meanings of whiteness in everyday life, scholars have exposed the codes of white culture, worldview of the white imaginary, and assumptions of the invisible marker that depends on the racial other for its own identity. In particular, the literature has helped educators understand the taken for granted, daily aspects of white privilege. This chapter takes a different approach toward the study of whiteness and argues that a critical look at white privilege, or the analysis of white racial hegemony, must be complemented by an equally rigorous examination of white supremacy, or the analysis of white racial domination. Although the two processes are related, the conditions of white supremacy make white privilege possible. As such, a critical analysis of white racial supremacy revolves less around the issue of unearned advantages, or the *state* of being dominant, and more around direct processes that secure domination and the privileges associated with it.

Chapter 6 critically appraises the literature on the strategies to either reconstruct or abolish whiteness. There are two significant camps regarding the uptake of whiteness: white reconstruction and white abolition. In the first, reconstructionists offer discourses—as forms of social practice—that transform whiteness, and therefore white people, into something other than an oppressive identity and ideology. Reconstruction suggests rehabilitating whiteness by resignifying it through the creation of alternative discourses. It projects hope onto whiteness by creating new racial subjects out of white people, which are not ensnared by a racist logic. On the other hand, white abolitionism is guided by Roediger's announcement that "whiteness is not only false and oppressive, it is *nothing but* false and oppressive." In opposition to reconstructing whiteness, abolishing whiteness sees no redeeming aspects of it and as long as white people think they are white, Baldwin once opined that there is no hope for them. Chapter 6 considers white reconstruction and abolition for their conceptual and political value as it concerns not only the future of whiteness but of race theory in general. In doing so, the book affirms *and* critiques studies of whiteness in order to observe the limitations in the first wave of whiteness studies, perhaps provoking a second wave.

Chapter 7 goes against the popular refrain that whites do not know much about race. In studies of race, the idea that whites do not know much about race is generally accepted. By virtue of their life experiences, white students and teachers are portrayed as subjects of race without much knowledge of its daily and structural features. This chapter, however, argues that whites do know a lot about race in both its everyday sense as a lived experience and its structural sense as a system of privilege. A critical reading of whiteness means that white ignorance must be problematized, not in order to expose whites as simply racist but to increase literacy about their full participation in race relations. Constructing whites as knowledgeable about race has two advantages: one, it holds them self-accountable to race-based decisions and actions; two, it dismantles their innocence in exchange for a status as full participants in race relations. Chapter 7 attempts to build a conceptual apparatus by which to understand white racial knowledge. It offers suggestions for anti-racist practices in education that whites as well as educators of color may appropriate when teaching racial content.

Chapters 8 and 9 engage race in the arena of educational policy. I follow through with the framework of a critical social theory of race, in particular whiteness, by analyzing No Child Left Behind, which I argue is framed by an unspoken white frame. Many studies of whiteness have provided insights of the informal aspects of white privilege, or the everyday cognates of a more general white structural advantage. In this chapter, I begin a discussion on the formal aspects of white privilege by analyzing NCLB as an "act of whiteness." The educational literature is replete with critiques of NCLB as it affects children of color, poor students, or immigrants. However, less attention is paid to the way it creates U.S. nationhood through the social construction of whiteness. In other words, how does NCLB construct and imagine the white nationhood? To answer this question, I analyze the racial context out of which NCLB arises, or the partnership between neoliberalism and color-blindness. To be more precise, NCLB does not represent a vulgar form of color-blindness due to its deliberate recognition of the four subgroups that name and implicate race. That said, NCLB is interpellated by a liberal form of color-blindness that names the symptoms, rather than the causes, of racial inequality. My main goal in this chapter is to suggest that NCLB should be historicized as an expression of its historical conjuncture, a sign of its racial times.

Chapter 9 flows from previous chapters by applying a race–class analysis to urban education and urban sociology. It ventures into the often strained relationship between Marxism and race critique signaled earlier in Chapter 3. The chapter attempts to build a more compatible study of race and class without economizing race relations, but by building toward a racialized class analysis and a class-informed race analysis. It discusses how "urban reality" is as much an *imagined*, in addition to a real, place. That is, the urban is socially and discursively constructed as a place, which is part of the dialectical creation of the ghetto as both a real and imagined space. The urban is real insofar as it is demarcated by zones, neighborhoods, and policies. However, it is imagined to the extent that it is replete with meaning, much of which contains contradictions as to exactly what the ghetto signifies. For instance, there are "urban" communities that are positively urban like the Upper East and West Sides of Manhattan, New York, but not Harlem or the South Bronx; Santa Monica and West Hollywood, California but not Compton or Echo Park. In other words, in light of power relations, "urban" may signify the hallmark of civilization and the advances it offers, or a burden and problem of progress. Both Chapters 8 and 9 entertain policy implications.

Chapter 10 expands race analysis into the global setting. With Charles Mills, this last chapter extends Du Bois' notion of the color line into transnational contexts. At the turn of the 1900s, W.E.B. Du Bois argued that the problem of the color line was the twentieth century's main challenge. Following his insight, this chapter suggests that the problem of the twenty-first century is not only the global assembly line but equally the *global color line*. Appropriating concepts from globalization discourse, which is usually concerned with economic restructuring, the chapter defines a global approach to race, in particular whiteness, in order to argue that the problem of white racial domination transcends the nation state. Using concepts from economic globalization, such as multinationalism, fragmentation, and flexibility, a critical pedagogy of whiteness promotes an expanded notion of race that includes global anti-racist struggles. The chapter concludes by suggesting that educators consider seriously the insights of the neo-abolitionist movement. That is, a critical pedagogy of whiteness poses the possibility of the abolition of whiteness as its ultimate goal. In effect, this last chapter wraps up the book's main concerns about racial domination, whiteness, and the possibilities of education.

As a political and intellectual project, the book showcases my main objective to understand the contours of racial domination and ways conceptually and practically to address it through educational research. As such, the book is also concerned with the possibility and necessity, rather than inevitability, of liberation from relations of domination. The book is an attempt to bridge disparate, competing, and apparently incommensurable perspectives, tying class/materialist, discursive, and racial analyses together. Like the narrative at the beginning of this Introduction, I hope the book helps illuminate the racial lessons in your everyday life, not more but also not less. I also hope you enjoy it.

1
Critical Social Theory
An Introduction

Critical social theory (henceforth CST) is a multidisciplinary framework with the implicit goal of advancing the emancipatory function of knowledge. CST is not a traditional discipline but maintains a quasi-disciplinary status in the academy, which is more accurately described as a convergence of existing disciplines. In education, CST promotes critical thinking, broadly conceived. Through the multidisciplinary framework of CST, quality education is proportional to the depth of analysis that students have at their disposal. Deprived of opportunities for historical analysis in its material and discursive forms, students experience their education in its alienated and abstract form; we could hardly call such an experience "quality" or "critical." However, with the benefit of CST, classroom discourse broadens students' horizon of possibility, expands their sense of a larger humanity, and liberates them from the confines of their common sense (Leonardo, 2003a). The multidisciplinary knowledge base of CST affirms the role of criticism as bound up in the definition of a quality educational experience. It also privileges the role of theory in critical education, not as something separate from practice, but its conceptual form. In fact, CST rejects the radical distinction between theory and practice as two separate poles of a dualism. CST does not promote theory for theory's sake, or what Althusser (1976) called "theoreticism," but encourages the production and application of theory as part of the overall search for transformative knowledge.

Critical social theorists have produced many generative critiques of educational processes, such as parental involvement (Lareau, 2000) and curriculum formation (Apple, 1990), as well as less formal aspects of schooling, like popular culture (Giroux, 1994). Critical social theorists have also broadened the influences impacting education, including insights on new constructions of identity within the postcolonial context (McCarthy and Dimitriadis, 2004). Without suggesting that critical social theory should become the new "tool kit" for educators, this chapter will focus on the usefulness of CST as a critical form of educational discourse, one whose contribution promotes criticism as the defining aspect of a quality education. By presenting CST as a form of criticism, I highlight its power to change the pedagogical process from one of knowledge transmission to knowledge transformation. After a brief genealogy of

CST, I proceed with a section outlining the contours of a language of critique, which is followed by a final section on a language of transcendence in quality education.

A Genealogy of Critical Social Theory

As a descriptor, critical theory finds its lineages in at least three lines of inquiry. In philosophy and literature, critical theory engages debates in aesthetic as far back as Greek thought, collected by volumes such as Hazard Adam's (1970) *Critical Theory since Plato*. There is another sense of critical theory found in the Frankfurt School's programmatic study of a Kantian theory of knowledge coupled with a Freudo-Marxist theory of modern society. It has been suggested that theory first became "critical" with the arrival of Kant's critiques of reason, ethics, and beauty. Under the leadership of Max Horkheimer during Nazi Germany, Frankfurt Critical Theory sought to make theory critical insofar as it exposed the dialectical tensions in modernity, such as between authoritarianism and enlightenment, summed up by Horkheimer and Adorno's (1976) *Dialectic of Enlightenment*. In a third sense, critical theory is a more general description of theory that is politically edgy, a form of "agitational theory" (Agger, 1992) concerned with institutional and conceptual transformations. Its project is centered on the function of criticism and its ability to advance research on the nature of oppression and emancipation.

Critical theory is related to social theory, which is a broader category of theoretical production than critical theory, including subsets like sociological theory, race and ethnic theory, cultural theory, and literary theory (see Lemert, 1993). Its multidisciplinary knowledge base is typical of both critical and social theory. Some scholars have synthesized critical and social theory into an overarching framework, such as Craig Calhoun's (1995) *Critical Social Theory*, which includes a chapter dedicated to the Frankfurt School, but goes beyond it to include discussions of Foucault, feminist standpoint theory, and nationalism. Bennett deMarrais and LeCompte's (1999) text on the sociology of education explicitly states that it proceeds from a "critical social theory" position and Morrow and Torres' (1995) *Social Theory and Education* brings a mélange of critical and social theories from the Frankfurt School to Nancy Fraser. Finally, Patricia Hill Collins' (1998) *Fighting Words*, her follow-up to *Black Feminist Thought* (2000/1990), contains a more explicit attempt to bridge critical and social theory with race and feminist theory.

Critical theory is known for its propensity for criticism, a tradition it arguably owes to predecessors, like Marx and Kant. Social theory represents an expanded set of criticism with the advent of more recent discourses, such as postmodernism and cultural studies. CST is an intellectual form that puts criticism at the center of its knowledge production. Through criticism, CST pushes ideas and frameworks to their limits, usually by highlighting their contradictions. In quality education, criticism functions to cultivate students' ability to question, deconstruct, and then reconstruct knowledge in the interest of emancipation. In this chapter, I will be less concerned with the question of *who* is a critical social theorist and more with *what* it is and *how* scholars have engaged its central themes. Choosing this path acknowledges that there exist bona fide critical social theorists that most scholars recognize—Martin Jay lists 50 critical theorists in the USA (see Agger, 1992)—but for this chapter it is more heuristic to assess how "critical ideas" have been received and engaged, even by non-critical theorists. In addition, I appraise both critical theory and social theory with respect to the functions of criticism, thus building a case for *critical social theory*. That said, CST is by no means a unified field and contains certain contentions, such as the productive debates between materialism and discourse analysis, identity and difference, and determinism and undecidability. The chapter forms the basis for the subsequent chapters on race, whiteness, and education, all of which draw insights from CST.

Theory is not new in educational parlance. In the mid-1800s, Horace Mann's idea of the common school theorized an educational experience that resembled both the humanist focus on core subject areas and the factory model of learning. Educational theory arguably reached its golden age with Dewey's pragmatism, enjoying not only engagement within the discipline but also with philosophical discourse in general. In the Deweyan sense, quality education was elusive until the empiricist tradition in educational research constructed a suitable theory of "experience" (Dewey, 1938). On the other hand, CST is relatively new in education, perhaps traceable again to Dewey's influence (see Sirotnik and Oakes, 1986), but popularized by the late Paulo Freire, or its "inaugural philosopher" (McLaren, 1999), who is "without question the most influential theorist of critical or liberatory education" (Weiler, 1994a, p. 13), and whose name "has become synonymous with the very concept and practice of critical pedagogy" (Giroux, 1993, p. 177). In education, CST is a contested terrain, not the least of which is captured by Ellsworth's (1989) interrogation of what she observes as critical pedagogy's overreliance on abstract rationality over lived contradictions. In addition, her essay brought to light the importance of positionality in the process of theory production, a process which Said (1979) describes as the imprint that an author leaves on his or her text.

Critical social theorists have tried to link up theory to the immediacy of lived realities. For example, in *Reflections on Exile* Said (2000) addresses the problem of theory production that detaches itself from the face of real, historical suffering, such as war, imperialism, and displacement. He notices, "Reading historiographers like Hayden White or the philosopher Richard Rorty, one finds oneself remarking that only minds so untroubled by and free of the immediate experience of the turbulence of war, ethnic cleansing, forced migration, and unhappy dislocation can formulate theories such as theirs" (p. xxi). Said favors *concrete* theory that foregrounds historical experience and the necessity of interpreting its source and insight. Said (1983) does not suggest that we forsake theory, but as he warns in an essay on "Traveling Theory," the critic must be resistant to theory that attempts to universalize its insights outside of the specificities of the history that interpellates it and to which the theory responds. Finally, the critical social theorist opens up interpretations of theories to human and social needs, thus making criticism possible in the first place. This is what Deborah Appleman (2000) was encouraging when she argued for the appropriate place of critical literary theories in high school English classes. Working with English teachers, Appleman documents her participants' attempts to teach adolescent students Marxist and poststructural literary theories in their engagement of the standard classics in literature. She may as well have been referring to Said when she argues that "critical theory can travel with adolescents from the literature classroom into the rest of their lives . . . [because] we want our students . . . to reflect a keen understanding of their location (and degree of complicity) within a variety of competing ideologies and possibilities" (p. 126). Both Said and Appleman affirm the role of theory to attest to as well as intervene into social relations that set the limits of student learning.

We can say that pedagogy first became critical with the arrival of Freire's work and soon after critical theory's cousin in critical pedagogy entered the educational lexicon. Although it would be accurate to appropriate Dewey as an *influence* on the development of CST in education, it is Freire's work that promotes ideology critique, an analysis of culture, attention to discourse, and a recasting of the teacher as an intellectual or cultural worker (see also Giroux, 1988). In Freire's life work, we find a challenge to the prevailing structuralism since Althusser, a qualification to the new sociology that emphasized personal autonomy, and an interrogation of radical indeterminacy popular among certain postmodern theorists. Without suggesting that Freire accomplished his goals before he died in 1997, his work became the fulcrum for a CST program in education that searched for a proper reconciliation between structural conditions and human agency. Freire gave education a language that neglected neither the effect of oppression on concrete people nor their ability to intervene on their own behalf, nor the terrorizing and structured consequences of capitalism and other social systems.

Building a Language of Educational Criticism

Educational discourse not only frames the way students experience learning, it may also empower them. Pedagogically speaking, quality education begins with a language of critique, at the heart of which is a process that exposes the contradictions of social life. Through critical classroom discourse, teachers assist students not only in becoming comfortable with criticism, but also adept at it. As understood in CST, criticism functions not so much as a form of refutation or an exercise in rejection (Leonardo, in press), but rather as a precondition for intellectual engagement with an ideological formation (Eagleton,

1976). For example, even when bell hooks (1993) takes Freire to task for his patriarchal referents, she reminds us that "critical interrogation is not the same as dismissal" (p. 148). Engagement is at the base of criticism because one could hardly be disengaged when performing a thorough criticism of an author's ideas. That said, in CST criticism is not valued in and of itself but as part of an overall project that aims at material or institutional changes, a process which begins with a language that penetrates the core of relations of domination, such as race, class, and gender (Leonardo, 2003b). As such, CST begins with the premise that criticism targets systematic and institutional arrangements, how people create them, and how educators may ameliorate their harmful effects on schools.

This platform does not negate individual instances of oppression, but in order to understand their pervasiveness, CST attempts to lay bare their social, rather than personal, sources. By social, I mean those objective arrangements that have a stolid existence outside of our ability to articulate them. By personal, I mean more accurately "personalistic" sources of suffering, which are in and of themselves difficult to overcome, such as students' family dynamics and interpersonal relations. When these conditions become part of the overall rationalization of society and how it functions, we can say that such personal histories become instances of social patterns, not determined by them but certainly inscribed by them. These "impersonal" structures affect actual people in schools and one does not have to look further than Kozol's (1991) *Savage Inequalities*, where he describes the degradation that minorities and poor students suffer as a result of racial stratification and capitalism. To mimic a phrase from Radical Feminism, we can say that the "personal is structural."

In another vein, Habermas (1989) has built a project based on the notion of an "ideal speech situation," a theme he expands upon in his two-volume critique of distorted communication (Habermas 1984, 1987). As a regulative concept, the ideal speech situation recognizes that communication is always a bit distorted, skewed this or that way because of personal agendas and the like. However, communication becomes ideological when it is *systematically* distorted, that is, when its distortion is socially structured and transcends interpersonal differences. Mannheim (1936) suggests as much when he distinguishes between the personal plane of ideology from its historical form, arguing that the first is more a product of personal manipulation whereas the second is a product of a historical formation, like capitalism. Although neither Habermas nor Mannheim transcend the tension between structural determinism and personal agency, which represents the bugbear for CST, they draw attention to the systems analysis that informs much of the field. This fact distinguishes CST from psychotherapy, the former focusing on social emancipation whereas the latter focuses on individual mental health. To the extent that CST locates the sources of systematic oppression and the traces they leave in people, we may call it sociotherapy.

In CST, understanding the nature of oppression is central to its internal logic. That is, it proceeds from the assumption that oppression is real and formidable. Said another way, oppression is simultaneously social and lived. This is ultimately what McDade (1992) found in her study of teen pregnancy, where social oppression was lived everyday by adolescents who were constructed as problem students and whose bodies were ostracized from the general student population (see also Luttrell, 2003). To address this, Pillow (2003) builds a case for school discourses and feminist genealogies about the body since policies are "all about bodies" (p. 146). Therefore, oppression is material to the extent that it directs and controls the behavior of student bodies, but it is discursive insofar as bodies in schools are culturally inscribed and normalized. In this sense, oppression forms the basis for entering discourse with other humans, its "given" as logicians might suggest. In other words, the reality of oppression is part of the human condition and its structures inscribe our pedagogical or social interactions. Although different forms of CST may debate the nature of oppression—such as economics in Marxism, discourse in Foucauldian analysis, gender in feminism, or race in critical race theory—they converge on the idea that social inequality is stubborn, the persistence of which subverts students' full learning potential. Thus, critical social theorists are not in the habit of justifying that oppression exists, but prefer describing the form it takes. Instead, their intellectual energy is spent on critiquing notions of power and privilege, whether in the form of cash or culture.

Readers of CST in education are accustomed to discourses strewn with overtly politicized phrases, such as "pedagogy of the oppressed" (Freire, 1993), "predatory culture" (McLaren, 1995), "ideology and curriculum" (Apple, 1990), "struggle for pedagogies" (Gore, 1993), "dancing with bigotry" (Bartolome and Macedo, 2001), "globalization of white supremacy" (Allen, 2002), "knowledge, power, and discourse" (Cherryholmes, 1992), "discourse wars" (Pruyn, 1999), "education under siege" (Aronowitz and Giroux, 1987), and "teaching to transgress" (hooks, 1994). In this portrait, critical education means having to confront the reality of inequality, one of its latest examples going by the name of neo-liberalism with its ability to create new spaces for capital around the globe. Confronting inequality means coming to terms with social arrangements that create structural disparities and understanding their sources. Critical education encourages students to become aware of, if not actively work against, social injustice, such as the damage that global decentralization wreaks when it works in tandem with the centralization of capital in the hands of multinational corporations. Confronting social inequality also means that students must have access to discourses that pose critical questions about the new world order, a process assisted by theory-informed perspectives on students' social experiences.

CST in education does not ask students to wait until answers to difficult social problems are available before they critique them, as if a person cannot point out a fire because she cannot extinguish it. CST does not always offer a blueprint solution to a given problem, like racism (how does one "end" racism?), but rather to pose it as a problem, to ask questions about common answers rather than to answer questions (Shor, 1993). In other words, part of the solution can be found in how the problem is addressed in the first place. One sees this kind of engagement in Darder's (2002) reinvention of Paulo Freire in the context of southern California's sociopolitical condition. In her book, we read eight educator's narratives about how they "lived the pedagogy" that they learned through their courses in critical social theories in education. We witness their battles for language rights for Latino students in schools, their confrontations with White privilege in fairy tales like Hans Christian Andersen's *The Ugly Duckling*, and the relevance of CST for children from working class backgrounds. The vignettes speak to the concrete ways that CST addresses the needs of communities for whom theory has become a political weapon.

Oppression is not just the notion that someone suffers from impositions, such as having to wear a uniform in school or being unable to find socks in one's size. Rather and to Althusser's disapproval, oppression arguably occurs when one's human essence is subverted. For example, in the case of a Marxist-inspired CST, capitalism alienates individuals from their labor or productive powers, which represent the core of their humanity. It is a different situation altogether to argue that one cannot find clothes that fit—as annoying as this might be—since it is not part of human essence to wear properly fitting clothes. Moreover, capitalism alienates both workers and owners of capital—despite the fact that it benefits the latter—because it subverts their ability to achieve solidarity with each other and divides society. Critical education would mean that educators expose students to the concept of ideology critique, or examine the ways that capitalism discourages, at the structural level, a materialist analysis of social life. CST introduces them to the concept of "oppression" (or its age appropriate cognates) in order to differentiate between misfortune, which is random and quite natural, and inequality that is structurally immanent.

Critical teaching in this sense means the ability to apprehend the dialectical relationship between the objective and subjective nature of oppression. That is, part of defining oppression as the subversion of essence means that oppression must be socially pervasive. It must have material consequences registered by human bodies, which is "the central factor of human work, the actual participation of peoples in the making of human life" (Said, 2000, p. 375). In saying this, pedagogues recognize that racism is not the problem of white supremacist fringe groups, but a general institutional arrangement created between whites and people of color; the social definition of exploitation is not found in the practices of individual GM executives or Microsoft's Bill Gates, but in the productive relations found in capitalism entered into by workers and owners;

finally, patriarchy is not defined only in terms of men's chauvinist attitudes but people's very creation of gender roles and expectations that limit women's choices and ownership of their sexual powers. In all, a full understanding of oppression in its subjective and objective helix necessitates a language of ideology critique, a tradition of criticism from which students may draw. Together, the objective and subjective components of experience represent the wholeness of human existence. In critical education educators build with students a discourse that reminds us that our actions are inscribed by the very structures that we created (Shilling, 1992). A practical agent who navigates these structures acts on them in order to exercise her own autonomy without suggesting that such autonomy happens in a vacuum outside of social forces. To the critical student this means that, when aggregated together, subjective agency creates conditions for objective or institutional changes.

Ideology critique is not merely criticism. As used in common (i.e., uncritical) discourse, criticism is the deployment of commentaries for political purposes, usually indicative of a Leftist-leaning teacher in the popular mind. In this sense, criticism establishes the superiority of the critic whose impugnity the audience often fears. Here critical social theorists must take some responsibility when their main concern is to become the "ultimate radical" rather than promoting dialogue. That said, mainstream audiences often mistake criticism for political agendas as opposed to engagement, as if only critics have an agenda. Criticism is (mis)construed as pessimistic, judged as a form of negativity, and not in the sense that Adorno (1973) once promoted. The teacher-as-critic may be perceived as aggressive if she teaches the idea that patriarchy is alive and well, as politically incorrect if she cites the white supremacist origins of the United States, and as homophiliac if she questions the soundness of heterosexual families. However, the teacher-as-critic understands that criticism is at the center of a critical education that values debate, openness to different ideas, and commitment to democratic processes. Moreover, pedagogical interactions are never severed from wider social relations that need to be problematized. In this sense, criticism is more a search for emancipatory forms of knowledge and less a contrived condition to honor the critic. Criticism is positioned here as a central process in promoting a critical education *even in the face of* an uneven and unjust world.

A language of critique is never simply about clarity, but is always bound up with a political project. The politics of clarity is particularly important in the reception of CST in education because of its dense theories and descriptions, and therefore warrants some critical attention. Over the years, the issue of clarity has been a sore point in the wider engagement of CST. But clarity is always a question of clarity for whom and for what? Clarity is too often an issue of conventions and a critique aiming solely for clarity takes for granted the reader's position (Giroux, 1995). This does not suggest that critique should aim consciously for vagueness and obfuscation. For confusion seems antithetical to the critical spirit. It suggests that critique is not an issue of either clarity or complexity but both/and. Also, it implicates clarity as an ideological issue, rather than a merely rhetorical one (Lather, 1996). For example, an uncritical literacy program perpetuates the importance of clarity over political purpose and denies the fact that people's tastes and dispositions toward language are socially motivated. As a case in point, language learning frequently intersects issues of race, forming what Hopson (2003) calls the "the problem of the language line." Hopson combines Bourdieu's concept of linguistic capital with Du Bois' thoughts on the "color line" and finds that language learning is never just about induction into mainstream schooling but a way to perpetuate linguistic racism, in this case through the hegemony of English (see also Macedo, Dendrinos, and Gounari, 2003).

Criticism launched against the apparently muddy descriptions of CST tends to valorize ordinary language. It is not uncommon that mainstream educators charge that critical educational language is "elitist" or "exclusivist." Its highly academic discourse is not only hard to understand, it seems to demand much previous knowledge from its readers. Though this particular criticism helps point to the important project of widening the interest in CST, it also misses the mark because critical education is proportional to the depth of one's analysis, part of which is the engagement with theoretical discourse. It assumes problematically that ordinary language is sufficient and non-ideological (Gouldner, 1976; Aoki, 2000). The argument valorizes common language as transparent when compared to the supposed opacity of critical language. In fact, there is much in ordinary language that leaves one searching for a better mode of critique in terms of providing educators, teachers, and administrators discourses for a deeper engagement of school processes and hence a critical experience. It is for this reason that Said prefers the phrase "historical experience" because it is not esoteric (therefore accessible) but not without its theoretical moorings that a critical social theorist like Said (2000) proceeds to unpack. Likewise, CST in education works to build a language of depth hermeneutics and as such maintains its critical edge while at the same time fashioning it out of people's concrete lives or lived experiences.

Towards a Language of Transcendence in Education

In forging a critical education, critical social theorists do not stop at a language of critique. In order to provide students with a sustainable education, educators are encouraged to forge a language of transcendence, or what Giroux (1983) calls a "language of hope" (see also Freire, 1994). A language of transcendence is the dialectical counterpart of a language of critique. Insofar as CST accepts the reality of oppression, it also assumes the possibility of a less oppressive condition. This is why Bowles and Gintis' (1976) groundbreaking work, *Schooling in Capitalist America*, received such strong criticism from the educational Left. It projected a world almost completely under the sway of the capitalist imaginary, smoothly reproducing its social relations through schools without encountering resistance or striking accords. In his research on teacher group formation, Kanpol (1991) finds that teachers develop a certain level of "good sense" that resists the totalizing picture of domination found in Bowles and Gintis' analysis. In addition, Kanpol lends empirical evidence and practical support to the otherwise theoretical analysis of resistance popular in critical pedagogy. Searching for a more complete theory of social life and change, CST promulgates ideology critique as well as utopic thinking, without which the nightmare cannot transform into a dream that wants to be realized (see Leonardo, 2003c).

Dreaming is not the idle activity that a realist and positivist schooling discourse may consider a sign of a mind gone awry. In Freire's conversations with Cabral, the revolutionary from Guinea-Bissau discussed the importance of dreaming in the process of real change, punctuating his belief with, "How poor is a revolution that doesn't dream!" (see Darder, 2002, p. 93). Here dreaming is less an idealist, illusory notion and more the necessary projection of the radical imagination. Kincheloe (1993) has suggested that educators can *teach* students literally to dream as part of teacher education courses. Dreaming spurs people to act, if by dreaming we mean a sincere search for alternatives and not the evasion of reality. It is not always an unconscious act, but a metaphor for social intervention that moves the critical social theorist from analysis to commitment. In a colloquium, James Banks lamented the way that schools have co-opted Martin Luther King's radical persona and transformed him into "the dreamer." In my ensuing conversation with Banks, he relates that King's message has become so diluted, some African American students no longer want to hear any mention of the "dream speech." To the extent that King was a radical dreamer, he died for his dreams and spurred on a generation of dreamers. For in the end, dreaming represents the cornerstone of utopia, without which a society lacks direction and a future (see Ricoeur, 1986).

Giroux's (1988) language of possibility is built around the premise that critical education revolves around the capacity to imagine an alternative reality for education. Educators note that Marx's contribution was contained not only in the several volumes of *Capital* where he performs a radical critique of capitalism; equally important were his collaborations with Engels on the notion of scientific socialism (Marx and Engels, 1970). Foucault's (1977) critiques of disciplinary society and the schools to which it gives rise must be understood in the context of his ideas on local resistance, rupturing regimes of truth, then establishing an alternative or counter regime, what Bakhtin (1981) calls a heteroglossic condition without finality (see also Popkewitz, 1998; Martin, 1992a). For Martin (1992b) and with respect to schools, we must excavate the constructions of knowledge, especially when they appear in the guise of objective scientific discourse and the legitimacy of textbooks. Finally, feminists such as Wittig (1993) perform unforgiving critiques of patriarchy and project a social formation where the category "women" (a sex class) would work against "woman" (a social creation). In education, Sadker and Sadker's (1994) sustained assault on the U.S. educational system from primary grades to professorships is based on the hope that critical educators can fight against gender oppression and improve gender relations.

To the casual observer, these authors appear unjustifiably angry, prone to exaggeration, and are wont to point out the dark side of schools and society. To the critical social theorist, however, they represent an "arch of social dreaming and a doorway to hope" (McLaren, 1991). They recognize the many faces of oppression, but acknowledge the history of resistance to dehumanization, from the Underground Railroad to the Combahee Collective. It must be made clear that dreaming of a utopia does not equate with idle fantasy. Utopia is the dialectical counterpart of ideology critique and we can go so far as to suggest that ideology critique contains a kernel of utopia, or the shattering of current reality. For this reason, it is significant that Martin Luther King spoke of a dream and not a fantasy, where the first maintains a continuity with reality by first explaining it and the second is largely out of sync with it. For a critical social theorist, dreaming represents less a wandering consciousness and more a refusal to surrender to despair.

As defined here, a language of transcendence is always a process and not a description of a state of affair. In post-enlightenment strains of CST, Marxism, Deweyan pragmatism, Freudian psychoanalysis, and a host of modernist philosophies have been criticized for their reductivisms, teleologies, and essentialisms. These critics, represented broadly by postmodernists and post-structuralists, fault enlightenment critical theorists for assuming a "true world," for depicting a social life explained by a singular cause, or for promulgating an educational condition that is ultimately knowable and controllable through scientific inquiry (see Leonardo, 2003d). Under this new criticism, critical education is less the search for a particular social arrangement but rather it is coterminous with the very process of criticism itself. That is, the forward motion of criticism is part of the good life. Social life is depicted as a "limit situation" in the Freirean sense, a process that exposes the limits so that they can be transcended. Insofar as emancipatory schooling necessitates posing the possible, critical education also requires a sensibility for the "impossible," of always preparing for the unfinished project of enlightenment (Biesta, 2001). The new criticism has succeeded in complexifying the search for critical education. It builds in a limitless sense of hope without suggesting that real limits do not exist in people's lives. It has broadened our concerns to include reforming educational language and discourse, teaching students to appreciate the politics of representation and production of meaning, and highlighting the narrative structure of educational processes, like curriculum formation.

Within CST, criticism does not surrender the search for emancipation so dear to enlightenment philosophers, but qualifies it as a never-ending process of liberation, of deferred and multiple emancipations. It gives up determinisms and inevitabilities in exchange for a conscious (re)making of the world (Freire, 1998). It is vigilant about oppression and takes its cue from Bell (1992) that racism is likely permanent, not as a pessimistic pronouncement, but as the ultimate act of defiance. In other words, although a socialist educational system may give rise to a condition free of labor exploitation, it cannot guarantee the disappearance of racism or patriarchy. A language of transcendence means that students learn the difference between fighting against oppression and projecting a utopia free of contradictions and strife. For utopia is always haunted by its counter-utopia, or a condition that subverts utopia from ever becoming a reality *once and for all*. Rather, the *idea* of utopia is integral to human and educational progress because it guides thought and action toward a condition that is better than current reality, which is always a projection. In fact, by definition utopia cannot exist. For once it has been realized, utopia graduates to the status of reality and loses its utopic characteristics. Critical education is no less than the search for a language of utopia.

To the extent that CST builds a language of criticism, it depends on a language of engagement with the social world that we make and that makes us. Thus it comes with a certain discourse of hope. Not only does it deploy the politically edgy phrases cited above, but critical social theorists are also accustomed to optimistic phrases, such as "pedagogy of hope" (Freire, 1994), "pedagogy of love" (Darder, 2002), "curriculum for utopia" (Stanley, 1992), "care of the self" (Foucault, 1986), "democracy and education" (Dewey, 1916), "school reform as if democracy matters" (Fraser, 1997), and "women teaching for change" (Weiler, 1994b). Critical social theorists have made it known that critical education is as much about teaching students the ability to read the world more critically (ideology critique) as it is imagining a better world that is less oppressive (utopian critique). For Dewey and Fraser utopia may represent the radical extension of a democracy built around the common good and a vital community over and beyond a form of government. Or as Fraser (1997) describes, the fundamental nature of democracy entails:

> the commitment to equality for all people, the commitment to individual liberty and the right of every citizen to give voice to her/his ideas, and most significant, the commitment to the building up of a better community for all people—beginning in the classroom and extending to the larger society in which the school is located and in which its graduates will live (p. 55).

If this passage smacks of early twentieth century Deweyan sentiments, it is because critical social theorists in education take seriously Dewey's thoughts on direct participation both in schools and society at large.

A pedagogy centered only on critique becomes a discourse of bankruptcy, a language devoid of resistance or agency on the part of students and educators.

In this sense, just as Dewey pronounced that education is not preparation for a future life but is life itself, hope is not a future projection of a utopic society but a constitutive part of everyday life. It is structured into the oppressive arrangements that critical social theorists aggressively analyze because oppressive conditions always produce resistance. Hope represents what Maxine Greene (1988) calls the "dialectic of freedom," which is not a given but a power on which we act responsibly in order to become authors of our own world. In her "search for a critical pedagogy," Greene (1986) insists that we make that search as specific as we can, which suggests that she agrees with Freire who encouraged educators to remake his ideas in the contexts in which they find themselves. Greene's search for a U.S. articulation of critical pedagogy asserts that hope is not only universal but specific to place, time, and culture. In the USA, she argues, it is informed by the broad and inclusive language of Whitman and Thoreau. In short, she suggests that living with difference is part of critical education.

CST is a recent innovation in education. If Freire is its founder and *Pedagogy of the Oppressed* its first text, then it has been around for only three decades. Although Agger (1992) finds it problematic that there are more "students of critical theory" than actual critical theorists, CST seems to be gaining currency across the disciplines. These developments have benefited from earlier preparations at the Frankfurt School and the Birmingham Center for Contemporary Cultural Studies, among others. The field of education has appropriated these insights, which by no means represent the mainstream in educational scholarship. That said, educational scholars from conservatives to radicals have responded to CST, sometimes with outright hostility, other times with healthy skepticism, and occasionally with unspoken advocacy.

An educational movement directed by CST attempts to build on the contributions as well as to address the limitations of its predecessors, one over-emphasizing structures, the other reveling in linguistic play. As Giroux never tired of reminding us, critical educators assist students in mapping the contours of oppression through criticism, a process that entails both a language of critique and hope. Through this double move, critical education fluctuates between the poles of ideology and utopia, exposing the limitations of our social formation and searching for interstices of possibility in institutions and agency in individuals. CST improves the quality of education by encouraging students and teachers to take up personally meaningful choices that lead to liberation. This move is accomplished through the practice of critique and a sense for alternatives, not as separate processes but dialectically constitutive of each other. As a discourse, CST is indeed challenging, but in the fifty years since the Brown decision, it remains to be said that critical education has never been achieved without a fundamental struggle for freedom. If oppression and emancipation are the two main concerns of CST, then its transformative knowledge base should also reflect their full and lived complexity. For answers are only as deep as the questions that educators and students are able to pose. In this sense, critical education is not something that teachers provide *through* CST. Rather, it is the product of a struggle during the pedagogical interaction where both teacher and student play the role of critic. If criticism is done appropriately and authentically, then educators put theory in its proper place within the process of education.

2
Ideology and Race Relations in post-Civil Rights America

In 1996, an edited volume devoted to Stuart Hall's work published the essay, "Gramsci's relevance for the study of race and ethnicity." Central to Hall's analysis (1996c) was Gramsci's deployment of the concept of hegemony. This chapter hopes to accomplish parallel insights on race by going through the concept of ideology as theorized by Althusser. A thoroughgoing and critical theory of ideology is currently missing from race studies in education. When ideology is invoked, it either goes through a Marxist refutation of the racial concept or it is posed as a problem that needs to be transcended rather than a constitutive part of the ideological struggle over race. Just as Hall reminds us that Gramsci's theory of hegemony must be taken in the context of Gramsci's Marxist problematic, this chapter notes that Althusser's theory of ideology must be taken in the context of his commitment to historical materialism. However, in order to analyze the relevance of Althusser's theory of ideology for the study of race (something which did not appear in Althusser's work), I appropriate his insights *sans* his problematic of historical materialism. Althusser's theory of ideology is useful for a study of race, which is as much a problem at the ideological level as it is at the material. Furthermore, Althusser's *discourse* on ideology enriches debates about race to the extent that his *general* insights on ideology are appropriate for such an analysis. In the following explication, I present a brief introduction to the multiple levels of Althusser's theory of ideology. Then, I appropriate his general insights and relevance, determining the most pertinent moments in his theory for the study of race. Last, I pose the problem of color-blind discourses on race.

A Brief Overview of Althusser's Theory of Ideology[1]

Althusser's theory does not represent a single or unified front on the concept of ideology, but rather several strands of his ruminations over some years (McDonnell and Robins, 1980). The theory contains at least four strands and draws from several traditions, from Marx, to Comte and Durkheim (see Ranciere, 1994). That said, Althusser's theory has a center of gravity from which the strands emanate. His first and most fundamental assertion is that ideology is opposed to scientific thinking, or is pre-scientific. This first moment of his critique undergirds the following three moments. Here, Althusser opposes theory to philosophy, the first a scientific undertaking and the second a speculative one. But to Althusser (2003), philosophy is not merely ideological, or the status of "sheer ideological illusion" (p. 257) to which the *The German Ideology* reduces it. It is ideological when it merely creates *new knowledge* based on existing scientific concepts without the development of *new theory*.

Althusser prefers theory over philosophy for the same reasons that Marx once criticized Feuerbach as merely interpreting, rather than transforming, history, but this is not meant to reduce the status of philosophy (and Althusser saw himself primarily as a Marxist philosopher). The task is to set philosophy on its feet, where politics finds its "theoretical expression," (Althusser, 1976, p. 160), and make it harmonious with science. It is in philosophy where the problematic is posed and in science where it is *realized*. Through philosophy, a new "position" is marked, a spatial metaphor that signals a new theoretical practice, the creation of new categories: the epistemological break. Althusser (2003) says, "All these [scientific] problems relative to the conditions for posing difficulties as problems deserve to be posed correctly in their turn. That task falls to philosophy" (p. 278). So here Althusser breaks the traditional opposition between philosophy and science and puts philosophy in its rightful place beside science in a sacred union.

To Althusser (1969), the second moment of ideology belongs to humanism. There are several reasons why humanism is neither politically sound nor scientifically correct. Humanism denies the fact that class struggle is at the forefront of the debate. It substitutes humans as subjects of history for the historical and objective position of the working class in a class-divided society. In fact to Althusser, Feuerbach seems more culpable as a philosopher than Hegel, the more "scientific" of the two and to whom Marx owes a debt for having established the idea of history without a subject (Althusser, 2003, p. 239). On the other hand, Feuerbach's atheist humanism represents something of a philosophical impasse. Feuerbach's humanist essentialism becomes an additional problem of anthropology and not merely of speculation, the former becoming a source of an epistemological obstacle through its insistence on Man rather than social formations or structures.

Althusser posits a third moment of ideology as like-the-unconscious. Ideology is as necessary to sustaining life as breathing and people depend on ideology as a way to make sense, albeit limited, of their lived experiences. Ideology is not an aberration to consciousness, which provides ideology's sense of autonomy, but rather an integral part of it embedded and unrecognized in the unconscious. As Althusser (1971) notes, whereas particular ideologies may have a history, ideology in general has no history and is eternal, like the unconscious. If ideology is a system of representations, of images that people use to create a portrait of the social formation for their own understanding, then ideology, as an imaginary relation, also enables them to imagine an alternative possibility, which is often an alienated form (see Hirst, 1994). In this sense, ideology serves a function despite the fact that it may distort, rather than describe, a reality (Leonardo, 2003b). It contains a practical dimension—the ability of people to construct a worldview—which is different from the theoretical function of producing real knowledge.

For Althusser, the fourth moment of ideology is related to the unconscious through our attempts to represent it in concrete terms. Or in Althusser's (1971) words, "[A]n ideology always exists in an apparatus, and its practice, or practices. This existence is material . . . where only a single subject (such and such an individual) is concerned, the existence of the ideas of his belief is material in that *his ideas are his material actions inserted into material practices governed by material rituals which are themselves defined by the material ideological apparatus from which derive the ideas of that subject*" (pp. 166 and 169; italics in original). In the last instance, ideology has a material basis because it becomes an object *for*, rather than *of*, scientific analysis. In order for Marxists to generate real knowledge *about* ideology, then it must be grounded in an empirical form. Or as Bernard-Donals (1998) puts it, Althusser found that "ideology has simultaneously a discursive/material component and an extra-discursive/material component" (p. 167). In other words, through Althusser we understand that ideology is not only limited to the realm of ideas, but has material underpinnings.

Ideology, Race, and Science: A Love/Hate Relationship

Race-conscious scholars have had a love/hate relationship with science and the scientific enterprise. On one hand, what passes off as science—e.g., eugenics—has been used to justify racial hierarchies (Stepan, 1990; Roberts, 1999). It would be tempting to assert that this mode of thinking is a relic of a cruel past. But Hernnstein and Murray's (1994) revisiting of eugenics-based arguments in their book, *The Bell Curve*, suggests that people, particularly Americans, are still obsessed with scientizing racial categories, especially when it is at the expense of blacks, or more accurately to the advantage of whites. Unlike other conservative scholars who discredit any study of race, Hernnstein and Murray informed the public that "race mattered" but because they accepted its consequences with little ounce of critical reflexivity, they reified the concept rather than demystified it. Despite the authors' mitigating ideas about environmental factors, they reaffirmed an old racist belief that whites (and Asians) are more genetically intelligent than blacks and they went about proving it "scientifically" or under the aegis of science. To Hernnstein and Murray, race was all too real yet their research hardly qualifies as race-conscious work. Scientific taxonomies of race have been guilty of reifying race as real based on physical characteristics (in this case genetics) rather than as social relations based on group power (see Watkins, 2001). For example, earlier the anthropological categories of Caucazoid, Negroid, and Mongoloid races made it possible to line up human remains next to each other and classify them by race based on physical traits. Critical of this development, Franz Boas (2000) and other anthropologists deemed "race" as unscientific and therefore was not the proper domain of anthropological research. This pronouncement had two consequences. First, "culture" graduated to the center of anthropology and now is co-extensive with the discipline itself (see Gonzalez, 2004). Second, Boas' decree was taken to mean that race is meaningless because it was unscientific.

In essence, science legitimated the *meaningfulness* (or lack thereof) of a concept, stigmatizing the study of race as merely ideological and made up, unlike its real counterpart: culture. Race has become an ideological concept without scientific merit, therefore not real. In Part I of a helpful film series on race, "Race: The Power of an Illusion," socio-biologists helped students conduct DNA experiments to jettison the idea that race is genetic if it could be proven that genetic variation within one race was at least as great as variation among racial groups. The analysis left the viewer craving an "ideological" perspective because a scientific one failed to account for the inner workings of race, despite its scientific inaccuracy. That is, if the belief in race is based on spurious (i.e., ideological) notions of genetic inheritance, then it stands to reason that a critical understanding of race requires ideology to explain how it works. The metaphors of "blood," "skin," and "DNA" represent the ligature of race that compels its subjects to believe in its reality, in its solidity. Race was never literally about these things *per se*, but the ontological power to define and distort perception in this new way, of accounting for bodies and then stratifying them (Omi and Winant, 1994). In other words, a scientific discrediting of race (absent of accounting for ideology) is insufficient because the racial mind is hardly scientific; it is ideological. In multiculturalism, this means that a theory of ideology is necessary.

Over the years, white students in education courses on race or multiculturalism have worked hard to maintain their ideological worldview, even in the face of scientific evidence to contradict their perceptions. For example, they have asserted that it is not only reasonable to avoid ghettos and *barrios* out of fear of crime, but that it is ultimately rational to do so for self-preservation. Despite the fact that it is scientifically inaccurate and sociologically insignificant (Winant, 1997) to be victimized as visitors of these spaces, white students mobilize these critiques because they maintain that victimization remains a possibility for them. To many whites, it is not convincing to argue that people who live in ghettos and *barrios* are the main victims of crime in their own neighborhoods, not the unfortunate visitor. That is, higher crime rates are mainly an issue for people of color who live in poor areas, not for the occasional white visitor. Whites might as well play the lottery in hopes of hitting the jackpot. Countering with scientific evidence an ideological mindset that criminalizes people of color becomes an exercise in futility because it does not even touch the crux of the problem, one based in fear and loathing. There is the added irony that blacks are the real victims of ghettoization, of a systematic racial segregation in its *de jure* and *de facto* campaigns orchestrated by whites to destroy the black community and full integration into American society (Massey and Denton, 1993). Blaming people of color for problems they did not create is like blaming the colonies for being underdeveloped and reduced to conditions many people would consider "uncivilized."

The same cannot be said for the fear that people of color feel when confronted with a mainly white neighborhood, *of all class levels*. The history of lynching, both as a white supremacist practice and a form of social control, bears out in a way that victimization of whites in spaces of color does not. For African Americans, lynching is impressed into their consciousness and collective memory. Although traditional lynching occurs much less than it used to, there are many ways to lynch a person. Historical examples of race riots incited by white rage, white mobilization of what Althusser once called the "repressive state apparatuses," like the police, to stamp out even the most peaceful and constitutionally protected expressions of protest, and the subversion of what many Americans would consider basic rights, such as voting, are patterns of treatment that make it rational for people of color to respond with fear and suspicion to their white counterparts. In other words, this fear is sociological and historical, not mainly psychological. For all the science that multiculturalists have at our disposal, there does not seem to be a path around ideology. *For as much as critical theorists have critiqued the ideology of science, we also need a science of ideology.*

This development is not unlike the recent claims of scientific Marxism, which eschews the concept of "race" and opts for "racialism," "racialization," or "racism" (see Miles, 1993). This is a critical point and deserves some attention. Racism, in particular, becomes a subcategory of class exploitation, an oppression not based on race but the antagonisms found in capitalism. In this case, economics—like culture earlier—is the real relation that unseats the four-letter word of race. Everything but racial structures seems to be more appropriate processes for a scientific understanding of the lives of people of color and whites. It would be reasonable to assume that the same argument applies to women when it comes to the equally reified notion of gender. To a race or gender-radical scholar, this becomes a bit of a challenge. In contrast to the Frankfurt School's critique of science as ideology's recent child (see Geuss, 1981), scientific Marxism discredits the concept (indeed the study) of race because it does not inhere objective status. Not only does historical materialism represent the way out of race, but class struggle is the trump card that will eventually make race struggle obsolete. However, it is worth noting that race scholars rarely suggest that race struggle cancels out class struggle. This silence may be explained for two possible reasons. One, much of race scholarship is driven by a bourgeois perspective that makes the problem of capital quite invisible. It could be asserted that race scholars are anti-racist but pro-capitalism, subverting their own claims to race liberation through an unrigorous critique of one of racism's partners-in-crime. Two, race scholars cultivate no illusions about canceling out class struggle through race struggle. In short, they do not posit the end of racism as the signal of the end of class struggle.

Concerning race, scientific Marxism invokes the terms racism, people of color, minorities, racialization, racialism, skin color without reference to the *term* race, despite the fact that it is obvious the *concept* of race is invoked. That is, avoiding the term-race does not guarantee that one is not wrapping one's argument in the concept-race. In fact, this is what Bonilla-Silva (2001) discovers when he interviews white workers about their perceptions concerning their work conditions. Although they seem to avoid any mention of blacks or other people of color, struggle to remain color-blind, and work excruciatingly to stay away from racially insensitive comments, Bonilla-Silva reports that most white respondents said something racially problematic sometime during the interviews. So it seems that scholarship from both the Left and Right share a common suspicion for the concept of race as a power structure or explanatory framework *in its own right*. In the case of the scientific Left, race does not matter either as a relatively independent social relation or a determining principle in the lives of both whites and people of color. It is explainable instead as a reflex of the capitalist mode of production.

In his book, *Althusser's Marxism*, Alex Callinicos (1976) makes the distinction between determining and dominant principles. Whereas many superstructural features, like the political or ideological fields, may be dominant and contribute to the overall complex unity of a mode of production, they are not determining principles. One could deduce that race may be dominant in the social formation but not determining, which is reserved for the economy in the last instance. Following Althusser, ideologies such as race have an autonomous and even material existence but scientifically lack the determinations that one finds in the economy. What seems to need some explaining is the presence of race in several modes of production, such as capitalist, communist, and mixed economies. Although communism certainly removes much of the brutal material basis in the racism from which people of color suffer, it has not succeeded in eradicating racism altogether. In fact, communist regimes have not guaranteed the obsolescence of race and instead intensify other forms of oppression, such as bureaucratic relations and other leadership arrangements. In the USA, Marxists may even blame the race concept for fracturing class solidarity. It is curious to note that a concept becomes the culprit for compromising the class movement: not white working class racism, not the actions of white proletarian leaders to marginalize blacks from full participation in socialist organizations. All of these developments suggest that race does have a determining and autonomous existence that is complexified by and cuts across different economies. We may go so far with Giroux (1997), who says, "As a central form of difference, race will not disappear, be wished out of existence, or somehow become irrelevant in the United State and the larger global context" (p. 294). Said another way, despite its unscientific status, race is a structural formation that maintains an interdependent, co-determining, and heteronomous relation with the economy and other social relations.

That being established, science has been used by sociologists and other social scientists to map out the modes of existence of race despite the fact that the concept was an invention (see Lott, 1999). Countless social scientists from Allen and Farley (1989), to Oliver and Shapiro (1997), Bobo and Kluegel (1993), Snipp (1996), and Bonilla-Silva (1997) have relied on the scientific method to sketch the racial landscape, determine its features, and map out its consequences for whites and people of color. In other words, although race may not be a scientific concept, determining its effects requires the help of science. For instance, it took a racially-critical form of science to debunk eugenics and its ideological corollaries. Althusser's first and most determining moment in his theory of ideology (i.e., that it is unscientific) is an insufficient principle on which to base a theory of racial ideology because it problematically elevates science to the status of a color-blind theodicy. Critical work on race has good reasons to be suspicious of such a move, for it discounts the racial motivations of "scientific research" (Hunter, 2002a).

On that note, radical work on race within multiculturalism cannot forsake ideology or an ideological critique of racial formations. Critical work on race does not only study its real manifestations and deems everything else ghosts of the real; it must critically understand its imaginative (i.e., ideological) dimensions, or how people imagine race in their daily lives. For example, no amount of scientific data will convince white supremacists that racism exists to benefit them and disadvantages people of color. Only an ideological shift makes this change possible, both at the individual and structural level. Racism is not a scientific mindset; on the contrary, it is quite irrational, which does not suggest that it is uncalculated or unpredictable (Feagin, Vera, and Batur, 2001). Racist ideology is driven by fear of, misinformation about, and distance from the other. As a result, science alone seems lacking as a conceptual apparatus to explain a very unscientific racist process. Instead, it requires a thorough ideological understanding of how whites distort certain facts about the world and history. A theory of racial ideology must come to grips with contradictions that seem to defy reason and scientific understanding. However, the discourse of science represents a common and public language that often begins the discussion about what does or does not exist. Race scholars utilize the scientific discourse to support the first premise of race analysis: that it matters in people's lives, that it unequally benefits whites, and that it is as real as its institutions. It is through science that one goes about making a case that a racist formation does exist. Based on these dynamics, race-conscious work must neither elevate nor forsake science.

Race and Humanism: "I Belong to Only One Race, the Human Race"

That race is an illusion is common to humanist interpretations of society. Race was created to impose a detour to a true understanding of a more fundamental human experience. It is a foil used to confuse people that they are humans of a particular skin color rather than human beings with the universal stamp of the species. On this point, there is agreement between humanists and race-conscious intellectuals. Likewise, ethnic affiliation creates cultural divisions between people who would otherwise share political or material interests. In this sense, humanism has been successful in pointing out the limitations in racial or ethnic classifications. However, it has also been used as an ideological tool to derail our understanding of the specificity, the particularity, or the historical nature of relations such as race. Its shortcoming comes from its failure to explain why a society looks *this way* and is organized with *these consequences.* It asserts universal human rights despite race rather than accounting for it. Like humanists, race-conscious intellectuals acknowledge the often arbitrary nature of race and ethnicity, who belongs in a said group, or what it means to be part of a group. Others may even go so far with humanists to consider race as fundamentally divisive, having been created in order to stratify the world according to skin color. In pursuit of Althusser's theory of ideology, we are warranted to ask: "If race has real effects, how can it merely be false? How is it merely illusory?" To the extent that race produces real effects, it accomplishes its task through allusion as much as illusion. It alludes to real processes that impact various groups in different and unequal ways.

Humanist ideology cannot explain why the structures of modern race evolved out of the colonial period and capitalist expansion because it regards "skin color experience" as something other than "human experience" rather than considering *skin color as an organizing principle for society as a whole.* In this sense, Althusser's second critique of humanist ideology is applicable for a study of race because it exposes humanism's inability to deal effectively with the "race question." Because it projects Man as the primary element of its problematic, humanism forsakes the valuable critique of racial formations or structures. With respect to gender relations, this humanist fallacy has been pointed out (see Weedon, 1997). *Race and racism are not at all about humans; they are struggles among racial groups.* In its rush to assert the universal human, humanism neglects the particular and racialized human, which it considers a block to accessing true human experience.

Humanism's search for an originary, or genetic, human experience, is quickly betrayed when, upon deconstruction, human experience appears cultural or racial (usually Euro-centric or white) and not universal. So what initially appears as general becomes a front for the universalization of a particular racialized experience, which is the lynchpin of humanist ideology. Transforming an event into something "human" when it is racial in nature has been a staple of white humanism's inability to come to terms with people of color's concrete experience. On the concept of origin, which has religious roots in *filiation* (i.e., tracking), Althusser (2003) has this to say:

> [O]ne has at last sighted the guilty party, the Originary Individual; he has been identified, he makes "tools" of some unspecified sort, he lives in groups: *he's the one, all right. We've got him this time.* It is enough to "tail"[*filer*] him, to track him, not to lose sight of him, since one is sure that at the end of this manhunt [*filature*], one will rediscover both the *1844 Manuscripts* and *Capital*! (p. 294; italics in original).

This genetic penchant in humanism makes it difficult to engage the structural conditions of a racialized society that constructs specific humans, such as whites and blacks. In fact, this is perhaps the most difficult aspect of teaching about race. Many whites as well as people of color who identify with whiteness find it difficult to accept that racism is mainly a white problem. They are either more accepting of and accustomed to the claim that racism is a human tragedy (therefore everyone's problem), or worse, that people of color impede their own social advancement. By saying this, one notices that humanist-minded students are no longer using race analysis, the first premise of which is that life looks quite different for whites compared to people of color. If we follow this line of argument, then racism is simply not a "race problem" anymore but a "human problem." Racism is redefined as any form of hatred based on race, regardless of its effects. It is assumed that structural white racism in the post-Civil Rights era has been all but erased/eraced. Martin Luther King's speech is reduced to his utopia without his critique (Toji, personal communication). Compared to the slave and Jim Crow eras, racism today has a human face (pick your group), not a white one. Forty years after the Civil Rights Movement, racist America has finally rid itself of this blemish in its history, this shameful 250 years of slavery and 100 years of Jim Crow, this embarrassing contradiction in American "democracy." Interpersonal racial attitudes have improved over time and it is time now to move on to bigger and better things: American humanization.

Cynicism aside, Althusser clearly saw the limitations of humanism and anticipated the poststructural movement that took humanism to task for its inability to explain why humans labor under specific conditions. Regarding race, race-conscious people also recognize the possibility of human experience before or after the concept of race, but they are dogged by the constant reminders of the complete racialization of daily life. Race-conscious scholars may be "against race" (Gilroy, 2000), that is, *anti*-race, but they may find it difficult to be *ante*-race. Trying to recapture a time before race after centuries of racialization is like trying to remember how a conversation *in medias res* got started in the first place. Too much has been said and too much has been done. The task is grounded less in escaping such vicissitudes of a race-based society and more in confronting their limitations, explaining why they exist, and countering their negative effects through rigorous examination. Because a misinformed humanism does not contain within its discourse a sufficient race critique, it bypasses an explanatory framework that many "humans" use to make sense of their lives. Moreover, humanism thwarts its own goals of achieving complete humanization when it fails to confront and help dismantle those structures responsible for the dehumanization of people in the first place: in this case, institutional racism.

As an organizing principle, race is the justification of an entire social edifice, from schooling, to jobs, to marriage. It is not only or mainly, according to Bonilla-Silva (2001), a relation of attitudes between individuals. This problematic sentiment is common enough and leads some people to assume that every group is an equal opportunity racist because whites do not have a monopoly on racial animosity. Rather, race is a structure in which these attitudes become meaningful, which otherwise are not meaningful in themselves; in other words, the racial structure gives them meaning. It is a process of marking, of hailing human subjects into the racial formation as subjects of its apparatuses, such as schools. The humanist ideology conveniently forgets that in a racist society, asserting humanity by default means asserting whiteness since whites seem to represent what it means to be human; the same can be said for men, heterosexuals, and the bourgeoisie. Textbooks, the media, government, and civilization in general all bear the marks of whiteness, which begin to suggest that "human" equates with "white," as Victor Lewis reminds us so eloquently in the film "Color of Fear." In fact, the humanist argument or liberal insistence on individuality becomes a form of rationalization for the way a society is racially structured since it fails to analyze social organization in terms of group interests. This does not suggest that humanists do not recognize the existence of racism, even at the structural level. But its discursive universe does not define the problematic as a question of structure but one of humanization. And as long as humanist ideology, according to Althusser, defines the goal as a perpetual search for Man's essence (filiation) rather than the continuous development of social structures, then it becomes difficult to combat the strongest investment in race via group affiliation.

Humanization is no doubt the goal, if by that we mean a more free or less oppressive society. A more humanizing education system, a more humanizing society, and approaching students' full humanity—these are all worthwhile endeavors. But these goals cannot be accomplished before the ethical imperative of "doing the right thing." That is, whites have not been able to relinquish their racial privileges because it is the humanizing thing to do for others, let alone that they also become humanized in the process. Fighting against racism is galvanized less by a humanist sentimentality and more by an ethical imperative, in Kant's sense of it. Anti-racism is not a commitment because one *gains* in human terms, although this certainly is a product of it. For whites, it actually means *losing* their position in the racial structure, of giving up their lion's share of resources. Ultimately, this is also Althusser's bone of contention with humanism: its penchant for individual improvement, whether this individual is represented by the person or as a metaphor for humanity at large. Meanwhile, in the case of race, it misrecognizes the racial formation and how it *functions*, how it subverts solidarity across races, and how humanism makes it difficult to define human experience without the qualifiers white, black, Latino, Asian American, Native American, or Arab. Althusser's second moment in his theory of ideology is quite applicable for a study of race and multiculturalism because it exposes the racial evasions in humanism. It suggests that far from being the autonomous reasoning individual, the subject of racial formations is motivated by the interpellations of its structures. Being human in a racial formation is inescapably bound up with being part of a racial group and subject to its shifting, intersecting, but determining effects.

Racial Ideology and the Unconscious: "I don't have a Racist Bone in my Body but . . ."

Althusser's third moment—that ideology is largely unconscious—is arguably the most resonating and most relevant portion of Althusser's theory for the study of race and racism. It has been suggested that racism (and therefore race) seems to have a permanent status (see Bell, 1992), not unlike the unconscious for Althusser. For example, if we survey American racial history, we note transmutations and transformations in race and racism but would not receive the general impression that they are about to go away. In fact, there is little to suggest that race is declining in significance, to William Julius Wilson's (1978) chagrin. In the USA, we have entered a new racial predicament since 9/11, where religious race (in conjunction with skin color race) complexifies our racial categories and meanings. In the face of all these developments, one would be hard pressed to show optimism that race and its problem of racism will one day diminish; instead they assume the guise of foreverness. Althusser (2003) writes:

> Only a "subject presumed to exist" is ever interpellated—provided with his identity papers so that he can prove that he is indeed *the* subject who has been interpellated. Ideology functions, in the true sense of the word, the way the police function. It interpellates, and provides the interpellated subject with/asks the interpellated subject for his identity papers, without providing its identity papers in return, for it is *in the Subject-uniform* which is its very identity (p. 55; italics in original).

The ideology of race and its concomitant discourses interpellate *every* human individual into the racial formation. She is signified and brought into the racial universe, which gives her a racial label, white or otherwise. Of course, this is not a literal process of hailing someone down the street, but an unconscious hailing that is part of self-recognition, or misrecognition to be more precise. Once the hailing begins and provides racialized subjects with their identity, it never fails to record a response, "Here I am!" This process does not yet speak to the eventual goal of eradicating race—which is a possibility I discuss in Chapter 4—but points to the difficult task of countering racial identification.

Consistent with Althusser's theory, the more rigorous social scientists become in their systematic understanding of racial stratification and institutions, the larger the ideological field of racial common sense becomes. As the criteria for a systematic understanding of race become more precise (e.g., what it is or is not), the field of distortions becomes more comprehensive. As race, especially its commonsensical meanings, takes hold of more people, they begin to define their experience through reified notions of race, such as "it is about blood, genes, or biology." It becomes the ubiquitous but unexamined marker. Race is an intimate part of how people represent/understand themselves and others. Racial ideology may distort their scientific understanding of social life, but it also functions for people in a daily way, and not always in a positive sense. It gives them a threshold for comfort as they choose their friends, decide where they want to live, and deliberate on who is or is not moral. The *collective racial unconscious* includes even the most "enlightened" person who presumes to think "outside" of race. For *racial ideology has no outside* and the person or society immersed in race cannot think outside of it, which represents the racialization of reality and the realization of race. Either a society is completely racialized or it is not; there is no such thing as "a little bit racialized" or "this or that nation is more racialized than another." South Africa is not more racialized than China; Sweden is not less racialized than the United States. They are all racialized societies, but race has assumed a particular form in each of their history, Apartheid in one and Jim Crow in the other. Since racialization and white supremacy have reached global proportions (Mills, 2003), it is becoming impossible to find pockets of non-racialized societies. There is no island on which Robinson Crusoe could land.

The unconscious nature of racial ideology is especially pertinent when discussing racism. The racist is always the other, never the self; another society, never one's own. A racist, even the most rabid, rarely admits or recognizes that he is racist. It produces an ironic condition of "racism without any racists" (see Bonilla-Silva, 2003) since racism is like a flatulent that someone else always releases in the room. The first realization a race thinker confronts is that all but a few whites admit to their racism. Groups who appear as "obvious" candidates of white supremacy invert reality by claiming to be victims of "reverse racism." Rather than indict white advantage, white supremacists indict people of color for wanting too large a share of the "American pie." In this section of the chapter, I would like to discuss the role that white women play in the maintenance of racism: particularly, through discourses on affirmative action, interracial dating and marriage, and racial politics of sexuality. White men's racial atrocities are well-documented, but as a result, they have become alibis for a more general white supremacy. Less is known generally about white women's racism although critiques of feminists of color have made them more visible (see Mohanty, 1988; hooks, 1984; Anzaldua, 1999). In the case of white women who oppose affirmative action, they claim that it disadvantages them as white people. With respect to white mothers of mixed race children, this decision goes against their very own children's structural chances for advancement. First, this belief is belied by the fact that white women have been one of the largest beneficiaries of affirmative action policies (Tatum, 1997; Marable, 1996). When they oppose such corrective mechanisms, they subvert their own personal (immediate) interests as women while acting in accordance with (long-term) racial supremacy. They are involved in a performative contradiction and in the process unwittingly show us their racial cards. Second, this dynamic dispels notions of white women's innocence from racism based on the belief that they are oppressed by patriarchy and therefore share interests with other oppressed people, that is, their oppressed status gives them epistemic privilege.

The racial interpellation of white women is a feminized form of racism that complexifies the patriarchal myth of women as protectors of the family, captured in the saying "blood is thicker than water." That is, it is assumed that women choose family first. Because racism makes sense only in the context of group interest, white mothers of mixed-race children are torn between race and family (Horton and Sykes, 2004). As split subjects, they may vacillate between the two poles. If blood is thicker than water, then sometimes *skin is thicker than blood.* At crucial junctures where white power is threatened, such as the debate over affirmative action, white mothers of mixed-race children could just as easily choose race over family, identifying with the former rather than the latter. This largely unconscious act is motivated by supra-individual desires, which does not suggest that white women do not know what they are doing. They may not know the extent of their participation in racism, but they are not dupes of it either. As investors in race, they know that their decisions matter, whether or not they understand the implications. As interpellated racial subjects, white women indeed answer the call but record different responses than white men. In other words, they occupy a different post in the racial army as whites defend the territory, real and imagined.

Because racism assumes a gendered form, white women play a distinct role in promoting their race, usually through the detour of mothering. It may appear in the form of discouraging their children away from inter-racial dating in efforts to "protect" them from the criticisms and challenges that await them. Here we note the racial unconscious at work through the detour of "caring." The critique does not suggest that white women are less caring than before, but that this caring contains racial contradictions. White mothers who discourage their children from interracial dating or miscegenation reassert the ideological purity of whiteness through the purity of "blood." Such forms of caring are a result of patriarchy to the extent that women have been socially constructed and have evolved as the caring gender. But because this process occurs in the context of race and racism, it contains racial dimensions. On the surface, the scenario appears like an instance of choosing family over race, of protecting one's child. But a closer look reveals some contradictions.

Choosing one's partner is one of the most important choices that adults make and, along with career choice, is definitive of a person's level of happiness. Protecting the family suggests that the child's ability to gauge with whom he will share his happiness is promoted, thereby increasing the overall happiness of the family unit with the assumption that all concerns but race are favorable. When this choice is thwarted because of race, resentment and guilt usually occur. Protecting a child from the "pain" of interracial dating or miscegenation overlooks the richness of two different worlds coming together, exposing the reified notion of racial coupling, a process which has different purposes for different races. Furthermore, it exposes the myth and ideology of love when race complexifies the match. It is a popular belief that people marry their "soul mate." When inter-racial dating and marriage are discouraged, a large portion of the dating world is outside the field of consideration. This condition is hardly conducive to finding one's soul mate.

Objectification is not only a matter of gender relations under patriarchy, it is also a racial problem. When white women objectify men of color, they participate in the upkeep of white supremacy. Often, they are informed by the assumption that sexual comments about men cannot be branded problematic in the context of patriarchy and existing power relations between men and women. Although this distinction is important, it also shows white women's racial consciousness. In other words, to some white women, *sexual comments only concern gender.* They fail to notice that although their comments are not sexist, they are both racial and racially problematic. That is, they are examples of feminized forms of racism and recall the centuries of sexual domination and manipulation of men *and* women of color by white men *and* women. They are evidence of white women's ability to assert their racial privilege and power through sexuality even in the face of their own sexual oppression. Moreover, white women's objectification of bodies of color represents an instance of their solidarity with one another as racialized subjects. White sisterhood shares something with white men through their unconscious collaboration in racial supremacy, but the former takes on a specific historical appearance that differs from the latter. On this point, men of color have been reticent to enter the fray over the gendered articulations of racism, perhaps out of fear of appearing gendered in the process. However, the entrance of men of color into a critique of gender/race ideology is important because it represents their solidarity with women of color, as bell hooks (1984) reminds us.

Following Lacan's extension of Freud, Althusser reminds us that although we cannot directly experience the unconscious, it exists through its effects—in the discourses of everyday life, experience, and dreams. It would be too much to claim that the unconscious is real, but its effects are as real as the dream is to the dreamer. To the extent that racial ideology, like the unconscious, is not real, its modes of existence or manifestation are real (see also Macdonell, 1986). The racial unconscious produces functions, one of which Althusser (2003) calls the "subject-function" (p. 53), which produces a "subjectivity-effect" (p. 48). The ideology of race has produced racial discourses that recruit racialized subjects who find their sense of self through them. Althusser (2003) explains, "It solves the problem evoked in the old complaint of military men—what a pity soldiers are recruited only among civilians—because the only soldiers it ever recruits are already in the army. For ideological discourse, there are no civilians, only soldiers, that is, ideological subjects" (p. 55). A racial formation only recruits from its citizens, which by default are the only candidates for racial subjects. Racial subjectivity is fundamentally unconscious because it always leaves a bit of itself unbeknownst to its subject. Racialism is always a remainder. And as the standards for a critical reading of race increase, more of the social field succumbs to racial ideology. That is, it engulfs its subjects to the point that they no longer imagine a non-racialized horizon. Even when they resist race at every turn, it betrays them in the end.

Ideology and Racial State Apparatuses: "Race is Real, Race Ain't Real"

Ample controversy has been thrown into the cauldron of race concerning its status. To the extent that race as a concept is not real, its modes of existence are real. Its racial subjects are real; likewise, schools, the workplace, and families are institutional forms of race. There is good reason to believe that race is not a scientific concept, which is not reason enough to reject its study but necessitates a multiple framework that includes ideological and materialist perspectives. As opposed to production, for which Marx found a suitable language to attach, race was an invention originating in the Occident. Unlike production, which humans did not have to create but discovered, race was invented in order to accomplish certain social goals. In order to rationalize their place in the world and then justify the treatment of others, white Europeans invented a classification system that put people of darkest skin tones at the bottom of the human hierarchy and lightest at the top. This position makes inequality central to the concept of a racial order and questions the notion that racial orders exist because of the mere presence of racial difference. Bonilla-Silva (2001) clarifies, "[W]e can speak of racial orders only when a racial discourse is accompanied by social relations of subordination and superordination among the races" (p. 42). The ideology of race was born and spurred on the development of the world in a direction that its creators could not have anticipated. It is in this sense that enables us to forward the thesis that race is not real because whites gave it an existence it did not already have. To the extent that monsters are not real, the giant we call race is likewise unreal. It is tempting to respond that the "race is real or not real" debate is energy not well spent, that it circumvents the more important work to be done describing how race functions and how racism can be subverted if not eradicated. However, defining correctly the conceptual status of race is part of unseating whiteness, depending on how race-conscious scholars set the terms of the debate over race.

That race is an ideology has led to the conclusion that it is not worthy of invoking because doing so further reifies what is already unreal. In that case, David Duke's sense-making of race is just as problematic as Cornel West's, each taking a different bite of the fruit from the same rotten tree. But just as Althusser warns against reducing philosophy to the status of mere ideological illusion, so we can say that race cannot be reduced to mere chimerical status devoid of material underpinnings. For example, as a racial state apparatus (RSA), school is a material institution where race takes place, where racial identity is bureaucratized/modernized, where people are hailed as racialized subjects of the state. In schools, teachers take roll as they hail students in homeroom as much as teachers hail them to answer when their race is called. Schools usually never fail to receive an answer for either one. It is one important place where race takes on an empirical form: from tracking practices, to resource disparities, to different rates of achievement. Therefore, race has material underpinnings and cannot be reduced only to ideological status (in the classical sense), or relegated to the realm of pure ideality.

Be that as it may, race-conscious work engages the ideological dimensions of race and links them to the material world and its racial organization. It is not based on skin color *simpliciter* but more accurately on the racialized imagination, of how *skin groups* exist and are reinvented over and over again. For example, through miscegenation and race mixing some African Americans are lighter skinned than South or South East Asians, but the American ideology of race neither constructs South and South East Asians as black nor do darker skinned Indians, for example, consider themselves black for that matter. The racial imagination, or the ideological process, is largely responsible for these group assignments. Even Bonilla-Silva (2001), whose structural model arguably approaches most closely the Althusserian paradigm of race studies, did not avoid the ideological dimension when he reports white workers' racial attitudes towards blacks, an ideology that serves practical functions. Bonilla-Silva (2001) favors a materialist examination of race relations and:

> reserve[s] the term *racial ideology* for the segment of the ideological structure of a social system that crystallizes racial notions and stereotypes. Racial ideology provides the rationalization for social, political, and economic interactions among the races (p. 43; italics in original).

Consequently, material institutions and their resources are modes of existence of an ideological process that requires a deep racial sensibility if undoing them remains a possibility.

Althusser's multi-pronged analysis of ideology is perhaps his greatest contribution to Marxist studies of society. Although not without its problems in the form of structural overdetermination and some theoretical excess, Althusser forged a discourse on ideology unmatched in recent debates. His thoughts represent a watershed in the debate between the real and ideological, representing genuine insights on their synthetical and recursive relationship with each other. Although a materialist in the last instance, Althusser always considered the ideologico-political battle as important theoretical and practical nodes in the warfare against bourgeois philosophy and capitalism. I have attempted to import his general findings for a study of race and ethnicity in order to illuminate the ideological contours of our current racial and cultural formation. I found that the third moment of Althusser's theory of ideology—a deployment of Lacan's theory of the imaginary and the unconscious—most directly intersects the racial problematic. It projects a clear picture of how racial ideology actually functions or works on a daily basis. Although we must mitigate the thesis that racial ideology is *completely* unconscious, to use Althusser's language, *racial ideology is unconscious in the last instance.* The three other moments in Althusser's theory provide supporting discourses to the third moment, lending the theory a sense of cohesion rather than unity. As the land of racial understanding becomes more solid, the sea of racial mystifications spreads. This is not meant to be a pessimistic statement about the future status of race and its hirsute companion, racism. On the contrary, it projects the importance of critical reflection over race and the strength of the ideological effort that such a process requires.

3
Marxism and Race Analysis
Toward a Synthesis

So far, I have shown how race and class analysis could be used together to generate insights on the nature of social oppression and liberatory interventions. In doing so, I have not explained the precise and intimate relationship between the two frameworks. In educational theory, orthodox Marxism is known for its commitment to objectivism, or the science of history. On the other hand, race analysis has been developed in its ability to explain the subjective dimension of racial oppression. The two theories are often at odds with each other. This chapter is an attempt to create a theory by integrating Marxist objectivism and race theory's focus on subjectivity. This suggests neither that Marxism neglects the formation of subjectivity nor that race theory ignores material relations. It is a matter of emphasis and the historical development of each discourse. In attempting to integrate them, intellectuals recognize their frequent appearance on the historical stage together. As a result, both Marxism and race analysis are strengthened in a way that maintains the integrity of each discourse. This benefits educational theory because praxis is the dialectical attempt to synthesize the inner and external processes of schooling.

Heidi Hartmann (1993) once argued for a more progressive union in the "unhappy marriage" between Marxism and feminism. Along the same lines, this chapter argues for a similar union between race and class analysis in education. Often, when Marxist orthodoxy takes up the issue of race, it reduces race relations to the status of a reflex within class dynamics. In short, orthodox Marxism economizes the concept of race and the specific issues found within themes of racial identity, development, and representation become subsumed in modes of production, the division of labor, or worse, as an instance of false consciousness. On the other hand, when race analysis takes up class issues, it sometimes accomplishes this by reifying race as something primordial or fixed, rather than social and historical. Indeed, in the social science literature there is both a general consensus that race amounts specifically to skin color stratification with black and white serving as the litmus test for other groups and more generally as a proxy for "group" that includes any social identity under the sun, which could be construed as a race. The former perspective has been criticized for its dichotomizing tendencies whereas the latter is guilty of too expansive of a definition of race. Moreover, uncritical engagement of class issues within race discourse fails to incorporate the historical explanations found in Marxism and ends up projecting the "naturalness" or "foreverness" of racial categories. In this chapter, I attempt to maintain the conceptual integrity of both Marxist and race discourses through a synthesis of their strengths, the first a material, objective analysis, the second through an analysis of subjectivity, or how the historical conditions of class are lived in existentially racial ways. In order to advance the theoretical understanding of educational analysis, I will pursue the historical and conceptual integration of race and Marxist discourse.

It is now a well-acknowledged social scientific fact that class status remains one of the strongest, if not the strongest, predictor for student achievement. In short, there is a positive correlation between the class status of a student's family and that student's success in schools. The higher the student's family class status, the higher the chances for school success. It is also an equally well-acknowledged fact that people of color disproportionately comprise the working class and working poor groups when compared to their white counterparts. In schools, Latino and African American students face the interlocking effects of racial, economic, and educational structures. From the outset, this establishes the centrality of both class and race analysis concerning school outcomes and policies designed to address them (Leonardo, 2003e).

The field of orthodox Marxist studies is dominated by the elucidation of the objective conditions of capital at the expense of the subjective, or ideological, dimensions of race within capitalism. It covers racism, not as a field of contestation among racial groups for power, but as an ideological distraction from the inner workings of capitalism. In short, racism is not at all about race but capital. With the advent of western Marxism, especially under the influence of Lukacs' (1971) humanism, Gramsci's (1971) notion of a cultural revolution, and Frankfurt critical theory, Marxist concepts about subjectivity came to the fore. In contrast, in race theory analysis of the subjective experience of race has been developed at least as much as studies that map its institutional, material basis. Du Bois' (1989) concept of "double consciousness" and Fanon's (1967) psychology of race are invoked as widely as talks of institutional "discrimination" or "segregation." Du Bois' search for the "souls of black folk" signals his concern for the subjective existence of a people whose worth is "measured by the tape of another world" through a school system that denies their true participation as intellectual citizens. Similarly, Fanon's journey into the essence of the black psyche, or his appropriation of Aimé Césaire's concept of negritude, finds this subjectivity routed through the distorting effects of a colonial education. Orthodox Marxism is conceptually silent on these issues because it brackets the subjective in order to explain the objective, much the same way Piaget brackets the objective to explain the subjective development of the child (Huebner, 1981). Marrying Marx with Piaget, Huebner introduces a brand of "genetic Marxism" as a way to bridge the objective and subjective correlates of history. It is through this synthesis that critical pedagogists arrive at the political economy of curricular knowledge. Huebner does not address the racial form of genetic Marxism but he is instructive in addressing the blind spots of orthodox Marxism and Piagetian epistemic theory. The marriage between objective and subjective analysis represents the cornerstone of educational praxis since at least as far back as Dewey.

Links between Orthodox Marxism and Race Critique

In the field of educational theory it is apparently unfashionable to revisit Bowles and Gintis' (1976) original insights because of the assumption that theoretical knowledge has advanced beyond their conceptual monism. The return to Bowles and Gintis is a fashionable *faux pas* as out of step as disco is in today's dance clubs, although one can expect the Gap clothing company to exploit it for nostalgia. In addition, with the popularity of various post-ism's, post-al's, or posties, Marxist structuralism appears imperialistic and conceptually flawed by its determinisms. Raymond Williams (1977) puts it best when he says that Marxism without determinations is a useless theory, but, were it to retain them in their current forms, Marxism would become a crippled intervention. That said, Marxist resiliency seems alive and well, judging from McLaren's (2000) reinvigoration of it in his book on Che Guevara and Paulo Freire; *Cultural Logic*, an online education journal dedicated to the vision of Marx; and a *Village Voice* online article's claim that despite the marginalization of Marxism in academe, it maintains a privileged status as a revolutionary explanation and intervention. The neo-conservative, neo-liberal, and postmodern attempts to displace the global critique of capitalism seems only to reinvigorate Marxist commitments to a perspective that responds with a vengeance, much like a boomerang that returns to hit its thrower in the face (see Buroway, 2000; San Juan, Jr., 1999; Eagleton, 1996; Ebert, 1996; Harvey, 1989). No doubt, post-Marxism would be more attractive in a world of post-exploitation. But for now, Marxism is, like blue jeans, refusing to fade away.

Under the structuralist wing of orthodox Marxism schools are said to reproduce the social relations of labor through the correspondence between school and work structures (Bowles and Gintis, 1976). Schools neither add to nor take away from economic inequality at large; they reproduce labor relations through homology. Like a factory, schools welcome students as inputs to the juggernaut of capitalism, where they learn dispositions necessary for the reproduction of capital, then leave the school site 12 years or so later as outputs of the system. Bowles and Gintis share Althusser's (1971) theory of the reproduction of the relations of production. They provide an innovation within Marxist theory by emphasizing the state apparatuses' ability to reproduce the division of labor, not so much through material processes but through ideology. Although critiques of reproduction theory abound, this fact does not refute that it occurs (Leonardo, 2000a).

Students take their place in the work world and the economico-educational process that puts them there is depicted as relatively smooth and uninterrupted. Although they differ in their orientation toward economic determinism, such that Althusser believes the superstructure rebounds and affects the economic infrastructure (i.e., overdetermines it), Bowles and Gintis and Althusser commit to the science of Marxism, earlier defined by Lukacs (1971) as the "scientific conviction that dialectical materialism is the road to truth" (p. 1). Dubbed as "critical functionalism" by Carnoy and Levin (1985), Bowles and Gintis' correspondence principle differs from the functionalism of Durkheim (1956, 1973) and Dreeben (1968) insofar as Bowles and Gintis are critical of capitalist structures and the general division of labor. However, critical functionalism shares a common conceptual assumption with structural functionalism to the extent that both discourses assume schools serve a predetermined social function. Although Bowles and Gintis focus on the school as their primary unit of analysis (a superstructural feature), they privilege the industrial labor force as the necessary, causal mechanism that gives form to school structures. It is for this reason that their perspective belongs to Marxist orthodoxy.

The role of race or racial groups in orthodox class analysis is significant but secondary, at best. The racial experiences of African Americans, Latinos, and Asian Americans are determined by the economy, reduced to reflex status, and fragmented by the effects of ideology. As Bowles and Gintis (1976) observe, "Blacks certainly suffer from educational inequality, but the root of their exploitation lies outside of education, in a system of economic power and privilege in which racial distinctions play an important role" (p. 35). It would be a mistake to conclude that the authors trivialize the structures of race and racism; as Bowles and Gintis say, they play a "role." But as in a play, race and racism are not the star of the show. In effect, Bowles and Gintis conceptually dissolve race into class relations, a move common to other Marxists not necessarily from the Bowles and Gintis school of thought. Other Marxists may be more graceful in their uptake of race but nevertheless share Bowles and Gintis' problematic and commitments. It becomes clear that race relations are products, effects of, and determined by the objective laws of economic processes. Though not usually perceived as a Marxist, Oakes (2005) later modifies this position through her studies of tracking by suggesting that "school matters." She finds that the institutional practice of tracking exacerbates, at times creates, class *and* race differences. She confirms Cornel West's (1994) simple but straightforward contention that "race matters." From this, we can infer that working class students of color face "double jeopardy" as they confront the specific interlocking conditions of class exploitation and racial stratification. Orthodox Marxist analyses of schooling pay respect to race as an important "distinction," but not a decisive, certainly not a determining, one. Thus, they forsake the racial concepts that would otherwise help students make sense of their racialized class experiences.

The racialized experience, while possessing an objective character because it finds its form in material relations, strengthens the subjective understanding of class relations. In effect, race is a mode of how class is lived (Hall, 1996b). As such, class is lived in multiple ways, one of them being racial. Students of color, like many scholars of color, find it unconvincing that they are experiencing only class relations when the concepts used to demean and dehumanize them are of a racial nature. As Fanon (1967) finds, "A white man addressing a Negro behaves exactly like an adult with a child and starts smirking, whispering, patronizing, cozening" (p. 31). Thus, it is not only understandable but reasonable that the orthodox branding of the racial imagination as "false consciousness" does not sit well with non-white subjects. It occludes white power and privilege, and the interests that maintain them. It is conceptually misleading as well.

In Ladson-Billing's (1998) studies of colonial education from "Soweto to South Bronx," African Americans experience daily psycho-cultural assaults that cannot be explained purely through economism because it does not propose a convincing explanation as to why African Americans and other students of color should be the targets of deculturalization (see also Spring, 2000). This has led Fanon (1963) to the conclusion that "Marxist analysis should always be slightly stretched every time we have to do with the colonial problem" (p. 40). Fanon's (1967) endorsement of Marxist critique is very clear when he says:

> If there is an inferiority complex, it is the outcome of a double process:
> —primarily, economic;
> —subsequently, the internalization—or, better, the epidermalization—
>   of this inferiority (p. 11).

Stretching the conceptual tendons of orthodox Marxism makes it flexible in accommodating the subjective experience of students of color as they navigate through an educational system hostile to their worldview. Although Fanon was speaking of the decolonization struggle during the 1950s, his insights are valid today because internal colonies like ghettos, *barrios*, and reservations bear the material and psycho-cultural marks of colonial education within a nation that daily reminds their subjects of the rightness of whiteness.

Like Hartmann's (1993) charge that orthodox Marxism's conceptual universe is "sex blind," one can lay a similar charge that it is also "color blind." Marxism lacks the conceptual apparatus to explain who exactly will fill the "empty places" of the economy. Its discursive structure does not provide compelling reasons for women's relegation to housework or non-white over-representation in the working class, buttressed by an educational system that appears to reproduce the dispositions for such a sorting of workers. Regardless of their class status, students of color show an incredible amount of resilience in an educational process that undervalues their history and contribution. Economic analysis conveniently forgets that when labor organizes itself into a subject of history, this subject is often constructed out of the white imagination

(Roediger, 1991). In other cases, white labor organizes to subvert the interests of people of color, as in the case of the Irish choosing their whiteness alongside their working class interests, elbowing out blacks for industrial jobs. It is a sense of naturalized entitlement that white laborers, even against the objective and long-term interests of the white working class, choose whiteness in order to preserve their subjective advantage, or what Du Bois (1998) calls whites' "public and psychological wages" (cited in Roediger, 1991). White skin advantage is so pervasive, it is well-represented even within non-white communities. Hunter (2005, 1998) finds that the "lighter the berry" the more privileges one garners, such as higher rates of education and status. In addition, lighter skin-toned African American and Mexican American women bear the privilege of being regarded as beautiful, as in the case of *la güera*, or "fair skinned." Here, "fair" takes on the double entendre of light and pretty. Of course, the point should be clear that they are not regarded as white subjects, but approximations of whiteness.

Race theory is not the only discourse to critique orthodox Marxism. With the development of neo-Marxist educational theory, Marxist economism becomes a target of cultural materialism. Arising out of the conceptual space that emphasizes the superstructure rather than the base in historical materialism, neo-Marxists like Bourdieu (1977, 1984) and Lareau (2000, 2003) mobilize concepts, like "cultural capital" and "*habitus*," to explain the conversion of economic capital to cultural practices that favor the life chances of middle to upper class students. Here, the focus is less on the objective structures of labor and more on the rituals and cultural repertoire that reify class privileges. Said another way, neo-Marxism is concerned with cultural reproduction in schools rather than the social reproduction previously described by Bowles and Gintis. Thus, a latent correspondence principle is still at work and discursively in place, this time with culture as the operating principle. For example, Lareau documents the difference in school participation between modestly middle and upper middle class parents. Appropriating Bourdieu's framework, Lareau finds that among other consequences, modestly middle class parents lack both the institutional confidence and cultural pedigree to influence the school bureaucracy during school activities, like Open House or parent–teacher conferences. In contrast, upper middle class parents possess the cultural repertoire and resources that position their children in advantageous ways in school, such as the academic ability to help them with homework or having the occupational credentials that put them well above teachers in terms of status. Such an innovation provides scholars information about a much-ignored group within Marxist theory: the middle class, broadly speaking. Because public schools serve mostly working and middle to upper class students, the cultural relationship between the "have some" and "have not" becomes an important site of understanding.

By and large, "the haves" send their children to private schools and thus do not interact with their working and middle class counterparts. Bourgeois parents do not directly work with working or middle class people because they have associates they can deploy to deal with management concerns. As a result, everyday interactions in public schools and other public places are waged between working and middle class families, and the Bill Gates of the world can afford (or pay) to avoid the fray. Thus, they become even more abstract to the working and middle class. In short, the capitalist class remains out of sight, out of mind. There are two concerns that strike the interests of this chapter with respect to the increased, conceptual attention toward the middle and upper classes. First, when conflict between working and middle to upper class becomes the focus of analysis, the original contradiction formulated by Marx with respect to the working and capitalist classes shifts or is displaced. Therefore, one may receive the impression that the primary contradiction is now between the working and middle class. It is indeed the case that middle class students receive curricular matter fashioned in their image. Their linguistic capital and cultural codes form the basis of pedagogical knowledge and legitimate interactions in the classroom.

Now regarded as an apparatus of the middle class, public schools reproduce the value system of their privileged clients, who hold a monopoly over the legitimate power to correct others who fall out of line with "the middle." Bourdieu (1991) describes:

> Through its grammarians, who fix and codify legitimate usage, and its teachers who impose and inculcate it through innumerable acts of correction, the educational system tends, in this area as elsewhere, to produce the need for its own services and its own products, i.e. the labour and instruments of correction (p. 61).

In the institutional context of schooling, middle class codes and values form the standard of correct *habitus*. It is at this point that the relational character of Marx's stress on the primary conflict should be invoked. The middle class may receive benefits or may even be the hegemons of the public schools, but this is different from saying that they benefit from the economic system at large and in an absolute way. With much of the analytical focus falling on middle class privileges, the productive power of the capitalist class is obscured. Despite their relative power, the middle class is not the main problem within a divided labor force. They may be the favored sons, but the father still controls the house. No doubt, as Marx reminds us, the middle class does not represent the revolutionary impetus for change but neither are they the main target of critique. In fact, the everyday existential battles between the working and middle class over issues such as vouchers and other choice programs detract from a greater understanding of the role of the capitalist class in the educational system. Again, they remain out of sight, out of mind.

That said, like Bourdieu and Lareau, neo-Marxism finds a productive ground on which to develop, in a dialectical way, the relationship between objective structures and their sedimentation on parents and students' subjectivity, which is the central concern of this chapter. In particular, they provide direction for a study of the body because a theory of *habitus* explains the way institutional arrangements become grafted directly onto the embodied perceptions and dispositions of students. However, a second problem arises when one considers the issue of race. Bodies are not just material deposits of class relations; they are also racialized bodies. In his unrelenting critique of the Racial Contract, Charles Mills (1997) asserts that traditional contractarians project a social understanding of the world that is race-blind. He proposes a theory of the Racial Contract that explains states and state apparatuses, such as the school, as mechanisms of white power in a herrenvolk democracy where the dominant white group experiences liberty at the expense of subordinate racial groups. Furthermore, he criticizes Marxism for its projection of a "colorless class struggle" (p. 111). Bourdieuan analysis of schooling benefits from an integration of the race concept in order to provide an analysis of parental involvement, for example, that asks the extent to which parents of color feel intimidated by white teachers or feel tentative during parent–teacher conferences and Open House night, even when both groups represent the same class. This would enrich Lareau's findings by modifying Bourdieu's influential concept of "cultural capital" in terms of race.

Racism and the Problem of Exploitation

As Cornel West (1988) proclaims, "The time has passed when the so-called race question, or Negro question, can be relegated to secondary or tertiary *theoretical* significance in bourgeois or Marxist discourses" (p. 18: italics in original). In the history of class–race relations in the United States there have been three conceptual ways to define the specific place of African Americans in the social formation. One, African Americans are subsumed into the working class. This strain ignores the specific experiences of African Americans outside of industrial labor or the workplace. Two, African American specificity is acknowledged within particular practices in the economy, such as discrimination. This perspective is not as reductionistic as the first but shares its economism. Three and most influential, African Americans suffer general class exploitation within a national context. This acknowledges the importance of black nationalism, is antireductionistic, and antieconomistic. Although West is concerned with the specific plight of African Americans, he acknowledges its common features with other oppressed groups, such as Chicanos, citing Mario Barrera's (1979) powerful work, *Race and Class in the Southwest*.

As we settle into the new millennium, race and class critique becomes more complex and specific. It is more complex because we must apply Marx's original insights to an economic system that is increasingly post-industrial, especially in first and second world nations. It is specific because the race question accounts for some of the unevenness in the economy, especially when we take into account the internationalization of the labor force. The development of race critique benefits from Marxism's general focus on objective, historical developments. In particular, its emphasis on the "real" provides race critique with a conceptual arm that guards against reification of the race concept. For example, Manning Marable's (1983) early polemic against racial essentialism blasts black men and the black petty bourgeois for their sexism and complicity with the exploitation of black women. Marable exposes the spurious myth behind the suggestion of a "black capitalism" or "black bourgeoisie," citing the fact that, in the beginning of the 1980s, only 200 black entrepreneurs account for the corporate core of American capitalism. Despite this, black men occupy positions in the sexualized economy that far outrun the mobility of their female counterparts. The abuse of women, especially by certain sectors of the subproletarian world controlled by black men, does not warrant all black men an assumed racial solidarity with black women because they contribute to the economic exploitation of women. This suggests that racial grouping does not equate with racial belonging.

That people of color exploit each other on the basis of a subgroup's economic interest subverts the notion of an essential group affiliation based on identity. Exploitation is an objective phenomenon that does not ask questions about the color of its perpetrator. On some level, the exploitation that people of color suffer at the hands of whites or other people of color bears a material mark that looks and feels the same. On the level of meaning, the exploited person of color may rationalize the exploitation as different, depending on the identity of its source. This perception may even attenuate the subjective experience of exploitation (i.e., soften it, because of a sense of self-identification that the exploited feels toward the exploiter). This rationalization is reasonable because it attests to the specific historical relationship between people of color and whites as opposed to inter-minority politics. However, conceptually it is problematic and reifies the concept of race because it posits an essential subject of identity such that it performs an *a priori* assumption about sameness between members of a "like" group. Exploitation by my sibling objectively alienates me as much as it would if it came from a complete stranger. If anything, the first case seems more of a betrayal than the second since there exists an assumed familial contract that is broken.

In light of this quandary, it is consequential that educators' definitions of racism become as complex as their subject matter. There are at least two ways to define racism: as a system of privilege or a system of oppression. In the first, a system of privilege depends on identity, or as Beverly Tatum (1997) explains, people of color can harbor racial prejudices, but do not earn the title of "racist" because they possess neither the institutional power nor the means to enforce it. Within this discourse, only whites benefit from racism in a direct and absolute way because they possess both racial power and institutional means. This is not untrue. People of color can be just as hateful as whites and perpetrate random acts of violence toward them, but they cannot be called racists. This definition has several advantages. It makes power central to the system of race and its problem: racism. Also, it makes clear who benefits from a racist formation: whites. Moreover, it distinguishes between temporary, relative benefits from absolute benefits.

In education it is widely touted that Asian Americans, as a group, represent the model student (see Nakanishi and Nishida, 1995). They are characterized as studious, obedient, and educationally oriented. As the racial middleman group, Asian Americans act as a buffer between whites and blacks. As the buffer, Asian Americans may receive additional benefits, such as positive representations as the "good minority." First, I am not here to debunk the construction that Asian Americans, by and large, are studious. However, that this studiousness is due to their racial make-up—genetic, cultural, or otherwise—is another matter. It is a known fact that Asian immigrants arrive into the United States already occupying a different class status when compared to their Latino or black counterparts (Portes and Rumbaut, 1990). Second, the relative benefits that Asian Americans receive as the favored child of U.S. paternalism keeps them at bay with respect to race relations. In fact, this may explain why many Asian Americans resist applying racial analysis to their life experiences, choosing instead to hunker down and remain silent. Also, Asian Americans may avoid race analysis because this would put them closer to the more vocal African American discourse on race and thus become more closely associated with black and receive harsher punishments from whites. In the final analysis, the case of Asian Americans shows how relative success is used to discipline Latinos and African Americans on the "fairness" of the U.S. educational system since a minority group is apparently able to rise in ranks (see Wu, 2002). Asian Americans benefit from this arrangement but, as Tatum suggests, this does not translate into institutional power.

Tatum's definition accomplishes its task, but not without conceptual trade-offs. It leaves underdeveloped or unexplained the responsibility and accountability of people of color who do not help the cause of racial emancipation, or worse, perpetuate racist relations, such as Marable's discussion of the subproletarian economy. An alternative way to define racism is to demarcate it as *a system of racial oppression*. This differs from Tatum's identity-dependent definition because it is a politics unguaranteed by the agent's identity. It is not merely a discussion about the agent's inauthenticity and more about racial consequences and the upkeep of race relations. Just as Ebert (1996) makes it possible to call Camille Paglia a "patriarchal feminist," it is also possible to say that the *actions* of people of color are racist when they participate in the maintenance of a racist system. This does not suddenly put people of color on par with white subjects because Euro-white atrocities toward the other is more comprehensive, far-reaching, and unparalleled (Said, 1979). Also, attention to racist acts as opposed to racist people should not be confused as saying that all racist acts are the same, as if to call a black person a "nigger" is somehow the same as calling a white person "honkey." A sophisticated conceptual analysis arrives at the historically divergent material source of the meaning of each term—both are derogatory but different in force.

As an insightful student of mine once commented, phrases such as "white trash" should not be mistaken as only a class-related slur disconnected from race. She reminds us that white trash is a stand-in for "bad whites," a descriptor that assumes the existence of "good whites." By contrast, even "good nigger" is a slur scripted through an act of distancing, of differentiating between frightful, militant-seeming black students ("bad") and an accommodating black student ("good"). Both "types" of student belong to the discourse of distantiation through its construction of the generalized, rather than concrete, black figure. They come out of a discourse of fear. In short, as another student concludes, Denzel Washington is still a "nigger" in the white supremacist imagination, and for that matter, Jackie Chan just another "chink," and James Edward Olmos another dreaded "wetback." Again, it should be clear that the speaker of racist semantemes matters, but this does not exonerate the act. Snoop Doggy Dogg or Tito of Power 106 on the Los Angeles music airwaves can just as easily act to perpetuate these structures.

When Tito recounts the top four songs at 4:00 of any given afternoon with an exaggerated Mexican accent while black and white disc jockeys alike have a hearty laugh, it is not conveniently set aside as an act of a colonized mind. Millions of students in the Los Angeles basin inhale these negative messages as they do the smog in the air. The speech act belongs objectively in the space of white supremacist discourse. As David Theo Goldberg (1990) describes, racism is a field of discourse. It consists of expressions, acts, consequences, principles, institutions, and a set of texts associated with subjects but not guaranteed by them. In other words, following Foucault, we may say that racist discourses maintain a certain autonomy from the subjects who utter them. Though it would certainly be a contradiction to discuss racism without reference to any racists, discursive analysis establishes the possibility that racist discourses work as easily through whites as people of color, even if it works against the latter's interests. Certainly, we may bring capitalism into the fold as a reminder that racism sells and financially benefits Tito and his co-conspirators. But selling crack also sells and no self-respecting person of color is rushing to encourage its promotion.

The discursive turn in social theory informs us of the social construction of identity. In a reading of identity as text, Stuart Hall (1996b), explains the fragmentation of identity into ethnicity, sexuality, and race. As such, the essentialist reading of identity in the forms of Negritude or radical strains of feminism are compromised and filtered through the articulation of several formations within a given context. Rather than offering a stable and overreliable notion of selfhood, Hall offers certain articulations of difference that are inflected through a constellation of competing discourses. In other words, there is no universal subject of race that is not already interpenetrated by overlapping ways of being, like gender, ethnicity, or class. This does not suggest that identity is neither meaningful nor useful. In fact, this does not prevent strong calls for the politicization of identity as a basis for social movements. It is this variegated sense of politics that Gramsci, read through Hall, describes as the "relations of force" that must be taken into account when applying Marxism to a particular social formation. Here we see the pragmatic suggestion of multiple levels of race analysis that resists its reification as an identity formed once and for all. Rather, through a *specific* engagement of the objective, historical conditions, Marxist race scholars understand that racialized subjects are inflected by a set of discourses struggling to define them. First and last, their determinants are not economic but a combination of material and ideological forces within a given social formation. For instance, the invention of postmodern racism is a material context where schooling becomes a denial of dialogue and becomes conscripted in incommensurable worldviews unable to connect on important issues, like equality (Flecha, 1999). The specific application of Marx's insights to the current objective conditions advances our understanding of an educational milieu fraught with decidable features, such as inequality.

Productive (rather than productivist) readings of race avoid the pitfalls of two positions: traditional identity politics and beyond identity politics. Identity may not be real (i.e., material) like the economy but it produces real consequences as racialized subjects act *as if they were real.* When white teachers act in patterned ways toward students of color through tracking practices or the like, they behave in ways that produce real and racial consequences. Some students face these behaviors on such a consistent basis that they become formidable, material forces in their educational lives. When students of color resist "official" school culture because they consider academic success as "acting white" (Fordham, 1988), they reproduce racial patterns in school outcomes. In short, racial politics exist, even if they are not real in the orthodox Marxist sense of the word. They exist as a material force that is objective and outside of individual control. The traditional sense of identity politics has been all but discredited in mainstream social theory (Leonardo, 2000b). That identity *is* politics is a form of guarantee that even Walmart cannot redeem. However, this does not suggest the end of all talks of identity politics. In fact, something curious has happened to the discourse on identity.

On one side, Marxists reject the postmodern attempt to fragment class struggle into green politics, gay and lesbian liberation, or multiculturalism. On the other side, postmodern theorists announce the annihilation of the unified subject at a time when the said groups were gaining momentum as social movements. Clearly, one receives a disjointed and confused picture. It is a bit like blaming the messenger for delivering someone else's message. Identity politics is quite old as discourses go; it was not created by postmodernists. In other words, as a response to postmodern theorizing the call for getting "beyond identity politics" seems both conceptually muddled and historically misplaced with respect to race and/or ethnicity. On identity politics, Lipsitz (1998) has this to say:

> [W]ork often derided as identity politics . . . [finds that] attacks on immigrants and on affirmative action amount to little more than a self-interested strategy for preserving the possessive investment in whiteness, a politics based solely on identity. Conversely, the best ethnic studies scholarship . . . [is] aimed at creating identities based on politics rather than politics based on identities (pp. 56, 66).

Race scholars informed by a non-reductionist reading of Marx provide some of the best insights for analyzing the material basis of race, racism, and ethnocentrism. By marrying Marxist objectivism with race critique, insurgent educators provide a language of critique that locates, rather than obscures, the beneficiaries of inequality in all its forms.

Towards an Integrated Theory of Marxism and Race Critique

Without a critical language of identity politics, policy educators cannot answer convincingly the question of, "Who will fill the empty places of the economy?" With it, they can expose the contradictions in the "beyond identity politics" thesis, which is dependent on the concept of identity in its re-assertion of the Euro-white, patriarchal, capitalism. However, without economic principles, educators also forsake an apprehension of history that maps the genealogy of the race concept. It is not uncommon that students of education project race into the past and equate it with the descriptor, "group," rather than a *particular way* of constructing group membership. For that matter, the Greeks of antiquity, Trojans of Troy, and Mesopotamians each comprise a race, much like today's African Americans or the African diaspora. Of course, this makes no sense. There is enough consensus between social scientists about the periodization of race to disprove this common sense belief (see Goldberg, 1990; Mills, 1997, 2003).

A progressive union between Marxist concepts and race analysis allows critical educators to explain that race is a relatively recent phenomenon, traceable to the beginnings of European colonization and capitalist expansion. As a concept, race is co-extensive with the process of worldmaking. Edward Said (1979) has explicated the process of orientalism, or how the Occident constructed the *idea* of the Orient (or Near East) through discursive strategies in order to define, control, and manipulate it. This does not mean that the Orient did not exist in a material sense, but that it was spatially demarcated and then written into a particular relationship with the west through scholarship and industries invested with economic resources. Cedric Robinson (1983) has mobilized a parallel oeuvre in what Robin Kelley (1983), in the foreword to *Black Marxism*, characterizes as a version of black Orientalism, or how Europe constructed the idea of the black Mediterranean. In this sense, race is a process of co-creation— it creates an external group at the same time as it defines its creator.

Another popular reaction to race discourse is the preference for the concept of culture. Rejecting the race concept as purely socially constructed, educators opt for the cultural analysis route as a substitute. In short, whereas race is an abstraction, culture is real. Culture is comprised of rituals, practices, and artifacts, whereas race is an idealist categorization of people based on phenotypes. Marginalized people have created rich inventories of culture, whereas race is imposed by white domination. Fearing the further reification of race, some scholars and students of education avoid the term altogether. They prefer race as ethnicity, race as class, or race as nation (see Omi and Winant, 1994). In other words, opposite race as an essence, race becomes an illusion. The cultural discourse benefits from a language of racial formation within a given historical context, or what Omi and Winant (1994) describe as "the sociohistorical process by which racial categories are created, inhabited, transformed, and destroyed" (p. 55). Broadly speaking, racial formations evolve in the field of representations, or racial projects. Racial projects are also objective material processes that compete for the distribution of resources such as educational credentials.

Other problems arise when we override, rather than integrate, race with culture. First, the real/non-real pairing between race and culture appears dichotomous, as if they were at odds with each other. With respect to certain groups, culture and race maintain such a close relationship that some forms of culture would not have evolved had specific racial structures been absent. In the case of African Americans, cultural practices such as slave narratives, blues, and secretly jumping the broom at weddings evolved from the "peculiar institution" of slavery. Cultural practices such as these are only real to the extent that they arose from the objective context of enslavement, the objectification of humans as chattel, and material arrangements such as Jim Crow. Jumping the broom existed in Africa, but the context of its surreptitious practice in the USA has a particular meaning related to the institution of slavery. Second, in order to make real their social experiences, slaves and their descendants objectified them in cultural forms thereby producing history through material practices. The privileging of culture divorced from racio-economic evolution may regress to a feel-good concept that is at once celebratory and forgetful that "More Americans are ill-housed, poorly educated, and without health care that ever before. The condition for the racial minorities of course is twice, even three times worse than for the general population" (San Juan, Jr., 1994, p. 60).

In fact, one finds this tendency in mainstream multicultural practice. San Juan, Jr. (1994) does not mince words when he writes, "One outstanding example of multiculturalism in practice is the apartheid system in South Africa where racist theory and racialist practice insist on the saliency of cultural differences . . . where the hegemonic ideology valorizes differences to guarantee sameness" (pp. 70–72). When multicultural education does not pay critical attention to the commodification of culture via racist signification, it robs students of the liberating aspects of cultural training. A materialist outlook on culture and race understands that too much *pluribus* and not enough *unum* takes for granted differences that only lately walked onto the scene. That is, although a multiculturalist should surely fight against what Memmi (2000) calls "heterophobia," or fear of difference, he or she should surely also reject differences that were constructed in order to create differences, rather than merely to observe them.

It is on this last note that I want to end this essay. Spickard (1992) has acknowledged the illogic of American racial categories by pointing out its shifting meaning, blurry lines, and sometimes inconsistent application. However, he admits that people of color find meaning in race because it gives them a sense of common struggle based on a denominator of historical maltreatment. This brings up a question with respect to the future of the race concept, which I take up more fully in the next chapter. If the creation of race is dubious and coterminous with exploitation, then it begs the question: "Why keep it?" A progressive education must risk the possibility of transcending the race concept only by going through it and not over it, just as, for a Marxist, it behooves us to transcend the class system. Martin Luther King's dream is, after all, David Duke's nightmare: a society free of racial strife only after full disclosure of its racio-economic essence.

4
Futuring Race
From Race to post-Race Theory

The concept of race and utility of race analysis have been staples of social theory and education for quite some time. One can hardly read or write about the challenges of education without confronting the "problem of race." This does not mean that scholars wholly embrace race; some actively avoid and denigrate its study. However, it suggests that while race studies may not have reached mainstream status in most disciplines, they have made an impact that significantly changes the trajectory of most disciplines that have spoken to matters of race. Gatekeepers of the disciplines, including education, who wish to uphold "excellence" rather than "diversity" have launched their battlecry in what is now familiarly referred to as the "cultural wars," as if the former were not a racial project (Symcox, 2002). That said, the race concept has been left relatively untouched, sometimes left as a proxy for the vague identity of "social group," sometimes conflated with ethnicity sometimes nationality. Particularly in the USA, race has become common sense and sometime loses both its specificity and edge. Loic Wacquant (1997, 2002) interrogates not only the utility of this move, but also the questionable, folk-knowledge status of race that passes as scientific or analytical. Or worse, Wacquant fears that with the reality of U.S. imperialism enacted at the level of theory, "American" race analysis is exported as a general world analysis rather than a particular set of assumptions. With the arrival of post-studies in the form of poststructuralism and its varieties, new opportunities for analysis, insights, and ambivalences have made it possible to ask fundamental questions about the status of race. As I have outlined in Chapter 3, it also returns to the fold more established discourses on race, such as Marxism.

This chapter delves into the recent advancements in race theory that prognosticate the future of race. Admittedly, this is not a simple task and is liable to make one an intellectual punching bag of critics from left to right. On one hand, race scholarship that forsakes a conceptual engagement of its own premises takes for granted the naturalized status of race. Questioning its solidity now seems unreal, caught up in unnecessary solipsistic arguments about the ostensible and unquestionable fact of race. After all, race groups exist and race history is indisputable. Race is real. End of story. There are several limitations to this approach. First, race was an invention and its matter-of-fact existence today should not be confused with its objective reality without the daily dose of reification. It is worthwhile intellectually to debate the conceptual status of race if racism significantly depends on the continuation of a racialized mindset. This is perhaps what James Baldwin was referring to, when he claimed that as long as white people think they are white, there is no hope for them (cited by Roediger, 1994, p. 13). After all, it is difficult to imagine white racism without the prior category of race that is responsible for white *perception* concerning which groups deserve a blessed or banished life. Race trouble arrived at the scene precisely at the moment when people began thinking they were white. Second, conceptualizing race is intimately tied to performing it, which informs social actors of the mechanisms that oppress them and how these may be different from related but distinct social relations, such as class or gender. Perceiving race as real is then tied to acting on it. The upshot is that taking up the race concept asks the primary question, "What is race?" without which race analysis proceeds commonsensically rather than critically. For example, which collectivities constitute a racial group is still unsettled in the USA. In an extreme sense, one may be tempted to brand the inability to deal critically with the concept of race as evidence of a certain anti-intellectual tendency. But that would be inflammatory and in the end does more harm than good.

On the other hand, reducing the problem of racism to the conceptual status of race comes with its own difficulties, as if racism were caused by a concept rather than racially motivated actions, such as educational segregation and labor discrimination. A concept, not white supremacist institutions, like slavery. Not the attempt to kill off Native Americans. Not the limiting of Asian American mobility by curtailing their citizenship rights. Not the constant attacks on Latino cultural autonomy. Racism is not ultimately the problem of people who think there are races "out there" but the materially coordinated set of institutions that results from people's actions. Certainly these actions have their root in the concept of race but a whip in the hand seems more responsible for racism than an idea in the head. These arrangements do not continue merely by virtue of our investments in a concept but through historical contestations over power within a racialized field of understanding. We may go a long way with Marxists' distinction between ideas and substance but this makes it all the more ironic that for all their materialist analyses, they would rather emphasize race as an idea rather than a set of material practices (see Bonilla-Silva, 2005). It is not just that people *think* they are white, but that they *act* on it.

Race does not disappear because we alter conceptualizing each other as post- or non-racial *if we act on the world in a racial way and with racial consequences.* Brazil is a case in point, where the concept of a post-racial democracy is compromised by the stubborn reality of racial stratification (see Telles, 2006). Whether or not we conceptualize Brazilian power relations as racial in the U.S. sense of it, there is a clear color line among those who lead the country and those who follow. This is not to argue that people of color in Brazil are worse off than those in the USA, which is a legitimate argument. This is an empirical assertion with much veracity but is besides my point. The problem of race, or racism, cannot be reduced to the concept of race as much as religious warfare fails to be explained by divergent interpretations of sacred texts. Rather, racial contestation is decided by internal concepts (reified as they may be) externalized through social behavior and institutional arrangements. To race realists, placing the word "race" in scare quotes appears as unduly intellectual-ist, particularly when other social relations that are equally socially constructed are not put under a similar, bracketed scrutiny. It appears they have an axe to grind against racial analysis. To these analysts, for all the realness that Marxists, in particular, claim in the end they ultimately fail to "get real."

Having already extrapolated Marxism's relation with race analysis, here I engage two additional treatises on the viability of race as a structuring prin-ciple, a conceptual form of understanding, and a form of politics. I will limit the discussion to progressive, left-leaning discourses rather than include the obvious post-race implications in vulgar color-blind conservatism, some of which I take up in a later chapter on No Child Left Behind. That established, the progressive forms of post-racial analysis offer genuine insights that any race scholar may take to heart, something that its conservative iterations may not put on the table as they are more concerned with denying race rather than engaging it. Here, "progressive" takes on a slippery status and includes dis-courses that take race seriously as a marker of social difference, whether or not this takes on a determining status, as the Marxist case shows. In other words, the arguments that I showcase in this chapter do not assert that a post-racial condition has largely arrived, that race has somehow become irrelevant. The analysis is concerned less with the notion that race is declining in significance and more with posing the question, "What is the future of race?" In other words, what does race relations look like after the innovation of a race ambivalent analysis?

As we have seen, in Marxist theory race retains its ideological status and a racial cosmology inevitably subverts a clearer understanding of social life and the educational apparatus where race is learned as social practice. This does not mean that Marxism outright rejects race struggle but questions its scientific status and praxiological implications for change. In sociology, Robert Miles' (2000) work proves instructive; in history, Barbara Fields (1990) assumes prominence; and in education, Darder and Torres (2004), and McLaren and Torres (1999) have taken the lead. Instigated by cultural studies, post-race dis-courses distinct from Marxist orthodoxy provide an opportunity to ask new questions about race made possible by studies in the politics of representation. According to Gilroy (2000), post-race discussions signal an opportunity rather than something to be feared insofar as race understanding may be advanced in order that race may not remain standing. Like Marxism in the current conjuncture, post-race analysis is a politics that proceeds without guarantees, with race under possible erasure (see Hall on Marxism, 1996a). It is, as Gilroy (2000) punctuates, a politics of race abolition. It is a "crisis of raciology," enabled by "the idea that 'race' has lost much of its common-sense credibility because the elaborate cultural and ideological work that goes into producing and reproducing it" takes more than it gives, that race "has been stripped of its moral and intellectual integrity," that "there is a chance to prevent its rehabilitation," and that race "has become vulnerable to the claims of a much more elaborate, less deterministic biology" (pp. 28–29). By contrast, white abolition asks a different task of race theory to the extent that it prioritizes targeting whiteness in its uptake of race. Race is dependent on what Lipsitz (1998) earlier called the "possessive investment in whiteness" so any utopia without race must confront the strongest form of racial worldmaking that is whiteness. Their differences notwithstanding, post-race and critical studies of whiteness share conversations at the abolitionist table. In Chapter 6, I inquire into the conceptual status of whiteness in race studies but here I delve into the status of race within whiteness studies, specifically within the abolition movement. Race sits strategically at a crossroad that demands scholarship which is attentive not only to its declining or rising significance but to its very future as a system of intelligibility.

From the outset, I would like to be clear about my intentions regarding the invocation of post-race analysis. I want to avoid being misinterpreted as suggesting that race is declining as a structuring principle of society, particularly the USA. There are signs for this prognosis, as Gilroy clearly provokes, but they are inconclusive. Gilroy's argument does not depend primarily on its empirical veracity but its logical conclusions. On the contrary, one can make a good case that race relations pulses as strongly as ever, perhaps even more significantly than previous eras. As Mills (1997) asserts, there is neither a transracial class nor gender solidarity and therefore race remains axiomatic. In addition, I do not argue that a society may reach a post-race situation by downplaying race and racial contestation, as in policies that turn a color-blind eye to race in education in a desperate attempt to make the States united again, like "the good ol' days.". Downplaying race struggle will ensure that it continues at the level of social practice. Suggesting that race does not matter does not necessarily make it so, as Gotanda (1995) clearly shows in his debunking of the apparent color-blindness of the U.S. constitution. However, that race matters does not suggest that society should continue existing in a racial form, that race should keep mattering. That is, insofar as the USA is racially structured, skin color stratified, and somatically signified does not automatically recommend their perpetuity. So the task of this chapter is not only to promote anti-racism but to consider the post-race position, which is to say, the politics of being anti-race.

The futuring of race asks neither the question of race's current significance nor its real past but more important, its projected destiny. It takes from Nayak's

(2006) assertion that "post-race ideas offer an opportunity to experiment, to re-imagine and to think outside that category of race" (p. 427). To be more precise, post-race ruminations allow educators to recast race, even work against it, as Gilroy suggests, but this move cannot be accomplished with the pretense of thinking *outside* the category of race. As I argued in Chapter 2, in a racialized formation, race has no outside. We are caught up in racemaking at every turn and presuming access to its outside comes with dangerous implications, usually founded in color-blindness. Rather, it suggests the possibility of undoing race *from within* rather than from without, of coming to full disclosure about what race has taken from us to which we no longer consent. In this sense, the unmaking of race interests the oppressed races more than the master race, the latter arguably more invested in its continuation. Therefore the analysis does not make the audacious pronouncement that this move is plausible but asks whether or not it is possible and preferable. Given the bogus beginnings of race, this point seems warranted and within the realm of possibilities. Given race's omnipresence in U.S. society, it seems impossible. That is the problematic of this chapter, wedged as it is between the possible and the impossible, between the precept of and a preference for race.

Post-Race and the Insufficient Project of Race Signification

As Paul Taylor has suggested, the innovation of post-race analysis does not signal the end of race as we know it.[1] Rather, like the "post" in post-analytic philosophy, the same "post" in post-race analysis signals an opening, not the closing of race scholarship. It allows new questions, as products of intellectual and material development, to surface. Like the "post" in many schools of thought in extant, post-race is the ability of race theory to become self-aware and critically conscious of its own precepts. It signals the beginning of the end of race theory proper, which becomes impossible to continue in the same vein. A race theory that becomes self-aware of its own constitutive activity enters the next stage of development in a dialectical moment of the thought process. Race theory becomes post-race precisely for the same reasons that modern thought is challenged by postmodern theory. Modern theory still exists but only after it reckons with the postmodern. Likewise, race theory emerges as something different, if not new, through the filter of post-race.

I believe Taylor is right to frame the discussion in this manner. It avoids the otherwise vulgar suggestion that we are "beyond race" or have "transcended race" for usually unsubstantiated reasons. It acknowledges the debt owed to race analysis proper but propels it forward without jettisoning it. What do we make of society as we remake race in a daily way? Like one might ask about modern theories after the postmodern moment, what does race analysis look like after the arrival of post-race thought? For all of Baudrillard's ranting against modern teleologies and determinisms, he did not succeed in making them irrelevant before his death (see Leonardo, 2003d). However, he forced a response from modernist thinkers. As a carbuncle on their theories, Baudrillard and other postmodernists pushed social theory and their intellectual adversaries into different directions, if not forward. Post-race analysis accomplishes a similar move, forcing a hard and sometimes difficult look at race theory.

Race understanding stands at the uncomfortable street corner where our bodies meet their socially constructed racial identity and where we leave the same intersection unsure of what we have just become as a result of race. Gilroy (2000) writes, "[W]e always agree that 'race' is invented but are then required to defer to its embeddedness in the world" (p. 52). Nayak (2006) laments, "The problem that race writers encounter, then, is how do we discuss race in a way that does not reify the very categories we are seeking to abolish?" (p. 415). If race was a figment of the Occidental imagination, it is one of life's deepest ironies that people of color hang on dearly to a concept created in order to oppress them. Many centuries later, U.S. minorities find it hard to imagine a post-race society, either because they suspect that color-blind whiteness is up to its old tricks again or they are invested in a hard fought sense of an oppositional identity, the giving up of which means a fundamental loss of meaning. Or as Nayak (2006) observes:

> [F]or minority ethnic groups the erasure of race may equate with the obliteration of an identity and shared way of life . . . the concept of race, however tarnished it may appear, has provided an important meeting place for political mobilization, inclusion and social change (p. 422).

Although Nayak commits the usual slide between ethnicity and raciality, something he misrecognizes when he asserts that "whiteness is not homogeneous but fractured by the myriad ethnic practices," (p. 417), he is correct to note that race (not only racism) is a source of problem as well as a resource of meaning for racially despised groups. Yet he misses an opportunity. Whiteness is precisely homogenizing, wiping out ethnic differences in favor of racial solidarity, which I take up later in Chapter 6. For people of color, race is a condition of their being and to dispute its centrality in their lives violates their perceived right to be, and usually without the profitable returns that white ethnics gain as they shed their identity to ascend to white raciality. In the end, race may take away more from than it gives to people of color. It certainly benefits whites more than non-whites.

This does not mean that whites are eager to give up race but there is less of an ironic return for them. This point extends Nayak's (2006) claim that "It is precisely because whiteness is seen as an unmarked racial category that the loss of race for white theoreticians can appear inconsequential." (p. 422). We might distinguish between whiteness' discursive sleight-of-hand to conjure up a post-race reality and whites' general unwillingness to relinquish race privilege. Giving up race is consequential for whites for it is responsible for the lightness of their being, a sense of existential lack of tethers. Their sense of freedom and mobility is a direct and negative correlation with the restrictions people of color face. Their post-race attitude is belied by their racial behavior. A post-race situation is a threat to whites' very existence and can only come at a great loss for them, which may be greater than the loss of meaning for racial minorities. Racial recollections for minorities do not vanish with a post-race reorganizing, such as the South African case, but white domination and privilege is eradicated structurally, which does not suggest that it does not continue through ideology. Arguably, race memory serves as the constant reminder against the return of white supremacy just as Jewish remembering of the Holocaust guards against its repeat. Race comes with certainties for whites and it is precisely the lack of guarantees that accompanies post-race analysis that threatens their interests. Post-race arguments are intended to challenge white supremacy before they are designed to threaten the status of its victims. The latter becomes something to give up in exchange for the greater return in ending the former. Although post-race scholars do not underestimate this loss of meaning, they consider it worth the risk for it is a system of meaning that creates more problems than liberties. This loss, as Nayak suggests, can be turned into a gain.

To dispel further any notions that this model mystifies the inner workings of race, education under post-race assumptions makes it clear that it is made possible precisely by testifying to the inhuman tendencies of a racialized humanism. Gilroy (2000) contends that his "[planetary] humanism is conceived explicitly as a response to the sufferings that raciology has wrought," (p. 18) not its obfuscation. To Gilroy, the crisis in raciology represents less a crisis of identity and more the uncertain status and preferable (rather than inevitable) demise of race, not only at the level of signification but also at the level of social organization (see also Hirschman, 2004). The sweeping global changes in economy and diasporic movement complicate and compromise racial world-making, stripping it of previous guarantees and predictive value as an autonomous relation. New events in history, such as the apparent racial contest undetermined by skin color but mediated by somatic politics between Hutus and Tutsis in Rwanda, disturb our race-as-skin-color expectations. Although this case should not be overinterpreted as proof of the waning effect of skin color difference, for which we have more worldwide evidence, the Rwandan situation brings new insights to race analysis by introducing the reinterpretation of bodily differentiation through primary markers besides skin color. Even the multiracialization of beauty images, which includes increasingly more black and brown faces, signals new anxieties about race, but this time by disturbing its clear lines of demarcation rather than their enforcement. Whereas race thought was revolutionary in its own right, this new stage of development represents a revolution of the revolution, or the dynamic continuation of that transformation. To the extent that raciology introduced white subversion of the humanity inhered in people of color, post-race represents the attempt to subvert the subversion. Race changed some subjects into people of color; it may be time to change again. This neither suggests that racism nor racialization fails to exert its dominant imprint on social processes, subject formation, and State sponsored policies. However, it means that both race struggle and raciology may begin the day but in no way end it, giving way to the era of racial ambivalence.

I have no desire to overstate the case. Made clear by the stubborn standard of whiteness, from Tyra Banks, Halle Berry to Beyoncé Knowles, to Jennifer Lopez and Selma Hayek, light skin still approximates white beauty standards (see Hunter, 2005). But as colonized peoples challenge white supremacy across the globe and gain access to networks of power monopolized by whites, counting on race stratification becomes ironically ambiguous and upsets racial expectations. This is a condition not to be deplored ultimately as a sense of loss, at least not in the manner that one grieves the passing of a seemingly endless war that has given this life much meaning. Putting race to peace may open up possibilities for other ways of being that have been heretofore limited or closed, particularly for people of color. The loss should not be minimized but countered by a sense of clarity concerning the neuroses of race about which Fanon (1967) spoke so forcefully and which Gilroy calls the "rational absurdity of 'race' " (p. 14). Gilroy taps a certain post-racial suggestion in Fanon whose attempts to restore blacks in their proper human place represent black analytics, or negritude, in order then for blackness to vanish under its own weight (see also Nayak, 2006). Just how the problems of humanism fold into the refashioning of the human in a post-race condition remains contested, opening the door for Gilroy's pragmatic planetary and postanthropological humanism. Blackness, for example, may remain a culture and disappear as a racial category. Gilroy clarifies, "There will be individual variation, but that is not 'race' " (p. 42). This last point is worth elaborating.

Human differences continue but whether or not skin color variation should form the basis for social organization is the question. As a modern principle, race is a particular grouping of individuals into social groups. As embodied collectivities, these social groups could very well continue intact as we enter a post-race society, but they will no longer be considered skin groups once the race principle has been discredited. The bodies remain but they will be conceptualized differently as post-racial subjects. African Americans may continue as an ethnic group so blackness as a form of cultural practice may thrive in the absence of race where "skin, bone, and even blood are no longer the primary referents of racial discourse" (Gilroy, 2000, p. 48). It will neither sever completely its relation with blackness as a racial experience nor be reduced to it. Racial solidarity will be liberated from the "cheapest pseudo-solidarities: forms of connection that are imagined to arise effortlessly from shared phenotypes, cultures, and bio-nationalities" (Gilroy, 2000, p. 41). Of course Gilroy is speaking of both non-whites and whites, who desperately cling to identity as a visual confirmation of one's politics. For it is whites who, in their fetish of color, clearly profit more from racial politics as a form of interest consolidation than people of color who mobilize identity movements as a form of defense against white supremacy.

As race relations enters its late phase of development, its contradictions become riper and more obvious. Its logics hang desperately onto a world-view that becomes more anachronistic. This does not mean that race struggle becomes obsolete. On the contrary, post-race condition is reached precisely by exposing the myths held up for so long by a pigmentocracy that is whiteness, which people of color both love and hate because they have been taught for so long to admire the white and hate the black collective. For people of color, self-love in this instance is always uncertain for it is bound up with self-doubt. The possibility of ending race is the task of bringing back clarity to a situation that for so long has been clouded with the miseducation of racialized humans. This is the challenge of post-race thinking.

Critical Studies of Whiteness and the Abolition of Race

Whereas post-race sets the stage for the problematization of the race concept, studies of white abolition investigate the primary investment in a racial world-view known as whiteness. Race was created by European humanism, designed to limit theories of the human to those with white skin particularly, and those broadly conceived as white by the master race. Any talk of race abolition must contend with its strongest force of attraction for whites, for whom all the talk of "getting beyond color" becomes the most reifying contradiction when shifting relations of wealth and power enter the equation (Frankenberg, 1993). Like Forrest Gump, whites run from most serious discussions of race reconciliation and toward race as a default protection even for the most down and out whites. This means that race abolition is at the same time the abolition of the white race. The future of race is the problem of whiteness. But what does this really mean?

Race, particularly its U.S. iteration, is an opportunity structure for white ethnics. For whites who experience class or gender oppression, whiteness becomes a form of coping mechanism. This is not insignificant and means that race was created by and for whites. People of color recreate race as well but usually as a protective response to whiteness. In critical studies of whiteness, race is understood as a differential system of advantage that benefits all whites regardless of their class or gender status. However, race has been used as a contradictory mechanism *among* whites as well. For the white working class, the history of race is full of contradictions. At once, they are beneficiaries of race and victims of capital. They experience group exploitation but have the ability to denigrate any person of color above their class status by simply appealing to race superiority. Roediger (1994) finds that "whites are confessing their confusion about whether it is really worth the effort to be white. We need to say that it is not worth it and that many of us do not want to do it . . .

exposing how whiteness is used to make whites settle for hopelessness in politics and misery in everyday life" (p. 16). Here we have to contextualize Roediger's analysis as speaking directly to the experiences of poor or working class whites. Inserted into the racial opportunity structure known as U.S. race relations, previously denigrated white ethnics find their mobility by being articulated with white raciality.[2] They escape persecution from Europe or elsewhere to find their new belonging in U.S. race relations. But the white working class does not benefit from whiteness in an absolute way, often clinging to it as a protective shield from the cruelties of labor exploitation.

Race has been used as a mechanism of mystification for the white working class in order that they learn to accommodate the ravages of U.S. capitalism. A pedagogy of white abolitionism does not begin with the premise that whites should learn to own their whiteness but to disabuse themselves from the common perception that the white race exists. Again, we return to the conceptual rejection of race; moreover, the abolition movement mounts a practical rejection of race as well. They do not ask whites to engage whiteness but rather to disengage from it. Abolitionism is not built around an oppositional sense of whiteness, which by definition does not exist because whiteness has never existed for other reasons besides oppression. In other words, it is completely and utterly negative, which leads Roediger to make the provocative announcement that whiteness is *nothing but oppressive and false.* It remains to be seen if whiteness possesses any redeeming characteristics. If this is correct, then educators must replace "the bankruptcy of white politics with the possibilities of nonwhiteness" (Roediger, 1994, p. 17). Roediger is not particularly fixated on the wholesale rejection of race as a form of organization. He is much more concerned with whiteness as a form of violence that seduces the white working class against its own objective class interests, some of which they share with workers of color. But in following the logical conclusions of Roediger's ideas, we would have to link the future of race with the demise of whiteness since it occupies a focal and privileged place in race, without which its center would collapse.

To the abolitionist, arguing for the transformation of whiteness lacks both a theory and history of whiteness. It lacks a sufficient theory because it does not explain whiteness as a distinct category from white people but conflates them. Thus, it disperses whiteness in light of the observation that a variety of white people exist, which misunderstands race's *modus operandi* to concentrate difference rather than proliferate it. Arguing for difference within whiteness is tantamount to constructing differences that do not make a significant racial difference, more accurately falling under the domain of ethnic diversity. The Irish may be radically different from the English in terms of culture and political history, but in terms of race these differences are put aside in exchange for their loyalty to whiteness as the glue that binds them against people of color. Students may insightfully suggest that "real whites live in England," which is a point well taken. But it does not ask the fundamental question, "What is whiteness?" To the abolitionist, whiteness has existed for one simple, historical reason: racial stratification. Ethnic distinctions are not forgotten but sidestepped if the racial conjuncture demands it. Whiteness is the oldest child of race, which "is the empty and therefore terrifying attempt to build an identity based on what one isn't and on whom one can hold back" (Roediger, 1994, p. 13). It is nothing but oppressive.

If whiteness is false and oppressive, then it stands to reason that race is the source of that mystification. Rather than the common alibi that U.S. racialized minorities are trapped in a cult of ethnicity instead of furthering the general, national interests (Schlesinger, 1998), whites appear as the ultimate special interest group (Banks, 1993) for the perpetuation of race. As a result, Ignatiev and Garvey (1996a) encourage whites to break the codes of whiteness by challenging other whites (and people of color) who assume that the body they address in front of them is a white person. This repudiation is part of "unthinking whiteness" insofar as race enables people to think of themselves as whites. They function through a white ideology (whiteness) that must be undone. Race relations begins to unravel since white exists with its Other and both are burst asunder in the process. Without a privileged center, there can be no denigrated margin.

Ironically, the call to complexify white identity ends up reducing it to white ideology. By contrast, abolitionists claim that whites are not "stuck with whiteness" and have acted against it time and again. In this process, it has been noted that white race traitors still accrue white privileges even when then disidentify with whiteness (Alcoff, 1998; Kincheloe and Steinberg, 1998). That is, racial structures still recognize abolitionists as white, who cannot monitor every moment that privileges them. Howard (1999) recounts a critical race moment when he forgoes the purchase of a new car to protest the racist practices of a car dealership. In this instance, he recognized white privilege and acted against it. Yet of course, racist car dealerships are a dime a dozen and another one awaited Howard. As a cautionary note, this is a reminder of white irony in race radical movements that break with the "White club" (Ignatiev and Garvey, 1996a) or "White racial bonding" (Sleeter, 1996, p. 261) because they are followed by the shadow of their privilege. That being the case, this is not a criticism that applies particularly to abolitionism, but to any white participation in a race movement within a racist social system. They will be recognized as white despite their disavowal of whiteness. This is unavoidable even when whites claim to disinvest personally in their advantages.

Within a racial formation whites are not born but made. They are not conceived in the biological sense (pun intended), but in the social sense. Dissolving whiteness, both in the ideological and institutional sense, means that the category white would neither be powerful nor useful as a racial category. This is not just a conceptual change, as in thinking differently about whiteness but a practical undertaking at the level of social practice. In other words, renouncing one's whiteness is a speech act of revolutionary proportions. It is not guided merely with the pronouncement "I am not white," but by the commitment "I will not act white." "White people" becomes an oxymoron because classifying people as white is at loggerheads with the notion that they exist because whiteness depends on the desire to disappear. To the abolitionist, white people, like race, are an abstraction. What Fanon (1967) would have been tempted to call "the fact of whiteness" vanishes right in front of our eyes. Perspectives that recognize the existence of racial groups, as is common in multiculturalism, are doomed to reify a racial imagination that has no basis in reality. Abolitionists, like Ignatiev, urge us to forget race and instead remember our common humanity.

Despite the call for disidentification, white abolitionists may find themselves swimming against an impossible tide. Roediger (1994) admits that "there is a sense in which whites cannot fully renounce whiteness even if they wanted to" (p. 16). This point does not vitiate against promoting abolitionism because it is misconceived or misguided, but brings up serious questions about its political reception. It should not be rejected because its likelihood of succeeding is low or that it is unrealistic. Abolitionism is not wrong because it may not, in the end, work according to plans. Critical race theorists never tire of telling us that racial strategies that challenge the establishment often converge with white interests and so maintain white advantage. A racial strategy cannot be judged solely on the likelihood of people taking up its cause. Abolitionism's possibility rests precisely on its unreasonableness, its shattering of racial codes.

That said, a racial strategy that fails to compel people to act leaves something to be desired. In other words, dismantling whiteness is not only a conceptual problem, but a political one. White resistance is not the only issue. Whites may be the subjects who answer the call, but will not be the only ones to hear it. People of color will find it difficult to believe and support the abolitionist philosophy because they have good reason to be suspicious of any white-led movement that claims to solve the problem that it created. People of color have been disappointed time and again by white retrenchment, racial malaise, and general inability to develop a certain stick-with-itness for the racial longue durée. This is the radical nature of white supremacy to be able to withstand all kinds of challenges and continue, albeit in different, compromised forms (yes, even abolitionism!). In the end, whiteness is not rigid, but incredibly flexible, a fact that abolitionism may underestimate. This conundrum represents a fatal contradiction in Ignatiev's neo-abolitionist movement because race is not just a figment, but a "pigment of our imagination" (Rumbaut, 1996). In other words, race is a combination of real and non-real characteristics, ideological as a category but material in its modes of existence. It is both real and imagined.

In one fell swoop, Ignatiev seems bent on constructing race (and whiteness) as only an illusion or ideological chimera, a trope that makes it quite compatible with orthodox Marxism. In other words, Ignatiev is convinced that race and whiteness are illusions and *nothing but illusions*. It begs the question: How does this sound different from color-blindness? Miles (2000) sums it up and claims:

> There are no "races" and therefore no "race relations." There is only a belief that there are such things, a belief which is used by some social groups to construct an Other (and therefore the Self) in thought as a prelude to exclusion and domination, and by other social groups to define self (and so to construct an Other) as a means of resisting that exclusion. Hence, if it is used at all, the idea of "race" should be used only to refer descriptively to such uses of the idea of race (p. 135).

Miles' otherwise thoughtful analysis of racism boils it down to a problem of false beliefs. No credible race theorist would refute this claim. Many individual whites do believe they are superior to people of color, which is made possible by the first condition that they must believe themselves to be white people. The problem is that they collectively practice this false belief, which graduates from a mere idea to an indomitable, material force. It would have been enough had it remained only in their heads. But because whiteness is also in their hands, they have built a society after their own image. In other words, the idea of race is material in its modes of existence. Although race may not be real (particularly in the scientific sense), it exists in real terms, such as a racial economy and its institutions. That races *should not* exist is a different point altogether from saying that they do not currently exist.

Ignatiev does not show the parsing out of real and non-real elements of race and rejects the entire kit and caboodle. However, abolitionists are on to something because it is symptomatic that whites, who spend a lot of time and energy resisting racial identification, would now find a problem with a framework that sanctions this already existing tendency. In other words, why would whites resist the philosophy of abolitionism when they practice it daily through color-blindness? It suggests that whites really do cherish whiteness, and therefore race, if not in an active sense then at least as a source of meaning. Whites' knee-jerk reaction implies that they notice their whiteness when its elimination becomes an imminent threat and therefore must be protected. But is whiteness ultimately worth it for the general white population, and particularly for the white working class? Abolitionists do not think so. In this section, I have gone a long way with the new abolitionism and find that its focus on whiteness gets at the crux of the problem. Although it falls into the trap of regarding race as purely ideological and located in people's heads, abolitionism's relentless attack on whiteness and the white frame of mind begins race analysis on the right foot.

We live in a time when race is under intense questioning. It is not the first time as racial analysis of society, the USA in particular, is only tolerated if it cannot be obliterated. The difference in the current moment is that progressive scholarship has taken this situation and reversed people's normal expectations. Like judo, post-race analysis takes the otherwise reactionary implications of color-blindness and uses its momentum against itself. In a complicated dance with hegemony, post-race scholars strike a compromise that upsets the head-to-head confrontation that usually results in racial antagonism. There is something subversive in this move. Arguing for the moribund status of race, post-race proponents in its cultural and whiteness studies variations do not rehabilitate race but annihilate it. Where they differ from color-blind pretenders is their ability to go *through* race instead of *around* it. They are able to speak to race rather than about it.

5
The Color of Supremacy

In the last decade, the study of white privilege has reached currency in the educational and social science literature. In 2009, the city of Memphis, Tennessee hosts the Tenth Annual Conference on White Privilege. Concerned with the circuits and meanings of whiteness in everyday life, scholars have exposed the codes of white culture, worldview of the white imaginary, and assumptions of the invisible marker that depends on the racial other for its own identity (Frankenberg, 1993, 1997; Hurtado, 1996; Kidder, 1997; Rothenberg, 2002). In particular, authors like Peggy McIntosh (1992) have helped educators understand the taken for granted, daily aspects of white privilege: from the convenience of matching one's skin color with bandages, to opening up a textbook to discover one's racial identity affirmed in history, literature, and civilization in general. In all, the study of white privilege has pushed critical education into directions that account for the experiences of the "oppressor" identity (Hurtado, 1999).

This chapter takes a different approach toward the study of whiteness. It argues that a critical look at white privilege, or the analysis of white racial hegemony, must be complemented by an equally rigorous examination of white supremacy, or the analysis of white racial domination. This is a necessary departure because, although the two processes are related, the conditions of white supremacy make white privilege possible. In order for white racial hegemony to saturate everyday life, it has to be secured by a process of domination, or those acts, decisions, and policies that white subjects perpetrate on people of color. As such, a critical pedagogy of white racial supremacy revolves less around the issue of unearned advantages, or the *state* of being dominant, and more around direct processes that secure domination and the privileges associated with it.

Racial privilege is the notion that white subjects accrue advantages by virtue of being constructed as whites. Usually, this occurs through the valuation of white skin color, although this is not the only criterion for racial distinction. Hair texture, nose shapes, culture, and language also multiply the privileges of whites or those who *approximate* them (Hunter, 2002b). Privilege is granted even without a subject's cognition that life is made a bit easier for her. Privilege is also granted despite a subject's attempt to dis-identify with the white race.

"Race treason" or the renunciation of whiteness is definitely a choice for many whites (Ignatiev and Garvey, 1996b), but without the accompanying structural changes, it does not choke off the flow of institutional privileges that subjects who are constructed as white enjoy.

During his summative comments about racial privilege at an American Educational Research Association panel, James Scheurich described being white as akin to walking down the street with money being put into your pant pocket without your knowledge. At the end of the day, we can imagine that whites have a generous purse without having worked for it. Scheurich's description is helpful because it captures an accurate portrayal of the unearned advantages that whites, by virtue of their race, have over people of color; in addition, it is symptomatic of the utter sense of oblivion that many whites engender toward their privilege. However, there is the cost here of downplaying the active role of whites who take resources from people of color all over the world, appropriate their labor, and construct policies that deny minorities' full participation in society. These are processes that students rarely appreciate because their textbooks reinforce the innocence of whiteness. As a result, the theme of privilege obscures the subject of domination, or the agent of actions, because the situation is described almost as happening without the knowledge of whites. It conjures up images of domination happening behind the backs of whites, rather than on the backs of people of color. The study of white privilege begins to take on an image of domination without agents. It obfuscates the historical process of domination in exchange for a state of dominance *in medias res*.

Describing white privilege as the process of having money put in your pocket comes with certain discursive consequences. First, it begs the question: if money is being placed in white pockets, who places it there? If we insert the subject of actions, we would conclude that racial minorities put the money in white pockets. Of course, we could also suggest that other whites put money in white pockets but this would sound tautological and does not speak to the actual direction of accumulation. It does not take long to realize that this maneuver has the unfortunate consequence of inverting the real process of racial accumulation, whereby whites take resources from people of color; often they also build a case for having earned such resources. Second, we can invoke the opposite case. This is where Scheurich's narrative gives us some direction, but only if we put the logic back onto its feet and reinsert the subject of domination. It might sound something like this. The experience of people of color is akin to walking down the street having your money taken from your pocket. Historically, if "money" represents material, and even cultural, possessions of people of color then the agent of such taking is the white race, real and imagined. The discourse on privilege comes with the unfortunate consequence of masking history, obfuscating agents of domination, and removing the actions that make it clear who is doing what to whom. Instead of emphasizing the process of appropriation, the discourse of privilege centers the discussion on the advantages that whites receive. It mistakes the symptoms for causes. Racial advantages can be explained through a more primary history of exclusions and ideological practices.

During the annual meeting of the National Association of Multicultural Education (NAME) in 2001 in Las Vegas, Nevada, "privilege" was a hot topic. During a workshop led by Victor Lewis, Hugh Vasquez, Catherine Wong, and Peggy McIntosh, the audience was treated to poignant personal histories of people coming to terms with their male, heterosexual, adult, and white privilege, respectively. We might recall that Lewis and Vasquez were two central figures in the excellent film on race, *Color of Fear*. Known for her work in whiteness studies and anthologized in multiple books for having produced the essay with a list of over forty privileges whites enjoy (see McIntosh, 1992), at the workshop McIntosh spoke clearly about her coming to terms with white skin advantage. Admitting that the gender lens was at first more convenient for her academic work and teaching, she describes her own coming to terms with race as seeing fin-like figures dancing out of the water before submerging and disappearing from sight, a scene taken from Virginia Woolf's *To the Lighthouse*. Speaking personally about her process of becoming conscious of white skin privilege, McIntosh describes the process as similar to having glimpsed a fin, not sure what to make of it but knowing that beneath the surface something great was attached to it. In short, McIntosh had seen something significant and it became the work of a critical scholar to make sense of it.

Ostensibly addressing a white audience at the NAME workshop, McIntosh continued by saying that coming to terms with white privilege is "not about blame, shame, or guilt" regarding actions and atrocities committed by other whites in their name. Here we return to the notion I took up earlier in Chapter 2, namely that racism is always about other whites, in this case, whites outside the workshop. Likewise, in an invited lecture that I titled "Race, Class, and Gender: The Problem of Domination," I was tempted to begin my talk with the same sentiment. Upon reflection, I decided against the strategy because I wanted my audience to understand that despite the fact that white racial domination precedes us, whites recreate it daily on both the individual and institutional level. On this last point, there are several issues that I want to bring up, which I believe are coterminous with the discourse on privilege.

Domination is a relation of power that subjects enter into and is forged in the historical process. It does not form out of random acts of hatred, although these are comdemnable, but rather out of a patterned and enduring treatment of social groups. Ultimately, it is secured through a series of actions, the ontological meaning of which is not always transparent to its subjects and objects. When early Americans, or what patriots fondly refer to as "founding fathers," drafted the Constitution, they proclaimed that people were created equal. Of course, slavery, patriarchy, and industrial capitalism were inscribing forces surrounding their discourse of freedom. In short, "humanity" meant male, white, and propertied. For this reason, any of their claims to universal humanity were betrayed by the inhumanity and violation of the "inalienable rights" of people of color, women, and the working class. In this case, domination means that the referents of discourse are particulars dressed up as universals, of the white race speaking for the human race.

In another instance, the case of African slaves in the USA literally reduced them to a fraction of a human being when the government reduced slave representation to three-fifths of a person. Fearing a northern-controlled Congress, the south struck the "Great Compromise" thereby effectively increasing their population while controlling the tax on slave importation. We bracket this process of reduction as a reminder that claims to literation always contain a process of figuration, that is, a representation. The literal reduction of blacks to three-fifths invokes the parasitic figure of whites, the representation of masculinity, and the specter of the bourgeois class. It is easy to see that the white supremacist, patriarchal, capitalist subject represents the standard for human, or the figure of a whole person, and everyone else is a fragment. In this way, policies of domination are betrayed by their accompanying contradictions and tropes.

Although McIntosh's essay enters its third decade since first appearing, it is worthwhile to re-examine it since it still has such currency. In fact, I often include it in my own course syllabi. To the extent that domination represents a process that establishes the supremacy of a racial group, its resulting everyday politics is understood as "dominance." McIntosh superbly maps this state of privilege by citing the many forms of racial advantage whites enjoy in daily life. However, domination can be distinguished from dominance where the former connotes a process and the latter a state of being, the first a material precondition that makes possible the second as a social condition. It is possible to discuss conferred dominance (McIntosh, 1992, pp. 77–78) because there are existing structures of domination that recognize such benefits, albeit unearned as McIntosh correctly points out. Otherwise, it is meaningless to construct perceived notions of advantage when social structures do not recognize them.

Although they clearly benefit from racism in different ways, whites as a racial group secure supremacy in almost all facets of social life. The concept of race does not just divide the working class along racial lines and compromise proletarian unity. Racism divides the white bourgeoisie from the black bourgeoisie (a mythical group, according to Marable, 1983), and white women from women of color (hooks, 1984). In other words, race is an organizing principle that divides across class, gender, and other imaginable social identities. This condition does not come about through an innocent process, let alone the innocence of whiteness.

When educators advise white students to avoid feelings of guilt, we are attempting to allay their fears of personal responsibility for slavery and its legacies, housing and job discrimination, and colonialism and other general-ized crimes against racial minorities. Indeed, white guilt can be a paralyzing sentiment that helps neither whites nor people of color. White guilt blocks critical reflection because whites end up feeling individually blameworthy for racism. In fact, they become overconcerned with whether or not they "look racist" and forsake the more central project of understanding the contours of structural racism. Anyone who teaches racial themes has witnessed this situation. Many whites subvert a structural study of racism with personalistic concerns over how they are perceived as individuals. In a society that denies whites access to a sociological and critical understanding of racism, this is not a surprising outcome. Stephen Small (1999) advises:

> [I]t is not useful to approach ideologies by asking whether they are "racist" or "non-racist." It is more useful to acknowledge the varied ideologies, and to examine them for their "racialized" intentions, content and consequences. In other words, it is more useful to consider all ideo-logies and the outcomes they have or are likely to have, for different "racialized" groups (p. 56).

Looking racist has very little to do with whites' unearned advantages and more to do with white treatment of racial minorities. Said another way, the discourse on privilege comes with the psychological effect of personalizing racism rather than understanding its structural origins in interracial relations. Whites have been able to develop discourses of anti-racism in the face of their unearned advantages. Whites today did not participate in slavery but they surely recreate white supremacy on a daily basis. They may not have sup-ported South African apartheid, but many whites refuse interracial marriage (see Alcoff, 2000), housing integration (Massey and Denton, 1993), and fully desegregated schools (Kozol, 1991).

Teaching, addressing, and writing for a white audience is necessary insofar as whites require inroads into discourses about race and racism. Certain slices of the literature on whiteness, for example, are an attempt to create a discourse that centers on white subjectivity, psychology, and everyday life. Frequently employing ideological critique of white worldview, whiteness studies exposes white lies, maneuvers, and pathologies that contribute to the avoidance of a critical understanding of race and racism. As these authors correctly point out, none of these strategies of whiteness is innocent or harmless. They fre-quently serve to perpetuate white racial supremacy through color-blindness, ahistorical justifications, and sleights-of-mind. However, we arrive at one of the limitations of writings or teachings based on an imagined white audience.

Countless authors from Freire to Fanon have suggested that oppression is best apprehended from the experiences or vantage point of the oppressed. This is not to suggest that oppressed people, as individual subjects of domination, somehow possess the correct or true understanding of racial oppression. Many of them are just as confused as whites when it comes to an organic understanding of racism. Many people of color have shown their inability to perform critical analyses of the causes of their own oppression (Leonardo, 2000b). That said, critical analysis begins from the objective experiences of the oppressed in order to understand the dynamics of structural power relations. It also makes sense to say that it is not in the interest of racially dominated groups to mystify the process of their own dehumanization. Yet the case is ostensibly the opposite for whites, who consistently mystify the process of racial accumulation through occlusion of history and forsaking structural analysis for a focus on the individual. This is not to go down the road of essentialized racial subjects, be they black or otherwise, and an equally essentialized white subject, as Stuart Hall (1996d) has pointed out. The advantage of beginning our analysis of domination from the objective position of those who receive policies of domination puts educators on the side of the oppressed, or at least an understanding of history from their conditions. Even when critical analysis takes white experience as its unit of analysis, this must be subjected to the rigors of the analytics of the oppressed. That is, there is a difference between analyzing whiteness with an imagined white audience against an imagined audience of color.

When scholars and educators address an imagined white audience, they cater their analysis to a worldview that refuses certain truths about race relations. As a result, racial understanding proceeds at the snail's pace of the white imaginary. When McIntosh listed her privileges as a white woman, she came to terms with unearned advantages. White confessionals are helpful insofar as they represent a discursive strategy to recognize the insidiousness of structural privileges. They also articulate an attempt to side with racial minorities through their sympathetic appeal to undo the said privileges. Tim Wise (2002) is insistent on pointing out the pathologies and flights from reason in white rationalizations of the U.S. race situation. Wise's Center at Fiske University links our current assault on whiteness with the avatar of Du Bois, who taught at the same university. However, we must also recognize that recent white attacks on whiteness appeal mainly to a liberal white audience, the content of which has been previously articulated by scholars and activists of color, as Cornel West (1999a) is quick to remind us.

Ruminations on whiteness are not new to many people of color and have been available for white readership before whiteness studies arrived on the scene. Black women know that their skin color does not match store-bought bandages, Latinos know their language is not spoken by management in most business places, and Asians know that their history rarely achieves the status of what Apple (2000) calls "official knowledge" in schools. White audiences have had access to these traditions of criticism for over a century. As such, radical writings on the topic of white privilege are new to white audiences *who read mainly white authors*. Much like the popularization of black R and B music by Elvis and Pat Boone, critiques of white privilege are given credence by white authors whose consumers are white readers. Rap music has now reached mainstream USA through its all-time best-selling artist, white rapper Eminem. None of this disregards their contributions, which are helpful for students interested in "pedagogies of whiteness" (Kincheloe and Steinberg, 1997). There are exceptions. When Roediger (1991) launched his critique of the "wages of whiteness," he expressed his debt to scholars of color, such as Du Bois. That said, the literature on white privilege is indicative of the lag in white uptake of radical racial thought.

Ultimately this same lag limits the racial analysis in the popular film, "Color of Fear." Although it is one of the most graphic films on the topic of race relations, it suffers from the tethers of white imagination. Throughout much of the ninety minutes, the men of color labor to convince a white participant, David, that white supremacy exists. After a while, one senses that it is a bit like convincing neo-Nazis that the Jewish holocaust happened. Despite the great and memorable lines from the film participants, one can't help to be frustrated by David's discourse of refusals when he discredits black people's fear of white rage as "unfounded," that individual hard work (or lack thereof) explains the history of groups, and that being white is essentially like being black. When I have shown the film to my class, students of color felt a sense of vindication when Victor, an assertive black man, lashes out at David. They experience their history articulated with a rage they have often felt toward white supremacy and white people. However, the discourses of color expressed in the film are familiar to my students of color. The information is not new to them.

The newness comes in the form of its publicity, of its coming to voice for them through the film participants. Victor, Hugh, and the other men of color become surrogates for the centuries of oppression experienced by many people of color, which rarely gets articulated in public life. By contrast, the same information is new to many of my white students, some of whom feel attacked, others enlightened. Thus, the majority of the film's discourse is spent on the question, "What does it mean to be white?" and forsakes a deeper engagement with "What does it mean to be black, Latino, or Asian?" Delving into the meaning of whiteness is central to antiracism but many whites, like David, resist it. David's consciousness drives the discussion and frames the issues because he needs to be convinced of the first fact of racial analysis: mainly, that white domination is a reality. In short, even the progressive discourse of "Color of Fear" caters to the white imagination. It is inscribed by the rudimentary aspects of racial analysis incarnated through David.

There is a double bind at work here. Although it is crucial that whites "buy into" racial justice since they arguably possess the strongest form of investment in race (Lipsitz, 1998), they also have the most to give up in terms of material resources. Consequently, convincing them to appropriate racial analysis for their own lives runs into difficulties. This is what McIntosh inevitably attempts with her honest appraisal of her own privilege. However, she is led to construct her narrative in such a way that obscures some of the real processes of racial domination. This strategy might be necessary insofar as she avoids threatening her (white) audience to the point that they discredit her message. Anyone who has performed a radical racial analysis has faced a similar scenario where the messenger is dismissed because the message produces psychological dissonance between a white subject's desire for racial justice and her inability to accept radical change. Nevertheless, there are certain discursive costs.

Throughout her essay, McIntosh repeats her experience of having been taught to ignore her privilege, to consider her worldview as normal, and to treat race as the problem of the other. Deserving to be quoted at length, she writes:

> [W]hites are carefully taught not to recognize white privilege . . . about which I was "meant" to remain oblivious . . . My schooling gave me no training in seeing myself as an oppressor . . . I was taught to see myself as an individual whose moral state depended on her individual moral will . . . [a] pattern of assumptions that were passed on to me as a white person . . . I was taught to recognize racism only in individual acts of meanness by members of my group, never in invisible systems conferring racial dominance on my group from birth (pp. 71, 72, 77, 81).

First, notice the passage's passive tone. White racist thoughts are disembodied, omnipresent but belonging to no one. White racist teachings, life lessons, and values are depicted as actions done or passed on to a white subject, almost unbeknownst to him, rather than something in which he invests. Second, the passage is consistent with McIntosh's advice for whites to avoid feelings of personal blame for racism. But white domination is never settled once and for all; it is constantly reestablished and reconstructed by whites *from all walks of life*. It is not a relation of power secured by slavery, Jim Crow, or job discrimination alone. It is not a process with a clear beginning or a foreseeable end (Bell, 1992). Last, it is not solely the domain of white supremacist groups. It is rather the domain of average, tolerant people, of lovers of diversity, and of believers in justice.

If racist relations were created only by people in the past, then racism would not be as formidable as it is today. It could be regarded as part of the historical dustbin and a relic of a cruel society. If racism were only problems promulgated by "bad whites," then either bad whites today outnumber "good whites" or overpower them. The question becomes: Who are these bad whites? It must be the position of a good white person to declare that racism is always about "other whites," perhaps "those working class whites." This is a general alibi to create the "racist" as always other, the self being an exception. Since very few whites exist who actually believe they are racist, then basically no one is racist and racism disappears more quickly than we can describe it. We live in a condition where racism thrives absent of racists (Bonilla-Silva, 2003). There must be an alternative explanation: in general, whites recreate their own racial supremacy, despite good intentions.

There is the other half of domination that needs our attention: white investment. To the extent that racial supremacy is taught to white students, it is pedagogical. Insofar as it is pedagogical, there is the possibility of critically reflecting on its flows in order to disrupt them. The hidden curriculum of whiteness saturates everyday school life and one of the first steps to articulating its features is coming to terms with its specific modes of discourse. In an interview with Grossberg, Stuart Hall (1996e) defines "articulation" as "the connection that *can* make a unity of two different elements, under certain conditions. It is a linkage which is not necessary, determined, absolute, and essential for all time" (p. 141; italics in original). Articulating the possibility of "universal" white supremacy necessitates strategies that unpack discourses in particular school places, which coalesce, making it possible for white supremacy to thrive. One of its features that critical educators confront is the notion of investment. The forces of racial amnesia daily threaten both white and non-white students. School curricula are able to describe racial disparities but are often limited to their testable forms and standardized lessons. Critical discourse on the continuity between past and present, institutional arrangements, and the problems of color-blind discourses are forsaken for "correct" forms of knowledge.

Communities of color have constructed counter-discourses in the home, church, and informal school cultures in order to maintain their sense of humanity. They know too well that their sanity and development, both as individuals and a collective, depend on alternative (unofficial) knowledge of the racial formation. By contrast, white subjects do not forge these same counter-hegemonic racial understandings because their lives also depend on a certain development, that is, color-blind strategies that maintain their supremacy as a group. Like their non-white counterparts, white students are not taught anti-racist understandings in schools; both are cheated of a critical race education. But unlike non-whites, whites invest in practices that obscure racial processes. State sponsored curricula fail to encourage students of all racial backgrounds to critique white domination. In other words, schools may teach white students to naturalize their unearned privileges, but they also willingly participate in such discourses, which maintains *their* sense of humanity. White humanity is just that: humanity of whites. So it is not only the case that whites are taught to normalize their dominant position in society; they are susceptible to these forms of teachings because they benefit from them. It is not a process that is somehow done to them, as if they were duped, are victims of manipulation, or lacked certain learning opportunities. Rather, the color-blind discourse is one that they fully endorse.

White domination is the responsibility of every white subject because her very being depends on it. A discourse of absolution misses the mark on the actual processes of white supremacy, a process that benefits all white subjects but in particular ways. Poor or working class whites may be beneficiaries of white supremacy, but they are not signatories of it (Mills, 1997). That said, if whites do not assume responsibility for the history of white supremacy, then who can? The strategy of race treason asks whites to take personal and group responsibility for the predicament we know as structural racism (Ignatiev and Garvey, 1996b). This is undoubtedly an unpopular option because the situation is admittedly "more complex" than that. It is true that people of color add to or participate in their own oppression, but at most this is annoying, not oppressive, to whites. Often, it is a psycho-social result of the degradation of a whole race of people and how it compromises their self-confidence and produces apoliticized forms of resistance. We can also speak of maltreatment between minorities, or what I call "inter-minoritarian politics," which is different from white racism. As I explained in Chapter 3, it is even possible that non-whites act or speak in ways that rearticulate and reinforce racist relations.

When Stephen Steinberg (1998) criticizes William Julius Wilson for his "retreat from race," Steinberg, who brands Wilson as former New York Senator Patrick Moynihan's academic reincarnation, calls into question any universal or color-blind social policy as a backlash of liberal thought since the 1960s. Wilson's (1987) popular and generalist proposals for raising black educational skills and credentials puts the onus on blacks to disrupt the cycle or culture of poverty, rather than centering the problem of white racism and its legacy of school segregation and Euro-centric curricula, just to name a few. Steinberg also takes Cornel West to task when the otherwise insurgent philosopher attempts to uplift the spirit of the race by noting its nihilistic tendencies and rampant materialism (see West, 1994), thus deflecting the focus away from white supremacy. One should not confuse Steinberg for suggesting that these afflictions, as West describes them, are not real or that the black community does not have its *own* problems. It also may sound strange to pair two scholars with seemingly divergent political commitments, Wilson being a social democrat of a Weberian persuasion and West (1999b) a self-proclaimed "democratic and libertarian socialist" (p. 256). Wilson and West's political similarity ends with the alliteration of their names. In fact, one senses West discursively distancing himself from his former Harvard colleague who advocates a "bourgeois perspective" with respect to Afro-American oppression (West, 1988, p. 21).

Steinberg (1998) interrogates West, like Wilson and Moynihan before him, for a "politics of conversion" that announces black nihilism as "a problem *sui generis*, with an existence and momentum independent of the forces that gave rise to it in the first place" (p. 37), a cultural politics with a life of its own independent of political economy and white domination. Is this a return to the culture of poverty argument? Indeed, it is a bit telling that the trade book, *Race Matters*, arguably West's least radical compendium on race and racism, should strike such an enchanting chord with the public. Because *Race Matters* resonates with a white audience's imagery of blacks as pathological and nihilistic, its discursive consequences are such that the text becomes coffee table reading for the white imagination, despite its best intentions. This is the power of discourse to be inserted into the historical flow out of the hands of its creator. West also receives added criticism from Miles and Torres (1999) who question if "race matters," preferring a return to class struggle. On this note, West (1999a) does not negate the importance of class struggle in tandem with race struggle. That said, he seems less concerned that the economy assumes a determining effect on race and other relations, let alone an originary point of struggle.

The sheer amount of acts of violence or terror by whites toward racial minorities is overwhelming. However, following the format used by McIntosh, it is helpful to create a selective list of acts, laws, and decisions, if only to capture a reliable portrait of white supremacy.

1. In order to promote the "purity" of the white race, anti-miscegenation laws prevent diversification of the gene pool (Davis, 2001; Alcoff, 2000). White racism's claims to purity is an instance of its problematic humanist essentialism (Balibar, 1990).

2. Housing segregation limits black mobility and access to jobs and other kinds of networks. Abandoned in inner cities, blacks suffer the most enduring and complete ghettoization in American history (Massey and Denton, 1993).

3. The rule of hypodescent, or the "one drop rule," allows the creation of more blacks and hence more slaves, increases scarcity of white identity, and provides an "out" for white rapists of black women to claim responsibility for their children (Davis, 2001; hooks, 1981).

4. Segregated education for students of color creates substandard schools, lack of resources, and inferior education (Spring, 2000). Even after the 1954 decision following Brown vs. Board of Education in Topeka, Kansas ruled that "separate is inherently unequal," second generation, or *de facto*, segregation still mars the educational experience of many students of color in the USA (Kozol, 1991).

5. Anti-immigrant Laws and Exclusion Acts curtail the rights of many Asian immigrants on U.S. soil and place limitations or quotas on immigration from their home nation (Takaki, 1993). These laws negatively affect family development and life, psychological wellness, and increases experiences of exile in Asian immigrants.

6. Colonization of third world nations establishes white global supremacy and perceived white superiority (Fanon, 1963; Memmi, 1965). Much of the continents of Africa, South America, North America, Australia, frigid Greenland and New Zealand, and large chunks of tropical Asia and the Pacific Islands succumbed to the expansion of the white race (see Jordan, 1968).

7. The Occident creates its infantilized other through methods of

cultural imperialism whereby the other is constructed, controlled, and written into inferiority (Said, 1979, 1994). Through cultural imperialism, ideologies of the West make their way to the shores of the "heart of darkness," (Conrad's terminology) where the culture of the white race is consolidated into a dominant frame of reference for civilization, moral development, and rationality.

8. Job discrimination limits the upward mobility of workers of color and their access to productive networks (Feagin and Vera, 1995; Feagin, 2000).

9. Whites' genocidal efforts against Native Americans facilitate take-over of Northern American soil and the attempt to eliminate its indigenous population. Where a policy of elimination was not possible, whites produced a form of education violent to Native Americans (Dog and Erdoes, 1999; Grande, 2004).

10. Global enslavement of Africans produced profit for white slave owners, compromised African collective development, and established centuries of the master-slave relationship between whites and blacks (Jordan, 1968; Fanon, 1967).

11. U.S. internment camps for Japanese targets an Asian group as "traitors" of the nation state and brands them as "forever foreigners" on U.S. soil. The same treatment did not fall on other "enemies of the state" during WWII, like Germans or Italians (Houston and Houston, 1973).

12. Exoticization of the other, which masks the colonial policy of the degradation of indigenous culture, has turned colonial posts into commercial artifacts to be enjoyed by the white imagination. Colonized lands, like Hawaii, are now places thoroughly "tourified" for the pleasure of visitors to partake in its stereotypical, prostituted, cultural forms (Trask, 1999).

13. California's Proposition 227, and others like it, impose English as the only legitimate language in schools and the workplace, thereby devaluing non-white cultures (Nieto, 2003a). Although other European languages, such as French and German, are also unofficial, groups associated with them are not conveniently constructed as "aliens," or the common insult for Mexicans and other Latinos.

14. Appropriation of third world labor exploits the global work force for the profit of post-industrial first world nations and the benefit of the white global bourgeoisie. This increases alienation for both groups, with the third world suffering the brutal structures of exploitation, unsafe work conditions, and an imbalance in relations of power among nations (Davis, 1997).

15. Military installation of naval and army bases to "protect" third world nations from external aggression promotes a condescending

and patronizing relationship between the protectorate first world nation and third world nation whose sovereignty is compromised (Enloe, 2001).

16. Welfare reform legislation in the USA, reaching its height during the Clinton era, works against the interests of people of color (Neubeck and Cazenave, 2001).

17. Forced sterilization of women of color continues the curtailment of their human and reproduction rights (Roberts, 1999).

18. The Tuskegee syphilis study, and other unethical medical research projects like it, use minority bodies for medical experimentations without the participants' full awareness and consent. In this case, the U.S. government deceived 400 blacks by promising free treatment for their syphilis. Between 1932 and 1972, the researchers conducted their disguised study of *untreated* syphilis, from which 100 black men died (Spina, 2000).

19. Jim Crow Laws create American Apartheid whereby blacks and whites are treated unequally under the auspices of the judicial system (Morris, 1984).

20. Inheritance Laws favor whites, whose families benefited from free black labor during slavery. Centuries later, their children retain their parents' wealth. In general, whites bequeath wealth onto their children, whereas blacks often bequeath debt to theirs (Oliver and Shapiro, 1997).

21. IQ-Intelligence testing, eugenics, and phrenology construct the genetic inferiority of people of color (Stepan, 1990). The popular book, *The Bell Curve* (1994), revisits and reasserts eugenics assumptions.

22. Tracking practices in schools limit the educational mobility, curricular offerings, and positive interactions with teachers of black and Latino students (Oakes, 2005).

23. The systematic lynching of African Americans served as a tool of social control. Often couched in the fears of miscegenation, lynching was thought to be justified because African Americans violated the racial and social etiquettes of the South or for their civil rights activism, such as registering to vote (Davis, 1981).

24. Race riots against blacks were used as tools by whites to destroy black property and business districts, especially when they were flourishing. Riots were also used to enforce neighborhood boundaries that maintained racial segregation. Reparations to blacks, who lost their property during the riots, were never made. Moreover, city governments often never officially acknowledged that the riots occurred (Massey and Denton, 1993; Roediger, 1991).

25. Women of color are more likely to be raped than white women, but less likely to be believed. The USA has a long history of sexual abuse

of women of color, largely because of their lack of power and whites' hypersexualization of them. Sexual abuse and rape of women of color create a culture of violence toward women of color (Davis, 1981).

26. White imposition of Christian religion and forceful conversion of non-Christian peoples (Spring, 2000).

27. Whites subverted community reading programs and other educational practices by blacks, forcing them to create surreptitious literacy programs (Holt, 1990).

28. Union exclusion of blacks from the working class movement or from leadership positions in proletarian groups (West, 1999b).

29. Many blacks and Latinos live in forsaken neighborhoods with high levels of toxic pollution. As a result, they suffer from diseases related to these forms of environmental racism (Lipsitz, 1998).

Privilege is the daily cognate of structural domination. Without securing the latter, the former is not activated. A few examples should suffice. Whites have "neighbors . . . [who] are neutral or pleasant" (McIntosh, 1992, p. 73) to them because redlining and other real estate practices, with the help of the Federal Housing Agency, secure the ejection of the black body from white spaces. Whites can enter a business establishment and expect the " 'person in charge' to be white" (McIntosh, 1992, p. 74) because of a long history of job discrimination. Whites are relatively free from racial harassment from police officers because racial profiling strategies train U.S. police officers that people of color are potential criminals. Finally, whites "can choose blemish cover or bandages in 'flesh' color" to match their skin (McIntosh, 1992, p. 75) because of centuries of denigration of darker peoples and images associated with them, fetishism of the color line, and the cultivation of the politics of pigmentation. We can condense the list under a general theme: whites enjoy privileges largely because they have created a system of domination under which they can thrive as a group. The volumes of writing on the issue of domination testify that the process is complex and multi-causal. But the enactment is quite simple: set up a system that benefits the group, mystify the system, remove the agents of actions from discourse, and when interrogated about it, stifle the discussion with inane comments about the "reality" of the charges being made.

When it comes to official history, there is no paucity of representation of whites as its creator. From civil society, to science, to art, whites represent the subject for what Matthew Arnold once called the best that a culture has produced. In other words, white imprint is everywhere. However, when it concerns domination, whites suddenly disappear, as if history were purely a positive sense of contribution. Their previous omnipresence becomes a position of nowhere, a certain politics of undetectability. When it comes to culture, our students learn a benign form of multiculturalism, as if culture were a purely constructive notion absent of imperialist histories and examples of imposition. Encouraging white students to reinsert themselves into the underbelly of history does not always have to occur in a self-destructive context. There are ways to address domination that require very little from people who benefit from it.

A white student in one of my courses admitted that whites possess the ultimate power in the USA and it does not threaten him much as an individual to recognize this fact. He explained that he can take this first step and often wonders why other whites find it so hard to join him. After all, admission does not necessarily mean ending domination; yet, many whites find even this act of enunciation impossible. In a brave attempt to ameliorate historical wounds between Japan and the Philippines, Professor Tsuyoshi Amemiya of Aoyama Gakuin University in Tokyo, Japan works with his students to accept personal responsibility for Japan's imperialist past (Walfish, 2001). None of these students occupied the Philippines during World War II; none of them were involved in the killings during this military invasion; and none of them appropriated the Filipinos' labor. But they all have one thing in common: an inherited sense of history that belongs to, rather than taken from, them. These students are not admitting that they created Japan's imperialist past and current Asian hegemony. Far from it. However, they recognize that their daily taken-for-granted benefits are legacies from the decades of Japanese imperialist policies.

Likewise, Australians have discussed instituting a national day of grieving, a day of atonement for crimes against the aboriginal population. White Australians are encouraged to sign a "sorry book" to apologize to indigenous people and acknowledge responsibility for the history of colonization and its continuing legacies, like the lost generation of aboriginal people whom the Australian government took from their families and tried to assimilate into white culture. Such a gesture does not represent a radical solution but an official attempt to recognize white racial domination. In the United States, the effort to provide former slaves "forty acres and a mule" failed during Reconstruction. Whites resisted this expression of atonement, one that would have changed the landscape of racial relations. Free blacks would have come closer to Booker T. Washington's (1986) dream of economic independence and a rebuilding of black America. In the new millennium, the U.S. government is no closer to an official apology or plans for reparations.

The discourse on privilege has pushed critical education to ask crucial questions about the nature of "white experience" and the psychological and material benefits from an unearned position in society. To the extent that white audiences need a discursive space they can negotiate as safe participants in race critique, discourses on privilege provide the entry. However, insofar as white feelings of safety perpetuate a legacy of white refusal to engage racial domination, or acts of terror toward people of color, such discourses rearticulate the privilege that whites already enjoy when they are able to evade confronting white supremacy. As long as whites ultimately feel a sense of comfort with racial analysis, they will not sympathize with the pain and discomfort they have unleashed on racial minorities for centuries. Solidarity between whites and non-whites will proceed at the reluctant pace of the white imagination, whose subjects accept the problem of racism without an agent.

A discourse on supremacy offers whites and minority students a progressive starting point because it does not cater to white racial thinking. Racial minorities comprise its projected audience, whether or not this is literally the case. As a result, it recognizes the existence of minority subjects and affirms their history. It begins from their starting point, one which needs little convincing about the reality of white domination. Discourses of supremacy acknowledge white privileges, but only as a function of whites' actions toward minority subjects and not as mysterious accumulations of unearned advantages. In our post-September 11 global village, racism reaches into the hearts of more people, into the hearths of their homes and schools. Through discourses of supremacy the racial story unfolds, complete with characters, actions, and conflicts. More important, resolution of the plot transforms into a discreet and pedagogical possibility.

6

The Ontology of Whiteness

Race scholarship is witnessing a shift. In Chapter 4, I analyzed the status of race within whiteness studies; here I would like to explain the status of whiteness within race theory. In the past two decades, whiteness studies has penetrated what arguably has been the home of scholars of color who write for and about people of color. Circa 1990, whiteness studies burst onto the academic scene with three important publications, written by white scholars about, but not exclusively for, white people. In fact, we would not be far off to characterize whiteness studies as a white-led race intervention. Circa 1990, McIntosh's (1992) essay on white privilege, David Roediger's (1991) *Wages of Whiteness*, and Ruth Frankenberg's (1993) *White Women, Race Matters* arguably represent the beginnings of a focus on whiteness and white experiences. Since then, there has been a veritable explosion of critical work on whiteness across the disciplines (Morrison, 1993; Allen, 1994, 1997; Ignatiev, 1995; hooks, 1997; Winant, 1997; Dyer, 1997; Aanerud, 1997; Lipsitz, 1998; Brodkin, 1999; Warren, 2000; Thompson, 2001; Bush, 2005; Wise, 2007). In education, the impact of whiteness studies has been no less (Sleeter, 1995a; McLaren, 1995, 1997; Giroux, 1997a, 1997b, 1997c; Ellsworth, 1997; McIntyre, 1997; Apple, 1998; Kincheloe and Steinberg, 1998; Howard, 1999; Sheets, 2000; Allen, 2002; Thompson, 2003; Richardson and Villenas, 2000; Gillborn, 2005; Lee, 2005; DiAngelo, 2006). It should be noted that scholars of color previously took up the issue of whiteness, but as a secondary if not tertiary concern (see Du Bois, 1989), insofar as studying the souls of white folk was an afterthought to the souls of black folk. With whiteness studies, whiteness and white people come to the center in an unprecedented and unforeseen way. This is different from the centering that whiteness is usually afforded in Eurocentric curricula and writing. Indeed it would be problematic to recenter whiteness as a point of reference for civilization, progress, and rationality in order to relegate people of color to the margins, once again. In whiteness studies, *whiteness becomes the center of critique and transformation*. It represents the much-neglected anxiety around race that whiteness scholars, many of whom are white, are now beginning to recognize.

Whiteness studies is both a conceptual engagement and a racial strategy. Conceptually, it poses critical questions about the history, meaning, and ontological status of whiteness. For example, it contains an apparatus for the precise rendering of whiteness' origin as a social category. In other words, whiteness is not coterminous with the notion that some people have lighter skin tones than others; rather whiteness, along with race, is the structural valuation of skin color, which invests it with meaning regarding the overall organization of society. In this sense, whiteness conceptually had to be invented and then reorganized in particular historical conditions as part of its upkeep. Inseparable from the conceptualization of whiteness, whiteness studies comes with certain interventions or racial strategies. There are two significant camps regarding the uptake of whiteness: white reconstruction and white abolition (Chubbuck, 2004). In the first, reconstructionists offer discourses—as forms of social practice—that transform whiteness, and therefore white people, into something other than an oppressive identity and ideology. Reconstruction suggests rehabilitating whiteness by resignifying it through the creation of alternative discourses. It projects hope onto whiteness by creating new racial subjects out of white people, which are not ensnared by a racist logic. On the other hand, white abolitionism is guided by Roediger's (1994) announcement that "whiteness is not only false and oppressive, it is *nothing but* false and oppressive" (p. 13; italics in original). In opposition to reconstructing whiteness, abolishing whiteness sees no redeeming aspects of it and as long as white people think they are white, Baldwin once opined that there is no hope for them (as cited by Roediger, 1994, p. 13). This chapter will consider white reconstruction and abolition for their conceptual and political value as it concerns not only the revolution of whiteness but of race theory in general.

Neo-abolitionists argue that whiteness is the center of the "race problem." They go further than suggesting that racism is a "white problem." Rather, as long as whiteness exists, little racial progress will be made. In fact, leading abolitionists, Ignatiev and Garvey (1996a), argue that multiculturalism and general race theories that accept the existence of races, are problematic for their naturalization of what are otherwise reified concepts. To Ignatiev and Garvey, races are not *real* in an objective and ontological sense and therefore whites, for example, are not real either. They do not go as far as suggesting that white people do not *exist*, which is a different point. They exist insofar as structures recognize white bodies as "white people." But this recognition relies on the reification of a spurious category in order simultaneously to misrecognize certain human subjects as white people. Race treason encourages whites to disrupt this process by pledging their disallegiance to the "white club." Race traitors are white bodies that no longer act like white people. The investment in whiteness (Lipsitz, 1998) is the strongest form of investment because it is the most privileged racial identification. As long as whites invest in whiteness, the existence of non-white races will also continue. Hirschman (2004) has argued that as long as race exists, so does racism and it is anachronistic to imagine one without the other. The clarion call for abolitionists asks whites to disidentify with whiteness, leading to the eventual abolition of whiteness. I would also add that it leads to another consequence, which is the abolition of white people, or the withering away of a racial category and its subjects. In other words, if whiteness disappears, so do white people. I will have more to say about this last point below.

By contrast, white reconstructionists disagree with abolitionists in the former's attempt to recover whiteness. The disagreement falls within two domains: theory and viability. Theoretically, reconstructionists do not accept Roediger's maxim that whiteness is only false and oppressive because there are many examples of whites who have fought against racism, such as the original abolitionists. Reconstructionists argue that whites can be remade, revisioned, and resignified and are not merely hopelessly racist. Their search is for a rearticulated form of whiteness that reclaims its identity for racial justice. They acknowledge that whiteness is a privilege but that whites can use this privilege for purposes of racial justice and therefore contribute to the remaking of whiteness that is not inherently oppressive and false. In schools, reconstructing whiteness includes focusing on white historical figures who have fought and still fight against racial oppression. Reconstructionists consider this strategy as more viable than arguing for the abolition of whiteness, which most whites will have a difficult time accepting. The discourse of white abolition will only lead to white defensiveness and retrenchment and does not represent much hope for even progressive or anti-racist whites. To the reconstructionists, abolitionism is tantamount to promoting a certain self-hatred and shame among whites, guilting them into accepting a movement that does not recognize their complexity. Rather, they prefer to instill critical hope in whites.

Clearly, there has been a shift in race studies and whiteness has come to the fore much more visibly. It is driven by a complex yet plainly stated question: What to do with whiteness? The debate between white abolition and reconstruction is a fertile educational ground. It represents a neglected aspect in race studies, which is the future of a privileged people and how they can participate in undoing these same privileges. It also poses the question of, "What do whites become after undoing these said privileges?" Do they become new subjects of whiteness or do they obliterate a racial category beyond recognition when they commit what Ignatiev and Garvey call "the unreasonable act" of race treason? Just as we may ask what the modern looks like after the postmodern critique (Lyotard, 1984), what do whites look like, in the ontological sense, after the critique of whiteness studies? This chapter hopes to generate not only insights about this process, but a rather needed dialogue. It is less concerned with identifying who is a reconstructionist or abolitionist of whiteness (although one can certainly have a productive discussion that begins there), and more with assessing the interventions that each discourse provides.

White by Another Name: White Reconstructionism in Education

Before we begin, one caveat must be entered. By focusing on whiteness, Apple (1998) warns that scholars of whiteness studies may unwittingly recenter whiteness, insufficiently knocking it off its orbit. He writes:

> [W]e must be on our guard to ensure that a focus on whiteness doesn't become one more excuse to recenter dominant voices and to ignore the voices and testimony of those groups of people whose dreams, hopes, lives, and very bodies are shattered by current relations of exploitation and domination (p. xi).

Much useful work has been spent on decentering whiteness from its privileged son of God status. When the sun of whiteness has been centered the planets of color have suffered. However, the centering of whiteness has also been an example of a certain inverted understanding, a geocentric theory that mistakes the real dynamics of social life and development. Not only does whiteness encourage us to be "flat earthers" (Friedman's phrase), but it constructs a Ptolemaic universe that misunderstands a world it has created after its own image (Mills, 1997). As a privileged marker, whiteness assumed that the lives of people of color depended on white progress and enlightenment, whereas a heliocentric critical theory puts whiteness in its rightful place in racial cosmology, as largely dependent and parasitic on the labor and identity of people of color. By recentering whiteness here, we counteract what may be dubbed the superstitious beliefs in the rightness of whiteness and institute a more scientific explanation of how the social universe actually functions. In other words, if critical studies of race recenter whiteness, it does not do so in order to valorize or pedestalize it. Quite the opposite. A critical study of whiteness puts the social heavens back in order.

The rearticulation of whiteness is part of an overall emancipatory project that implicates a host of institutions from economic to educational. Discursive interventions in education to transform whiteness attempt to explain the whiteness of pedagogy as they encourage a pedagogy of whiteness. That is, shifting the white racial project from one of dominance to one of justice requires a pedagogical process of unlearning the codes of what it currently means to be white and rescuing its redeeming aspects. Giroux (1997a) writes, " 'Whiteness' . . . becomes less a matter of creating a new form of identity politics than an attempt to rearticulate 'whiteness' as part of a broader project of cultural, social, and political citizenship" (p. 295). In rescuing whiteness, critical educators insert hope in white people as hermeneutic subjects who may interpret social life in liberating ways and not as hopelessly stuck in the molasses of racism. It recognizes the multiple moments of white history as an attempt to complexify racial options for whites (indeed speak to its existing complexity). In the dialectics of whiteness, whites search for positive articulations in history as well as facing up to the contradictions of what it means to be anti-racist in a racist society. Seen this way, the current formulations of whiteness are racist, but whiteness itself is not inherently racist. Being white is not the problem; being a white racist is.

Dislodged from the hopelessness and helplessness of having to consider oneself as simply privileged (therefore racist), white students' humanity is affirmed as the ability to choose justice over domination. Here, abolitionists may agree that whiteness is a choice, at least with respect to the kind of white person one chooses to uphold. This new racial project asks:

> [h]ow students might critically mediate the complex relations between "whiteness" and racism, not by having them repudiate their "whiteness," but by grappling with its legacy and its potential to be rearticulated in oppositional and transformative terms . . . ways to move beyond the view of "whiteness" as simply a trope of domination (Giroux, 1997a, p. 296).

Questioning the essentialism of identity politics, Giroux projects a third space for whites, which neither valorizes their "accomplishments" nor over-states their complicity in relations of domination (see also Giroux, 1997b, 1997c). Their history is not determined by the originary sin of racism but rather a complex web of contradictions that make up what it means to be white in any given context. As such, educators recognize the anti-racist moments within white hegemony as well as the racist traps of white calls for racial justice. The abolitionist movement of the nineteenth century provides a glimpse into this dualism if we consider the fact that John Brown and his comrades fought to dismantle slavery while their white privilege made their installment in leadership positions possible over those of black abolitionists, like Frederick Douglass. A reading of the abolitionists as exceptions to the white rule (so common in history books and lessons) misses the way that white privilege works to favor even white abolitionists; equally, educators note how, by fighting against the institution of slavery, abolitionists were remaking what it meant to be white. It testifies to the fact that "*some* of the time, in *some* respects even when not in *all*, whites empathize and identify with nonwhites, abhor how white supremacy has distorted their social interactions, and are willing to make significant sacrifices toward the eradication of white privilege" (Alcoff, 1998, http://www.iupress.indiana.edu/journals/hypatia/hyp13-3.html). In short, they were able to "rearticulate whiteness in oppositional terms" (Giroux, 1997a, p. 310). To the extent that the abolitionists were racially privileged and that they used these said privileges to edge out black abolitionists in discursive and institutional positions of leadership, they were anti-racist racists. They were located in the cauldron of whiteness without being entrapped in its determinisms insofar as they were anti-racist without being anti-white.

Within this perspective, social domination is not the sole property of whites as there have been many examples of non-white forms of domination. As Gary

Howard (1999) might put it, whiteness is not the problem but rather certain interpretations of what it means to be white that lead to forms of domination. The theory of social dominance is too deterministic because it fails to recognize the multiple positions that whites take up in the race struggle. There are different ways to be white: from fundamentalist, to integrationist, to transformationist. Or as Ellsworth (1997) once put it, "It is more than one thing and never the same thing twice" (p. 226). Just as Christianity is not the source of a religious problem, but interpretations that encourage subjugation of non-Christian peoples, the ultimate meaning of whiteness is up for reinterpretation under concrete conditions of struggle as educators "disrupt the sanctification of whiteness" (McIntyre, 1997, p. 149). Rather than rejecting whiteness, Howard suggests "breaking" out of whiteness, "emerging" from it to become something else. This process should not be underestimated. Just as Lenin once remarked that whereas the proletariat must merely be educated and the bourgeoisie must be revolutionized (see Althusser, 1976), so must whites be transformed or experience a transformative education. In other words, although the social experiences of both the working class and people of color provide the basis for understanding the nature of their oppression, we cannot say the same for the bourgeoisie and whites who must be "reborn" like the phoenix (Allen, 2005; Freire, 1993).

Because whiteness is a social construction, a range of possibilities is opened up for white agency. Although durable, racial identity is also fluid and flexible. It fractures into different racial projects, some of which do not merely reproduce and reiterate white power. That said, reconstructionists suggest that struggling with whiteness is well within a racial project, not an attempt to get outside of it (see also Omi and Winant, 1994). In this sense, *racial ideology has no outside*. As Kincheloe and Steinberg (1998) note, "As with any racial category, whiteness is a social construction in that it can be invented, lived, analyzed, modified, and discarded" (p. 8), which echoes Omi and Winant's contention that racial projects can be created, modified, and even destroyed. For the moment, Ignatiev and Garvey (1996a) agree when they declare that "what was once historically constructed can be undone" (p. 35). More of an ideological choice than a biological destiny, whiteness is part of a hermeneutics of the self. Though not entirely up to the individual to transform, whiteness represents a constellation of differences articulated to appear as a "lump-sum" category (Pollock, 2004), when in fact "there are many ways to be White" (Kincheloe and Steinberg, 1998, p. 8). Of course there are masculine and feminine ways to be white, poor and rich ways to be white, straight and gay ways, liberal and radical ways as well, which speak to "the diverse, contingent racial positions that white people assume" (Giroux, 1997a, p. 309). In this sense, resignifying whiteness leads us to the "multiple meanings of whiteness" (McIntyre, 1997, p. 4) that, rather than viewing it simply with suspicion for the world it hides, may imagine the world it opens up in front of it (Ricoeur, 1981;

Leonardo, 2003a). A hermeneutics of suspicion promotes disidentification with whiteness as erecting a veil (à la Du Bois) that works against its transparency, whereas a hermeneutics of empathy reserves hope that whiteness may emerge as an authentic worldview. This means that "making whiteness rather than white racism the focus of study is an important pedagogical strategy" (Giroux, 1997a, p. 309). White racism is inherently oppressive but whiteness, seen through the prism of reconstructionism, is multifaceted and undecidable.

In rearticulating whiteness, educators offer students discourses that provide not only access to different ways of being white, but also strategies that counter the anxiety associated with current discourses of whiteness. Because essentialist discourses limit the range of possibilities for white students to relate with others, their daily upkeep of whiteness is marked with extreme forms of racial anxiety and inauthenticity. Whites traverse the social landscape, threatened of being exposed as bogus racial agents as they round every corner. They know few alternative forms of whiteness outside the colonial framework, where they are interpellated as the colonizer. As a result, the unbearable whiteness of their being overcomes their search for alternative subjectivities and they become paralyzed to act. Giroux (1997a) asks:

> What subjectivities or points of identification become available to white students who can imagine white experience only as monolithic, self-contained, and deeply racist? What are the pedagogical and political stakes in rearticulating whiteness in antiessentialist terms so that white youth can understand and struggle against the legacy of white racism while using the particularities of "their own culture as a resource for resistance, reflection, and empowerment?" . . . a theoretical language for racializing whiteness without essentializing it (pp. 310–311).

The question here is less about students unbecoming white and more about what kind of whites they will become. It suggests coming to terms with the production of "white terror," perhaps "unthinking whiteness," but certainly not the abolition of the self, which comes with obvious contradictions for whites (McLaren, 1995, 1997). It is not a move to promote historical amnesia concerning white atrocities against the other thereby promoting a certain white "innocence," but redeeming whiteness in order to come to terms with these crimes and develop a positionality against them. In the process, whites assert their humanity as beings-in-struggle and beings-for-others, rather than using others-for-their-being. In this search, Giroux is adamant about developing a "power-strategic politics that refuses to accept 'whiteness' as a racial category that has only one purpose, which is closely tied to, if not defined by, shifting narratives of domination and oppression" (Giroux, 1997a, p. 306). It is a call for living with difference that is the cornerstone of the pedagogical interaction that Lisa Delpit (1995) coined as "teaching other people's children." Because we know that much of the teaching force is comprised by and large with white women, the reinvention of whiteness becomes even more imperative if the educating population not only will reach, but equally teach, the learning population that is increasingly less white.

In articulating a white position against racism, reconstructionists transform white identity from a cul-de-sac formation of endless oppressive histories into a productive, even positive, subjectivity. Anti-racist whites may still be caught up in the contradictions of their own positionality and the privileges that come with it, but they can actively use their advantages responsibly to create an alternative racial arrangement that is less oppressive. To the extent that whites are unable to throw off years of racist lessons and are dogged by their racist unconscious, through self-reflection they inhere the possibility of developing into anti-racist subjects. Whiteness is not a hopeless disease and may be rehabilitated (McLaren and Torres, 1999). Thus:

> a key goal of a critical pedagogy of whiteness emerges: the necessity of creating a positive, proud, attractive, antiracist white identity that is empowered to travel in and out of various racial/ethnic circles with confidence and empathy . . . Traditional forms of multiculturalism have not offered a space for Whites to rethink their identity around a new, progressive, assertive, counter-hegemonic, antiracist notion of whiteness (Kincheloe and Steinberg, 1998, pp. 12, 20).

Developing a positive racial self for whites entails that educators open up pedagogical conditions for students to forge an intersubjective space wherein they are able to enter the other without becoming the other. Now it must be noted that whites already enter racial/ethnic circles with confidence. The phenomenon of racial exoticization and tourism already encourages whites to enter non-white spaces in a way that only a colonizer can, who always feels in charge even when outnumbered by the other (Memmi, 1965). From Elvis to Eminem, white privilege confers the mobility to travel in and out of communities of color despite whites' irrational (and ironic) fears about violence. Moreover, as Ingram (2005) suggests, it is not clear why whites must develop identities against racism through positive racial affiliations rather than through religious, secular humanist, or civic patriotic ones.

The operative concept here is "empathy." Rearticulating whiteness reminds whites that the ghetto and other concentrations of color were created by whites in order to fulfill the dictates of segregation, the hallmark of American apartheid (Massey and Denton, 1993). Empathy enables whites to become "border crossers" (Giroux, 1992) with the benefit of critical reflection and recollection. White border-crossers understand that transcending boundaries itself is a racial privilege. That is, the policing of people of color limits their mobility despite the fact that some trickle into white spaces. Border intellectuals recognize the difference between racial fetishism that addresses the other as abstract and solidarity that conceives of the other as concrete, albeit a concrete generalized other (Benhabib, 1987). Empathy is not a mode of desiring the other to be part of oneself through the process of enfleshment, but rather recognizing the completion of the self through the other.

A theory of white reconstructionism comes with certain interventions that make it a viable political movement. To the reconstructionist, it offers a way into whiteness rather than a way out of it. It encourages whites to own their whiteness rather than disowning it. Reconstructionism is not an idealist politics but a critical, pragmatic one. Kincheloe and Steinberg (1998) put it this way:

> We are not comfortable with the concept of a new oppositional white identity as a 'race traitor' who renounces whiteness. It is unlikely that a mass movement will grow around that concept, as oppositional whites still would have little to rally around or to affirm (p. 21).

Because reconstructing whiteness is likely to provide whites racial options that are more appealing and imaginable (without understating the difficulties associated with it), reconstructionism may find its way into education as a pedagogical principle. Just as it is becoming increasingly difficult for whites publicly to oppose multiculturalism insofar as the emerging question asks what kind of multiculturalism will be forged and not if multiculturalism is desirable (Buras, 2008), white raciality is becoming more difficult to avoid or deny. The question is no longer whether or not whites are racial subjects—clearly they are—but rather how this racial project will play itself out.

White teachers and students alike will find their humanity in whiteness rather than denying people of color of theirs through white deployments of power. Reconstructed white subjects "[d]evelop both theoretical and emotional support" (Kincheloe and Steinberg, 1998, p. 21) rather than wallowing in guilt, which can be paralyzing for even the liberal-thinking white person. In fact, opting out of whiteness is a racial privilege that people of color cannot enact. Kincheloe and Steinberg punctuate:

> Whites alone can opt out of their racial identity, can proclaim themselves nonraced. Yet no matter how vociferously they may renounce their whiteness, white people do not lose the power associated with being White. Such a reality renders many white renunciations disingenuous. It is as if some race traitors want to disconnect with all liabilities of whiteness (its association with racism and blandness) while maintaining all its assets (the privilege of not being Black, Latino, or Native American) (p. 22).

Disappearing is not something people of color can accomplish. To the extent that whites may desire it, it speaks to their power to make the other disappear and when desirable, make themselves vanish. A project of white reconstruction locates whiteness in order to change it, unlearn much of what passes as white normativity, and in the process reappear as transformed whites.

Kill the White, Save the Human: White Abolitionism and a Pedagogy of Zero Degree

To the extent that white reconstructionism is a more realistic and reasonable option to address the crisis of whiteness, the white abolitionist movement championed by Ignatiev, Garvey, and Roediger encourages whites to commit the "unreasonable act" of race treason. Committed to the understanding that the "key to solving the social problems of our age is to abolish the white race . . . so long as the white race exists, all movements against racism are doomed to fail" (Ignatiev and Garvey, 1996b, p. 10), white abolitionism takes its cue from a hybrid strategy melding both the original abolitionist movement's focus on nonparticipation and the inversion of a white supremacist charge that whites who disown whiteness are "race traitors." In other words, neo-abolitionists ask whites (particularly poignant for poor and working class whites) to opt out of their whiteness in search of a more accurate understanding of their social conditions and political interests; strategically, these new abolitionists favor appropriating race treason as their battle cry rather than their badge of dishonor. This is both an empirical as well as a theoretical injunction.

Empirically, whites have participated in race liberation movements, such as anti-slavery and Civil Rights, but this does not equate with acts of whiteness but actions by white subjects. In fact, white acts against racism are the very opposite of whiteness as a *modus operandi* insofar as acting against racism threatens whiteness. One might even go so far as saying that dismantling whiteness and racism leads to the eventual breakdown of white people as a social category. Against reconstructionism, abolitionism suggests that there is little empirical proof of a positive iteration of whiteness and searching for examples of positivity is as elusive as the holy grail. Or as Ingram (2005) puts it, "The attempt to save whiteness by reducing it to ethnic identity is futile . . . I therefore conclude that, although white persons need not feel guilty about who they are, they should not aspire to a positive ethno-racial identification in the way that blacks and other oppressed racial minorities might" (p. 247). It also leads Ignatiev (1997) to lay down the gauntlet:

> We at *Race Traitor* . . . have asked some of those who think whiteness contains any positive elements to indicate what they are. We are still waiting for an answer. Until we get one, we will take our stand with David Roediger, who has insisted that whiteness is not merely oppressive and false, it is nothing but oppressive and false" (http://racetraitor.org/abolishthepoint.html).

On one hand, this might appear like a performative contradiction and that race traitors want to have their abolitionist cake and eat it too. That is, even when whites commit morally supportable acts, these do not fall within the domain of whiteness but rather within otherness. Is this a double standard and part of racial entrapment? This is just the kind of fodder that frustrates many whites who may take it as an instance of "reverse discrimination." On the other hand, the sense hinges on a particular conceptualization of whiteness, which suggests that it cannot be reduced to a deterministic relation between actions and which racialized bodies commit them. Not all acts that whites commit are categorically part of whiteness. Sometimes, white acts are articulated with histories of color rather than whiteness.

Historically, transforming whiteness lacks any concrete example. When whites congeal into a skin collective (and people of color may join them), the results have been predictable. History shows that Irish workers picked race over class by edging out black workers, Californians voted against affirmative action (a staple of Civil Rights legislation), and suburbanization created the hypersegregation of blacks in ghettos. On the other hand, whites exist at the intersection of discourses that struggle for supremacy over their subjectivity. They exist in multiple worlds and have had to make decisions about traversing the racial landscape. Here one may insist on the varieties of white people without contradicting the assertion that whiteness exists solely for stratification. In history, whites may be and have been transformed. But as we shall see, even this assertion needs to be qualified since transforming whites may lead to their disappearance.

Transforming whiteness also lacks history because it does not come to terms with the function of whiteness—why it was created, where it has been— but rather projects an ideal image of whiteness (what it would like whiteness to be) rather than the concrete history that has constituted it. It wishes away whiteness through a discourse of white positivity that is nowhere to be found. Likewise, one can distinguish between Americanism and Americans, the former an ideology the second a form of citizenship (with all its contradictions). Whereas Americanism has been used in imperialist ways around the globe, Americans may fight against this project and establish some distance from it. Of course, even Americans who fight against American imperialism receive the benefits of being constructed as Americans. However unlike whiteness, we may argue that Americanism retains false premises and is quite oppressive worldwide, but it is *not only* oppressive and false.

When we define the ideology of whiteness as hopelessly bound up with what it means to be white, then whites are trapped into a particular way of making sense of their racial experience. Recalling Marx's (1988) words in *Theses on Feuerbach*, today's neo-abolitionists argue that *the point is not to interpret whiteness but to abolish it* (Ignatiev, 1997, http://racetraitor.org/abolishthe-point.html; italics in original). In other words, like the young Hegelians who were satisfied with describing the world rather than changing it, white apostasies short of abolitionism do not pose a real threat to the juggernaut of whiteness. In the same vein that a Marxist would abolish capital rather than reconstruct capitalism, the abolitionist sees little purpose in giving whiteness another chance. There is a difference between white bodies and white people. Beyond a structural determinism which signifies that white bodies are always conceived as white people, one can argue that white bodies (termed "white" here for convenience) only become white persons when they become *articulated* with whiteness. Certainly white bodies existed prior to race but were interpellated into its discursive structure roughly five centuries ago, articulated to appear a given that white bodies have always been white people. In contrast, white bodies are not always white people *every single moment*, particularly when they are conceived as "race traitors." Likewise and with its own specificity, people of color who side too close with whiteness have been labeled as inauthentic and implicated with whiteness. With a different force and outcome, both have been guilty of racial blasphemy.

In Roediger's (1994) understanding, poor and working class whites live a paradoxical relationship with whiteness. Suffering from capitalist exploitation, poor housing, health, and substandard education, lacking social and cultural capital, unrealized (as opposed to potential) political power, poor and working class whites desperately hang on to "the public and psychological wages of whiteness" in the face of grim realities (see Roediger, 1991; Du Bois, 1998). Interested in returning whites to their full humanity, Roediger opts for a racio-economic perspective and struggle. Understanding that class struggle is dependent on, without reducing it to, racial interpellation, Roediger makes sincere attempts to build a race/class analysis. He finds an absence that:

> [a]lmost no left initiatives have challenged white workers to critique, much less to abandon, whiteness . . . workers who identify themselves as white are bound to retreat from genuine class unity and meaningful anti-racism . . . If it does not involve a critique of whiteness, the questioning of racism often proves shallow and limited (1994, p. 13).

In exchange for a more accurate understanding of their class oppression, white proletarians cut themselves off from workers of color in order to invest in their whiteness, which is often all that they have (Alcoff, 1998; see also Willis, 1977). They are both oppressed by class exploitation and are beneficiaries of racism. As a result, they cannot galvanize a genuine class movement that fails to establish solidarity with workers of color, not to mention the problems associated with whites licking their economic wounds with white privilege.

The race/class problematic has proved to be the thorn in the side of whiteness. Roediger (1994) observes, "Rejection of whiteness is then part of a process that gives rise to both attacks on racism and to the very recovery of 'sense of oppression' among white workers" (p. 13). In the end, Roediger observes that their class struggle is intimately bound up with a race struggle; their way out of class is racialized. Ignatiev (1995) agrees:

It is not black people who have been prevented from drawing upon the full variety of experience that has gone into making up America. Rather it is those who, in maddened pursuit of the white whale, have cut themselves off from human society, on sea and on land, and locked themselves in a "masoned walled-town of exclusiveness (p. 21).

Abolitionists attract suspicion insofar as the dismantling of whiteness becomes a racial means to a Marxist end (Alcoff, 1998). In a Marxist project, whiteness is constructed as a distraction to class struggle, preventing white workers from seeing their true objective interests despite the fact that they inhere real, albeit contradictory, racial interests. It seems that a Marxist intervention has failed to galvanize a genuine class struggle because of racial divisions. Therefore, abolishing whiteness (and by implication, race) removes one of the obstacles so that the "real revolution" can get underway. This position may underestimate white workers' possessive investment in whiteness, which goes against Ignatiev and Garvey's (1996b) notion that most whites would "do the right thing if it were convenient" (p. 12). Whites of all economic classes cling onto their whiteness, which makes it inconvenient—and to some, inconceivable—to commit racial suicide. That said and the criticisms notwithstanding, abolitionists question the value of whiteness. Their intentions aside—and one cannot be certain here—race treason is about as disruptive to the established racial code as recently imagined.

Linda Alcoff does not offer textual evidence for her suspicions of the abolitionists' ulterior and Marxist motives, which no doubt would have made her objections more credible. However, it speaks of a history of suspicion from people of color concerning whites when it comes to their sincerity in race struggle due to their consistent lack of commitment to racial justice. Derrick Bell (1992) says as much when he writes of "interest convergence" and explains the fact that racial progress in the USA is bound up first with white interests and only second with black empowerment. In other words, whites have only accepted racial progress when their overall interest is observed and not threatened. In the case of abolitionists, dissolving whiteness may serve the ultimate end of the impending class abolition. If that is the case, is a movement problematic if it serves more than one end? If abolitionism accomplishes its goal of dismantling whiteness, which in itself is deemed defensible, why should it matter that it contains an ulterior, Marxist motive? If the ultimate goal is objectionable, that seems to be another point altogether but it does not seem self-evident that an ulterior motive would disrecommend the movement even if one accepts the premise but not the conclusion.

To the abolitionist, it is unconvincing to argue for the "rearticulation" or "transformation" of whiteness. Rather than rearticulating whiteness, abolitionists prefer to disarticulate it. Like science's claim to be self-corrective, transforming whiteness assumes that whites possess enough critical self-reflection and awareness to confront themselves. Searching for an identity that is both white and anti-racist, we may be tempted to conjure up a "new white American," a "transformed white global subject." But this suggestion lacks both empirical support and conceptual legs. It appears as the "last stand of whiteness" to assert itself into a history that has never existed or provides no example. Arguing for a transformed whiteness is appealing. Its limitation is that it substitutes proxy for praxis. It betrays a conciliatory posture toward the function and purpose of whiteness as a parasitic ideology and social practice. Whiteness exists in order to prey upon its racialized counterparts and *it has always existed in this manner*, according to Roediger. Whiteness has taken different forms in the evolution of societies: official Apartheid there, Jim Crow here, and genocide in another. But its face of oppression is unchanging.

On the other hand, white people have made many different choices in life, sometimes working against whiteness but more accurately as vacillating between ideologies of whiteness and the other, in differing and context-based choices, in various degrees of intensity and commitment. For example, when white teachers and educators question schooling's racial disparities, they are making a choice against whiteness *as* white people. They are not transforming whiteness into something positive because whiteness does not transform to become anti-racist. It is by definition racist. As whites dismantle racism, they eventually undercut the basis for their existence as supreme people. This signals the end of whites as we know it. There is no other side out of which to emerge as a different white subject. Just as tinkering with tracking to the point that one may imagine undoing its patterned and patent inequalities is hardly tracking anymore (Oakes, 2005), so we may argue that whites with little to no advantage are hardly white anymore.

Race is a figment of the imagination, a veritable monster in the proverbial hallway closet with whiteness as its most frightening expression. Under these assumptions, even anti-racism is doomed to fail because it acknowledges the existence of races. To Ignatiev and Garvey (1996a):

> The task is not to win over more whites to oppose "racism;" there are enough "anti-racists" enough already to do the job . . . when there comes into being a critical mass of people who, though they look white, have ceased to act white, the white race will undergo fission, and former whites will be able to take part in building a new human community (p. 37).

Although Ignatiev and Garvey may be faulted in their overestimation that there are enough anti-racist whites "to do the job," their point hinges on questioning the heuristic value of race, and by implication the political value of race struggle designed to perpetuate race. To be fair, Ignatiev and Garvey do not merely ask whites to "put up their hands" in desperation when it comes to racial identification, or to keep their hands down when racial interpellation hails their subjectivity. It is hardly subversive for whites to announce that they are not white. This is already their inclination. Race treason is not just a transgression involving personal identification, but falls completely within the realm of *behavior*. Through oppositional behavior, race traitors disrupt racial commitments and expectations. Ignatiev and Garvey (1996a) write:

> The need to maintain racial solidarity imposes a stifling conformity on whites, on any subject touching even remotely on race. The way to abolish the white race is to disrupt that conformity (p. 36).

Abolishing the white race does not only mean repudiating membership through annunciation ("I am not white"), but more important through denunciation ("I will not act white"). Denouncing one's whiteness both at the personal and group level suggests acting against its codes. It answers the call to do the work of race, to labor against racial consent. It requires that we "transform 'reverse racism' into an injunction (Reverse racism!)" (Roediger, 1994, p. 17). Again, we see here the ironic strategy of abolitionism to use white logic against itself, of inserting sense into senselessness (e.g., challenging the belief that reverse discrimination exists for whites).

For most whites, the opposite of abolitionism is more difficult and resisted: white racial ownership. Reconstructionists have a clearer sense of this first step by recognizing the need for belonging and not necessarily in the sense of loyalty to white supremacy, but to some kind of identity. In other words, outside of the call for a universal human identity for whites, abolitionists do not offer up a specific identity since abolition is precisely the assertion of a non-identity. It is possible that reconstruction may offer the means to an abolitionist end. Alcoff (1998) writes, "Rather than erase these inscriptions as a first step, we need a period of reinscription to redescribe and reunderstand what we see when we see race" at the same time that we may be able to project the emptiness of whiteness, "which unlike ethnic identities . . . has no other substantive cultural content" (http://www.iupress.indiana.edu/journals/hypatia/hyp13-3.html). That is, whites must first come to terms with what whiteness has made of them in order to consider the move towards abolitionism.

It is difficult to imagine whites, many of whom function through color-blindness, to take the radical leap of race treason. Because of their color-blindness, many whites may find it ironically convenient (and not in the sense that Ignatiev and Garvey predict) to use abolitionism as a way to further mask white privilege. By disabusing themselves of having to take responsibility for white atrocities, white abolitionists do not face up to whiteness, which sounds too familiar. But if after having participated in recognizing and then reconstructing whiteness, whites realize the emptiness of the category, the abolitionist position may not have started the story but would likely end it. So in the final analysis, there is a way that reconstructionism would provide the entrance into whiteness and abolitionism its exit.

7

The Myth of White Ignorance

In studies of race, the idea that whites do not know much about race is generally accepted. By virtue of their life experiences, white students and teachers are portrayed as subjects of race without much knowledge of its daily and structural features (McIntosh, 1992; Kincheloe and Steinberg, 1998; Dalton, 2002; McIntyre, 1997). It has been suggested that whites do not grow up with a race discourse, do not think of their life choices in racial ways, and do not consider themselves as belonging to a racial group. Gary Howard (1999) puts it best when he suggests that whites "can't teach what they don't know," an appropriation of a statement from Malcolm X to mean that white educators cannot teach about race if they do not have knowledge of it. As a result of this oblivion and apparent lack of race knowledge, many white educators and researchers avoid studying racialization because "Race is not 'their' project" (Greene and Abt-Perkins, 2003), a sentiment that Aanerud (1997) rejects when she claims that race affects and is fundamental to all our lives, including white lives. The challenge is often posed as the transformation of whites into knowledgeable people about race.

Arguing that whites are initially ignorant of race is helpful within certain parameters because it exposes their nonchalance and lack of urgency about its processes. Taken too far, it has unintended, but problematic consequences, one of which is that it promotes the "innocence" of whites when it comes to the structures of race and racism. It constructs them as almost oblivious to the question of race and therefore obscures their personal and group investment in whiteness (Lipsitz, 1998), as if racial oppression happens behind their backs rather than on the backs of people of color. This chapter, however, argues that whites do know a lot about race in both its everyday sense as a lived experience and its structural sense as a system of privilege. It attempts to "make race visible," (see Greene and Abt-Perkins, 2003), with the specific goal of "making whiteness visible." A critical reading of whiteness means that white ignorance must be problematized, not in order to expose whites as simply racist but to increase knowledge about their full participation in race relations. It also means that the racial formation must be read into the practices and texts that students and teachers negotiate with one another (see Harris, 1999) as a move to affirm educators' power to question narratives that have graduated to common sense or truth (Bishop, 2005), like the "fact" of white racial ignorance.

That whites enter race discourse with a different lens than people of color, such as a "color-blind" discourse (Schofield, 2005), sometimes called "new racism" (Bonilla-Silva, 2005), "laissez-faire racism" (Bobo and Smith, 1998), or "symbolic racism" (Kinder and Sears, 1981), should not be confused with the idea that whites *lack* racial knowledge. Moreover, that they consistently evade a racial analysis of education should not be represented as their non-participation in a racialized order. In fact, it showcases precisely how they do perpetuate the racial order by turning the other cheek to it or pretending it does not exist. Constructing whites as knowledgeable about race has two advantages: one, it holds them self-accountable to race-based decisions and actions; two, it dismantles their innocence in exchange for a status as full participants in race relations. If constructing whites as knowledgeable about race means they are full participants in racialization, then this means that race knowledge is shared between people of color and whites as opposed to the idea that the former are the fundamental "race knowers" whereas the latter are "race ignorant." This chapter attempts to build a conceptual apparatus by which to understand white racial knowledge. It offers suggestions for anti-racist practices in education that whites as well as educators of color may appropriate when teaching, particularly about race. I argue that anti-racist pedagogy cannot be guided by white racial knowledge for reasons I hope to make clearer.

The following account is an attempt to describe *white racial knowledge*, which is different from taking an inventory of *white people's racial knowledge*. Following Roediger (1994), we may assert that white racial knowledge is not only false and oppressive, it is *nothing but* false and oppressive. If this smacks of "conspiracy theory," David Gillborn (2006) reminds us that perpetuating racism does not require a conspiracy. If educators conduct schooling as usual, the results are predictable and consistent with racial stratification. If this sketch paints white racial knowledge into a corner and as seeming sinister, then it is in line with the argument that whiteness and anything that comes with it, is violent and bogus. Its history is filled with stories of genocide, enslavement, and the general process of othering. Its way of knowing partitions the world for racial domination; therefore, white epistemology is caught up in a regime of knowledge that is inherently oppressive. Willis and Harris (2000) enter the battle over epistemology in the field of literacy by remarking:

> The importance of the role that epistemology has played in the intersection of politics and reading research cannot be ignored. It serves as an explanation for how elite powerful groups, with shared interest in maintaining their status, have worked together to determine how literacy should be conceptualized, defined, taught, and assessed. Understanding

the role of epistemology also helps to explain how these groups have worked to convince others of the veracity of their claims by suggesting that alternative ways of viewing the role of literacy in society are invalid because they fall outside of their ideological conceptions (p. 77).

As an epistemology, whiteness and its hirsute companion, white racial knowledge, seem to contain little hope. They are bound up with a white ideology that simultaneously alludes to and eludes a critical understanding of racial stratification. Against the suggestion that whiteness may be reconstructed, the neo-abolitionist movement suggests the complete dismantling of whiteness, finding little redeeming value in it (Roediger, 1994; Ignatiev and Garvey, 1996b; hooks, 1997). Here, I am using ideology in the classical Marxist sense as an evaluative, rather than a neutral or descriptive, concept in order to assess group belief systems—that is, ideology as a set of concrete forms of social thought (see Shelby, 2003). In terms of a study of whiteness, this *critical moment of ideology* allows for race critique that highlights not just the descriptive properties of white racial knowledge but its *functions* and *consequences.*

However, white people's racial knowledge is not synonymous with white racial knowledge. As concrete and thinking subjects of history, white people have some choices to make regarding how they will come to know the world. Sometimes, this knowledge comes in the form of endarkened epistemologies (Wright, 2003; Dillard, 2000; Scheurich and Young, 1997), as ways of knowing that are generated from the historical experiences of people of color and then appropriated by whites. We often see this happen with anti-racist whites who, while acknowledging their own white privilege, denounce white racism (see Wise, 2002). Working against the invidious effects of white racial knowledge supports "teachers' ability to create a professional community [that] is integral to improving teaching and student learning" (Ladson-Billings and Gomez, 2001, p. 676), which makes the problem of whiteness central to the search for a counter-community. In this journey, we give up hope in whiteness as an oppressive racial epistemology but retain hope in white people as concrete subjects in the struggle against racial oppression.

White educators' epistemological framework is not *determined* by their whiteness, although there is certainly a preponderance of white people who interpret social life through white racial knowledge. For this reason, whites are the usual suspects of white racial knowledge, the usual subjects for its discourse. That said, even people of color may embody white racial knowledge. Through his comparative studies of Brazilian and U.S. race relations, Jonathan Warren (2002) found that many black Brazilians espouse a color-blind perspective that resembles many white Americans despite the fact that their structural positions in society differ greatly. This is a compelling argument against the notion that while certainly a powerful influence on one's epistemology, structural position *does not determine* how a person ultimately makes sense of that structure. Thus, the following argument is less an indictment of whites and more a challenge, a gift that requires a counter-gift as response.[1]

White Racial Knowledge: What Do Whites Know about Race?

It is understandable that studies of whiteness have evolved in a way that constructs whites as quite unknowledgeable about race, especially in light of the fact that they benefit from racial structures. In this sense, uncritical studies of whiteness have fallen victim to a hegemonic assumption about race, in this case, that whites do not know much about race and therefore must be taught about it. Usually, this means that people of color become the tutors for whites, the ones "tapping whites on the shoulder" to remind them how they have "forgotten" about race once again. Nieto (2003b) proclaims, "White educators need to make the problem of racism *their* problem to solve" (p. 203; italics in original). White racial knowledge is an epistemology of the oppressor to the extent that it suppresses knowledge of its own conditions of existence.

Making whiteness visible works against white racial knowledge's insistence on maintaining its own invisibility. It comes with the realization that "even though no one says it, race matters [sic]" (Enciso, 2003, p. 156). In her study of 4th and 5th grade classrooms, Enciso finds that "the real is mediated." Her evidence supports the idea that race is a structuring principle that must be interpreted in classroom interactions, not as a naturally occurring phenomenon but as part of the assumptions that ultimately inform how people construct their world. Furthermore, she resists the individualistic rendition of race as explainable ultimately through interpersonal relations and places it rightly in "systematic constructions of dichotomies, coherences, repetitions, and rationales" (p. 162), a condition that is additive to white students' education but subtractive for most minority youth (Valenzuela, 2002, 1999). Freire (1993) has insisted that when groups are involved in relations of oppression, the beneficiaries of their structures perpetuate a system whereby they are absolved of any holistic understanding of its processes. However, Freire asks educators to be critical of such myths in one of the first steps towards a "pedagogy of the oppressed."

As beneficiaries of racism, whites have had the luxury to neglect their own development in *racial understanding*, which should not be confused with *racial knowledge*. Whites forego a critical understanding of race because their structural position is both informed by and depends on a *fundamentally superficial grasp* of its history and evolution (see Mills, 1997). This fact does not prevent whites from *realizing* their position of privilege, which is a pedagogical task. It points out the possibility of being "pulled up short" (Gadamer's phrase) when life events "interrupt our lives and challenge our self-understanding in ways that are painful but transforming" (Kerdeman, 2003, p. 294). Taken racially, I am arguing that whites may experience being pulled up short in order that they experience a "loss [that] can be an opening to recognize perspectives that

[they] tend to dismiss or ignore when life is going [their] way" (Kerdeman, 2003, p. 297). Racially pulled up short, whites realize that they have forsaken a "clearer, more honest, and deep understanding" of race in exchange for a delusionary "condition of self-inflation." To appropriate Kerdeman, pulled up short counters a certain white *hidalguismo* (Rimonte, 1997), or son of God status, and opens them to the humble condition of human fallibility.

This pedagogical realization is arguably what makes McIntosh's description of white privilege so powerful. Its value lies in its ability to engage, even to surprise, whites in realizing the fact of their racial power. I would argue that many whites are surprised not because they did not know their power, but they did not realize that people of color knew it as well. That whites then understand and name the basis of racial power in white supremacy is another matter altogether, which requires an epistemology of color to the extent that this is possible for whites. A deep engagement of race and racism by whites contradicts their ability to enforce efficiently the differential treatment of people of color. Otherwise, whites would have to consider their benefits as unearned and arbitrary, and at the expense of people of color. Of course, this does not speak for all whites, but for the collectivity known as whiteness. As utilized in this chapter, the term whiteness refers to a collective racial epistemology with a history of violence against people of color.

Whites are the subjects of whiteness, whereas people of color are its objects. All whites benefit from racist actions whether or not they commit them and despite the fact that they may work against them. Bonilla-Silva (2004) uses the term "white" to denote "traditional" whites, such as established Euro-Americans, but also includes more recent white immigrants, and increasingly, assimilated white or light-skinned Latinos, and certain Asian groups. We may take issue with Bonilla-Silva's classifications, but he complicates the category of "white" by pointing out its flexibility to include and exclude groups based on the historical conjuncture of whiteness. One only needs to consider how Irish and British in the USA live in relative racial harmony despite their longstanding ethnic animosities toward each other (see Ignatiev, 1995). Consider also the racial position of Arab Americans, currently classified by the U.S. census as white, but whose racial affiliation has witnessed a shift since 9/11. In short, whiteness is an objective yet flexible racial force that is supra-individual and "destabilizing the category 'White' [sic] shakes the very foundation on which racial differentiation and inequality is built" (Dutro, Kazemi, and Balf, 2005, p. 102).

Whiteness is also vulnerable when knowledge about its unspoken structures is formulated and used to subvert its privileges. Such knowledge can come from whites themselves, but is not generated from their social position or experience. Rather, it comes from the experiences of people of color. This point does not suggest that people of color are "right" by virtue of their identity but that racial analysis begins from their objective social location. Even when racial analysis centers whiteness, it must do so from the analytics of the racially oppressed. Because white racial knowledge comes from a particular point of privilege, it is often evasive, which leads Margaret Hunter (2002c) to assert that, "Whites' unspoken knowledge works as a barrier to antiracist education because it denies the reality of racism and it maintains the invisibility of whiteness as a racial identity" (p. 257).

As white children are socialized into everyday life and schooling, they learn their place in the racial hierarchy. They begin to *know who* they are. By "knowing," I do not suggest a conscious, self-present mode of thinking, but rather a social condition of knowledge, sometimes buried in the unconscious, sometimes percolating to the level of consciousness. It is less an act by the knowing white subject and more of an awareness of one's racial condition that may escape critical scrutiny. For example, white children learn but rarely question history books that speak almost exclusively of their accomplishments, distorted as these accounts may be (Loewen, 1995), that literature breathes their civilized culture (Takaki, 1993), and that science verifies their superiority as a people (Stepan, 1990). Very quickly, they build a racial cosmology where they assume a place of selfhood whereas people of color pose as the other or as interlopers. From this learning, whites gain valuable knowledge about the racial order, such as with whom they should associate, play, and later date or marry. Whites' racial knowledge develops into a particular racial self-understanding that begins with a sense of belonging in two ways. One, whites are born into a world that is racially harmonious with their sense of self. In the film, "Color of Fear," Lauren remarks that whites do not have to think about their place in society because they exist in a world that tells them who they are, from day one. They do not experience the self-doubts about identity that many people of color go through in their search for belonging. Growing up white in America has its own challenges, but it is a development rarely bound up with the question, "What does it mean to be white?" because to be white means to belong. Two, it does not take long for white children to recognize that the world belongs to them, in the sense that whites feel a sense of entitlement or ownership of the material and discursive processes of race (see Van Ausdale and Feagin, 2001). From the means of production to the meanings in everyday life, whites enjoy a virtual monopoly of institutions that make up the racial landscape.

White knowledge is also about *knowing where* to traverse the social landscape. They know that blacks live in ghetto spaces, that *barrios* are replete with Latinos, if not Mexicans (in the case of Los Angeles), and that Chinatown has good "ethnic" foods. Often, whites avoid such spaces altogether either out of fear of crime or discomfort with a different cultural (sometimes third-worldish) repertoire. In the former, whites rationalize their fear of ghettos and *barrios* due to their higher crime rates compared with suburbs. In the latter, whites feel anxious about the "strange" sounding syllables of Asian languages or the informal economy of ethnic enclaves. They are indeed a long way from the confines of The Gap and Starbucks.

During a class exercise led by a group of my students, the presenters asked their peers, "What are the advantages to your racial identity?" Significantly, whites answered that they experience freedom in mobility. By and large, they confessed that they felt little prohibition from travel or neighborhood selection on the basis of racial considerations or fear of racial violence. White racial knowledge is the ability to imagine oneself in any space, untethered by the concern, "Will there be people like me (other whites) living there?" Of course, many whites cannot afford purchasing a house in particular neighborhoods or travel to expensive resorts, but these are economical, not racial, reasons. Furthermore, when it concerns white fears of minority violence, be it in the form of drive-by shootings or random crime, we have to consider the fact that such fears have little basis in fact since most violent crimes are intra-racial, such as black-on-black gang or drug activity.

Likewise, my students of color saw advantages to their identity, such as the ability to speak a language besides English in the case of Latinos and the strength of a group to withstand centuries of oppression in the case of African Americans. However, it was noted that although these examples are personally felt advantages, they are not necessarily structural advantages. In the case of bilingualism, a wave of anti-bilingual education initiatives is cresting over the nation, led arguably by California's Proposition 227. Latinos are constantly told where they can speak their language, from the work place to public schools. In the case of slavery and its legacies, for blacks there is no structural advantage attached to it. They are victims of explicit racial profiling and implicit cultural rules of etiquette and social behavior, such as interracial dating. Students of color recognized that self and group pride do not equate with structural advantage.

White racial knowledge is *knowing how* the world works in racially meaningful ways, but avoiding to name it in these terms. Whites know how to talk about race without actually having to mention the word, opting instead for terms such as "ethnicity," "nationality," "background," asking questions like "What are you?" or that most veiled of all euphemisms, "Where are you from?" When a person of color names a state (e.g., New York), the question is restated as, "No, where are you *really* from?" Moreover, knowing how to invoke the concept of racism without having to utter the word is a trademark of even the liberal white discourse. Manning Marable (2002) found common substitutions, like " 'the country's racial picture,' 'the overall racial climate,' 'relations between Americans of different races and ethnic backgrounds,' 'racial matters,' 'the race theme,' 'an incendiary topic,' 'this most delicate and politically dangerous of subjects' . . . 'the state of race relations,' 'the racial front,' 'black–white relations' " (p. 46). In fact, whites spend a lot of time talking about race, often coded/coated in apparently racially neutral, or color-blind, terms (Schofield,

2003; Myers and Williamson, 2001). In Bonilla-Silva's (2001) surveys of black and white racial attitudes in the Detroit area, he concludes that "whites avoid using direct racial references and traditionally 'racist' language and rely on covert, indirect, and apparently nonracial language to state their racial views" (p. 153). Moreover, his research team found, "Only a handful of white respondents did not say something that was problematic at some point in their interview" (p. 143).

Of course, things may change when whites are exclusively around other whites. David Roediger (1991) says as much when he describes his childhood experience in the Introduction to *The Wages of Whiteness*:

> Even in an all-white town, race was never absent. I learned absolutely no lore of my German ancestry and no more than a few meaningless snatches of Irish songs, but missed little of racist folklore. Kids came to know the exigencies of chance by chanting "Eany, meany, miney, mo/Catch a nigger by the toe" to decide teams and first batters in sport. We learned that life— and fights—were not always fair: "Two against one, nigger's fun." We learned not to loaf: "Last one in is a nigger baby." We learned to save, for to buy ostentatiously or too quickly was to be "nigger rich." We learned not to buy clothes that were bright "nigger green" (p. 3).

Roediger's suggestion is that white racial knowledge exists and is a particular way of knowing—rather than the absence of it—that is intimate with what it means to be white. White racial knowledge is comprised of a constellation of metaphors used to define whites' sense of self and group in opposition to a denigrated other: in this case, blacks (see also Giroux, 1997).

In Michael Moore's award winning documentary about gun violence, "Bowling for Columbine," Charlton Heston reasoned that we have such high rates of violence in the USA because of a long history of ethnic differences. Curiously, the NRA spokesman found that gun homicides were a result of ethnic differences, rather than a product of a fundamentally, racially divided society. To Heston, the existence of these differences was the root of such problems, with fantasies of a homogeneous white society coming through loud and clear. This episode also shows another aspect of white racial knowledge. While they may claim that they know very little about race, whites suddenly speak volumes about it when their racial ideology is challenged. This happens in university courses where whites become animated about race and assert their knowledge when their perceptions of the world are questioned. It may surprise the educator that for a group that claims racial ignorance, whites can speak with such authority and expertise when they do not like what they hear. Of course, as this chapter argues they are indeed experts and authorities on race.

Knowing how to act in racially "acceptable" ways is a form of knowledge that whites develop in their everyday life. For example, it is often touted that people of color "play the race card." When Johnny Cochran invoked the issue of race during the O.J. Simpson trial, whites were aghast at the suggestion that the case had anything at all to do with race, or at least that it was tangential to the proceedings. Cochran was accused of making the case racial when race was apparently irrelevant. However, one does not have to look farther than the *Loving* v. *Virginia* case of 1967 to understand that miscegenation, or interracial marriage, is a racially charged issue with most whites (Funderberg, 1994). Inscribed by a history of anti-miscegenation, the Simpson case was already racial; Cochran did not have to make it so (Leonardo, 2003f). Whites reacted in racially significant ways to the case, which showcased their racial knowledge. They projected racialism onto people of color, removing themselves as alibis, or non-racial spectators, rather than participants in the racialization process. In other words, whites often play the race card as a sign of their investment in whiteness and as a way to direct the public discourse in terms acceptable to them (Lipsitz, 1998).

In my courses, through much dialogue my students and I have discovered that whites live with race everyday of their lives. As in the movie, "American History X," some white students admit that they learn racial lessons in their daily interaction with the world, usually with their family. The challenge is finding a condition whereby this knowledge is made visible. In response to our readings of Toni Morrison's *The Bluest Eye* (1970), Frederick Douglass' (1982) autobiography, or Peggy McIntosh's (1992) essay on white privilege, white students confessed that they have memories of race that they rarely speak about or analyze. Given the discursive space, whites tell narratives about moments when dating a black man, for example, brought out the worst in their friends and family. That is, what was otherwise a "non-racial" home discourse became racial when a person of color was introduced as a potential, albeit unwelcome, visitor. In her essay, one student wrote a poignant story about having left her school and then receiving a letter from one of her former classmates, informing her that a "nigger" now sits in her old seat. Not to worry, the friend added, because the class would make sure she never felt comfortable. A selective group of white students reflected on their own investment in, experience with, and knowledge of race. However, not all whites respond to racial analysis in such an embracing way. Usually, resistance and evasion are more common.

In what might be called an "ideal type" in Max Weber's (1978) sense of it, a white student played the race card in the most prototypical way. During a class discussion, the student confessed to me that she had been feeling unaffirmed because of her peers' negative reactions to her ideas about race. She concluded that she felt this slight was due to her being a "non-minority," that is, her status as a white person. After I addressed her observations and offered some advice, she decided to complain publicly to the class during a subsequent session, the main thrust being that her thoughts about race were not treated seriously because she was white. She saw this as a problem if sensitivity about diversity included white participation. On this last point, she was on the right track.

Based on this incident and the concerns I have about white racial knowledge, I would like to offer some analysis.

First, the student should be commended for feeling empowered to confront her peers and communicate her feelings and observations about race. Dialogues about race are never easy and entrance to them is most awkward for whites. Her desire to confront publicly her peers is not a problem in and of itself. Second and more problematically, her racial assumptions are symptomatic of the way that many whites play the race card, an aspect of white racial knowledge. In this particular case, throughout the semester this student received criticisms from peers of all races. In fact, her most vocal critic was another, albeit radical, white student. That the student in question interpreted her "victimization" as resulting from her peers' racialization of her as a white woman begs some questions, one of which is, Why did she fail to observe that other white students in the class did not feel victimized on the basis of their race? In other words, how was she somehow singled out on the basis of her race, whereas other whites were not?

To address this question, it is important to remember that when *personally* confronted with a negative situation, whites interpret it as racial prejudice against the *group*. My student may have overlooked the more obvious reason for her peers' disagreements with her, that is, they found her ideas problematic. Her discursive reversal is not hard to imagine when we consider that whites, for example, oppose affirmative action based on the perception that it disadvantages them, rather than defining it as a historical form of corrective intervention. Whites are comfortable with constructing racial knowledge when they feel threatened. Racial knowledge here means that the person perceives the group victimized by another group (even if this may not be the case) and speaks out in explicitly racial ways. In other words, this incident is an instance of throwing the white race card. However, when situations are positive and preserve group power, whites claim that their advantages stem from individual merit, that is, non-racial, deserving, and neutral. This suggests that whites *know when* to invoke race in a manner that maintains their "innocence." In fact, it is at this point when white racial knowledge mysteriously transforms into racial ignorance. Whites suddenly become oblivious to the racial formation.

This case also points out another important element in white racial knowledge. When dialogue is without tension, whites are willing to enter racial dialogue. For example, they enjoy discussions about diversity. What educator wants to be perceived as anti-diversity these days? When discussions become tense or uncomfortable and people of color show some anger or outrage, whites' racial resolve wanes and opting out of race dialogue becomes convenient. It becomes too difficult, too much of a strain, and too dangerous. Their participation becomes strenuous and the journey arduous. People of color do not enjoy the same choice because understanding racism and formulating accurate racial knowledge are intimate with the search for their own humanity.

As Hurtado (1996) has found, whites selectively participate in racial dialogue when it serves their needs, which is more often driven by the desire "not to look racist" than by a real commitment to end racism through honest race work.

When threatened, whites play the "generalization card." That is, they challenge sociological knowledge of race with the notion that not all whites benefit from racism or that talks of white supremacy paint an otherwise complex group with too broad of a stroke. They may play the "exception-to-the-rule" card, or elevating individual people of color who have "made it" (Rains, 1997). They personalize what is at heart an institutional analysis. In these instances where race is named, whites transform into many of the charges they make against people of color (e.g., irrational, emotional, and using identity politics). In the beginning of a course, instructors may remind students that sociological analysis is not about them *per se*, as I do; but when discussions become tense yet insightful, whites perceive generalizations to be about them, as individual persons. Students of color also personalize institutional knowledge, preventing them from apprehending the racial totality, but the consequences are different when whites derail knowledge of racial patterns. When minorities resist sociological knowledge of race, they further their own oppression; when whites resist, they further their own supremacy.

In order to maintain their previous knowledge of race, whites may disrupt radical discussions of racism with exceptions-to-the-rule in efforts to redirect race discourse from an institutional knowledge base to a personal one. As a result, white racial knowledge constructs the formation on its head rather than on its feet. Rather than speak of patterns, it would speak of exceptions. Thus, it fails to understand the racist and pervasive underpinnings of white society. Rather than use generalizations as evidence of a significant, and sometimes growing, problem, white racial knowledge would characterize generalizations as part of the problem. Generalizations are branded "politically incorrect" since they smack of stereotyping. Rather than scrutinize specific forms of racism that need to be combated, color-blind whites would rather offer examples of "racial progress," as if the interrogation of racism were on the opposite side of progress. The most common instance of this last point is whites' refusal to engage seriously the fact of slavery because it ended over a century ago. Although American society has indeed changed and slavery is now outlawed, white knowledge fails to grasp the devastating effects of slavery on black communities, psyche, and lack of material prosperity today.

In order for white racial knowledge to free itself of erroneous assumptions, whites must be self-critical on a couple of fronts. First, they must disinvest in the notion that they do not know much about race. Second, they can critically decode much of what comes across as "race free" discourse and analyze the racial underpinnings of white knowledge. Third, whites must learn to be racially sensitive about contexts when race seems a legitimate theme to invoke and ask why it was relevant to them then and not other times. Finally, whites can participate in building an anti-racist pedagogy against white mystifications, and displacing white racial knowledge from its privileged position as the center of classroom discourse.

Notes on Anti-Racist Pedagogy: Decentering White Racial Knowledge in the Classroom

Anti-racist pedagogy is informed by a constellation of discourses and sets of concepts. It also inheres several targets for analysis, one of which is white racial knowledge. Although it certainly comes with teaching methods, anti-racism should not be thought of as a method, just as Ana-Maria Freire and Donaldo Macedo (1998) warn against treating Paulo Freire as a method. By portraying anti-racism as a discourse, I am suggesting that it comes with a certain family of concerns organized into an overarching project. Anti-racism makes white supremacy and its daily vicissitudes a central concern for educators of any racial background. In effect, anti-racism is the recognition and critique of white racial knowledge. It is informed by Hunter's (2002c) suggestion of decentering the often white and male standpoint guiding courses on race and ethnicity (see also Hunter and Nettles, 1999).

White supremacy is a specific form of modern racism and is the inscribing force that makes other forms of racism thrive. That is, whites benefit from race relations in absolute ways. Non-white racism is certainly a problem but to equate it with white supremacy is to forget that white hegemony is global and remains unmatched by either Japan's imperialist history or China's economic power in Asia. We can say that understanding white supremacy and under-cutting white racial knowledge form the problematic of anti-racist analysis and pedagogy. Anti-racism is first and foremost a political project such that it is a particular form of work and commitment. In other words, its essence is not a method, a profession, or a curriculum unit. Anti-racism is a project of neg-ation to the extent that its main target of critique is the condition that makes white supremacy a structured, daily possibility for many students of color (Leonardo, 2003g).

Whiteness should not be confused with *white ethnic cultures*, some forms of which may be benign or even critical. By contrast as a racial collective, white-ness is associated with colonization, takeover, and denial. We may go a long way with the white neo-abolitionist movement in asserting that the greatest prob-lem of our time is the white race but find it necessary to qualify Roediger's (1994) assertion that the white race does not have a culture (see also Ignatiev, 1997). A *white racial culture* exists, which is intimately linked with a certain way of knowing. If by culture, we accept Geertz (1994) and Erickson's (2005) defin-ition that it signifies the combination of material rituals, symbolic meanings, and sense-making strategies that a group shares, then whites as a race appear to have culture. It is summed up in this chapter as a way of knowing the world, an epistemology. We only have to point out that people do not seem to question the existence of black or Latino culture, but have a more difficult time naming *white racial culture.*

When we recall lynching practices in the USA, we name white racial culture whereby whites from young to old gathered to pose for pictures eerily circulated like postcards. From this cultural practice, it is convenient for white children and their parents and grandparents to read the event from the perspective of white racial knowledge; along with partitioning the material world, whites have also divided the epistemological world and segregated counter-knowledge from white common sense. It does not mean that whites do not harbor contradictory feelings about these and similar events like them in history, such as photos of boarding schools for Native Americans, but that the totality of white uptake of race relations informs and creates white racial culture and knowledge.

The concept of racism is central to understanding the American landscape and history. However, because of the distorting effects of whiteness I have found through teaching that it is paradoxically both underused and overused in education classroom discourse. It is underused for the reasons stated above, that is, guided by white racial knowledge race is perceived as divisive and therefore should be downplayed. In general, white students avoid it, fearing that it would make them a target for criticism from people of color. That said, after having established a level of rapport with my students and peeling away the stigma attached to the term, I noticed that it quickly becomes overused. By this, I mean that anything racist becomes branded as a form of *racism without distinctions.* In these instances, analysis of racism is stripped of its radical, objective thrust and differences between its forms are leveled and equated with one another.

For example, Latinos are deemed racist when they exhibit hostility towards whites (i.e., racial hatred). Asians are deemed racist when they express stereotypical assumptions about blacks (i.e., racial prejudice). Blacks are said to be racist when they argue for Afrocentric schools (i.e., racial segregation). As a result, every group is constructed as an equal opportunity racist and racism becomes the problem of all racial groups, not just whites. Of course, these situations represent symptoms of a racist society that educators must mediate and problematize. In my courses, I have found it helpful to make distinctions between "inter-minoritarian politics," minority-to-majority attitudes, and white supremacy in order to avoid confusing differences in kind with differences in degrees. White racial knowledge seduces students to equate these historical forms and anti-racist pedagogy differentiates them. White-to-minority racism is different in kind from the struggles found between groups of color or animosity from minorities to whites.

I make it clear to my students that although Latinos may harbor hostilities towards whites based on race, Latinos do not own the apparatuses of power to enforce these feelings. Of course, a critical educator would mediate these animosities in a historically sensitive manner by acknowledging their root sources. Likewise, I point out that when Asians express racial prejudice against blacks, although these actions must be denounced, it must be remembered that this is a result of the middleman social position that Asians occupy as a buffer within the historic black–white anxiety (see Leonardo, 2000b). In other words, as the "model minority" Asians are often used as a foil to discipline the black and Latino population. Last, Afrocentric or Native American-based schools are compromises within a public school system that fails to meet their needs. It would be inaccurate to call their attempts to address their own community's needs as a form of segregation, as many white students are wont to do.

If segregation represents a group's institutional attempts to maintain power relations, then efforts by racial minorities to address their own community issues through self-separation cannot be called "self-segregation" or "reverse segregation." Minority-based schools do not promote the same segregation we saw earlier when whites segregated blacks into their ghettoized neighborhoods and prevented them from integrating into the nation's schools (see Massey and Denton, 1993; Kozol, 1991). If segregation is an action perpetrated by a group on another in order to maintain group power, then it is difficult to claim that blacks are segregating whites through Afrocentric schools in order to maintain black power. In the same light, Native American nations, Latino-based organizations, or Asian American ethnic enclaves do not represent attempts by these communities to segregate whites into their own sectors, let alone ghettoizing them.

This color-blind sentiment is showcased in a statement made by Sharon Browne, the leading attorney for the California-based Pacific Legal Foundation concerning a Seattle lawsuit that has reached the Supreme Court (see Blanchard, 2006). The suit involves parents who question the school district's use of race as one of the determining factors in students' access to particular neighborhood schools. Browne remarks, "By using race as a factor . . . they're teaching our kids that race matters. That is just plain wrong, and it's not the type of teaching that our school districts should be doing" (p. A8). Only white racial knowledge could suggest that "race doesn't matter" and in the same suit invoke the Civil Rights discourse as a line of defense against using racial considerations in public policy. It takes the word, as opposed to the spirit, of the Civil Rights Movement to suggest the very opposite of its intent that race matters. In the same school district, former Seattle director of the Office of Equity and Race Relations, Dr. Caprice Hollins constructs a color-conscious website that names "cultural racism" as the normalization of rugged individualism and standard English, among other things (see Carlton, 2006). She receives criticism from Andrew Coulson, director of the Cato Institute's Center for Educational Freedom, for challenging one of the "founding principles" of the U.S. nation: mainly individualism. One wonders if the Institute would also consider slavery and genocide as founding principles of U.S. nation creation.

Through my teaching, I have found that the concept of white supremacy is helpful in making distinctions between different forms of racism. For instance, whereas racism has been relativized to mean any form of racial animus stripped of its comparative basis, white supremacy is less ambiguous at the level of terminology. This does not mean abandoning the concept of racism altogether, but points out the usefulness of invoking white supremacy in particular contexts. I go a long way with David Gillborn (2005), who deems education policy that does not make central the problem of racism as an act of white supremacy. He explains:

> This critical perspective is based on the recognition that race inequity and racism are central features of the education system. These are not aberrant nor accidental phenomena that will be ironed out in time, they are fundamental characteristics of the system. *It is in this sense that education policy is an act of white supremacy* (pp. 497–498; italics in original).

The concept of white supremacy names the group in question. It is unequivocal in its political capacity to name whites as the group enforcing its racial power. In contrast, the notion of black, Asian, or Latino supremacy lacks any solid historical reference. There is no such thing. Two, supremacy is also unambiguous; it signifies a group's attempt to establish absolute control. It is clearly a representation of both personal value systems and institutional behavior because it invokes images of Klan activity and white racial riots, but also whites' daily feelings of superiority. Here again, white racial knowledge becomes a challenge, for it constructs white supremacy as a thing of the past, or at least is as insignificant as Strom Thurman's outdated beliefs.

Concerning white privilege, it is common to argue that whites benefit from race structures in differing degrees. Because of other intersecting systems or relations, it is not unusual to argue that whites do not benefit equally from race (Mills, 1997; Newitz and Wray, 1997). On the level of empirical knowledge, this seems harmless enough. For example, there are poor whites, white women, and gay and lesbian whites who suffer oppression. However, it is conceptually misleading to suggest that certain white subgroups benefit *less* from race than their counterparts who are rich whites, white men, and heterosexual whites. It seems even more questionable to suggest that "white trash" is somehow a racist insult, as Newitz and Wray (1997) claim.

By contrast, I argue that *all whites benefit equally from race and racism, but they do not all benefit equally from other social relations*. People are instantiations of many relations grafted all at once on their bodies, which creates a nexus of power relations, an interdependent system of forces. Given this state of affair, it is still helpful to invoke a language of causality. Thus, we are warranted to suggest that white women, for example, are not less advantaged than white men with respect to race, but with respect to gender, which affects their overall relation to the totality of forces. That is, it is not white women's place in race relations that causes their oppression but rather their place in gender relations. Likewise, the phrase "white trash" is a denigration of poor whites' economic and cultural location rather than a derision based on racial positionality. It is true that "white trash" contains a racial component. But structurally speaking, the exploitation that working class whites suffer is ameliorated by what Du Bois (1998) once called their "public and psychological wages" (see also Roediger, 1991). No doubt social relations intersect one another and a shift in one alters the overall relation of forces. Failing to provide students a language of causality, educators forsake a compelling explanation for the particular benefits and burdens that a racial structure produces. This distinction is different from arguing that whites do not benefit equally from race.

Another point that I teach my students is that anti-racism is historically self-reflective. It fully appreciates the role that history plays in shaping today's milieu. The legacy of slavery, apartheid, anti-Coolie laws, immigration exclusion acts, territorial takeovers, and other crimes against racialized subjects of history are regarded as events from a hundred years ago as if they happened yesterday. As anti-racist educators, my students understand that our racialized present was not dropped from above by a Euclidian observer, but rather that our current conditions were made possible by continuities in white treatment of people of color. On this point, I often take sports as an example. More than ever, today's black inner city youth are seduced by the spectacle of success in sports (see James, 2005). Many kids believe they can "be like Mike" (Jordan), move like Randy Moss, and swing like Sammy Sosa. In my courses on diversity, I link sports with slavery by explaining that during slavery, Africans were treated as depositories of white anxieties. Fearing carnal desires, the white imaginary invested the African body with sexual prominence and promiscuity. This spectacularization of the black body happened in conjunction with the exploitation of African labor. During Jim Crow, blacks filled white void by assuming the stage with white faces in minstrel shows. Again, blacks provided a convenient spectacle for white audiences. Today, basketball, baseball, and football are no minstrel show but they function in similar ways to showcase the spectacle we know as the black body.

Critical scholars and pedagogues face particular issues when teaching about race and anti-racist work. They understand teaching anti-racism to be a social condition that they navigate aggressively and yet tenderly. Aggressively confronting the theme of racism is important because it does both student and instructor a disservice when we fail to name its contours in the most direct and demystifying way, much like white racial knowledge. Thus, in my courses I try to enter the discourse of race and critique its consequences with plain talk. By that, I do not suggest a discourse of transparency (see Aoki, 2000; Lather, 1996; Giroux, 1995). Instead, it is time to suggest that it is quite normal to overtly discuss race, over dinner at the restaurant to activities in the classroom, from the home to homeroom. For too long, race discussions have been stifled because of the conservative and even liberal notion that any talk of race is, by default, recreating the problem of race, that is, it reifies what is at heart a social construction. Of course, this is a mystification in itself because it mistakes invoking race with its fetishization. Discussions of race may fetishize the concept, but this is a risk worth taking and on which any critical work reflects.

Whenever I discuss the topic of race, I make sure that I do not stammer or speak in a hesitating manner, whisper when I say "black" or "white," or act incredulous when I cite or hear examples of racism as if surprised that certain acts of hatred persist in our post-Civil Rights era. Like other academic subjects, race is part of normal classroom discourse: as normal as Newton in physics or Shakespeare in English. I have tried to remove the "controversial" stigma that white racial knowledge puts on race discourse. Whether or not I have been successful is another matter. However, I have also noticed that it means something different for a scholar of color to invoke race and this is where certain distinctions would help. When a minority scholar speaks plain talk about race, she may be constructed as militant, as needlessly angry about relations that are, after all, "on their wane." Thus, white racial knowledge constructs scholars who speak with such plainness about an *existing* problem as part of the problem because it assumes that the most functional way to deal with the situation is to focus on the "positive" relations between the races, not their insidious past.

Because race taps into students' affective investments, I have found that it touches tender histories in their lives. This is what I mean when I say that I tread tenderly on the topic of race at the same time that I aggressively analyze it. For white students, it should be painful to hear that the white race has colonized and constructed a world after its own image. It is not easy for them to read that, as Massey and Denton (1993) assert in their book, *American Apartheid*, whites have *intentionally* segregated and ostracized black people into ghettos. Many white students in education consider themselves decent, egalitarian people who believe in racial equality. However, they also frequently have a superficial understanding of race. Likewise, students of color are surprisingly deprived of a classroom discourse that extends beyond essentialisms. That said, students of color have the experiential basis to understand the effects of race on their lives in a way that white students, who often claim no racial affiliation or knowledge, do not. The various examples mentioned here are hard for students of color to hear as well because they jog memories passed down from their parents and communities. Sometimes they may even resist Massey and Denton's argument that blacks have been ghettoized in such a complete and enduring manner like no other group in U.S. history for two reasons.

First, they refuse to be classified as "ghetto," the image of which has been source of shame and embarrassment when spoken outside of certain black contexts. Second, because they are college or graduate students, they are a selective group of people who have "made it out of the ghetto" and believe it is a discrete possibility for others who work hard. Of course, we know from Kozol's (1991)

Savage Inequalities that housing segregation leads to paltry material conditions in schools for predominantly black populated areas. We can extend a similar argument for Latino *barrios*, and inner cities with Asian refugees. Here we see that teaching anti-racism necessitates a simultaneous sensibility for class relations, or race's material cognate, especially when we recognize that capitalism has wreaked havoc on people of color.

Race is completely socially constructed, but we have invested it with material institutions. In its modern sense, race does not mean "group," although some students would like to construct it that way. If the concept of race were to equate with the notion of group—the idea being that groups have always oppressed each other throughout history—this would effectively cancel out the particularities of our current racial formation. If race were to equate with the common-sense understanding of it as "group difference," then the Trojans were another race from the Greeks, the Romans just another race of people. In its modern sense, race is the creation of what many race scholars refer to as skin color stratification. That is, although it is possible to refer to race as a trope in biblical times, this is not its modern sense. The basic question of "What is race?" must be asked, something that white racial knowledge assumes is a relatively settled issue. Race is not just a figment of the imagination, but what Ruben Rumbaut (1996) calls a *pigment of the imagination*. Its genealogy is co-terminous with the creation of science and its eugenics movement, its "enlightenment" philosophy of the other from Kant to Kierkegaard, its cultural imperialism of orientalist proportions, its colonization of the Americas and Africanization of slavery, and its global exploitation of non-white labor for unimaginable profits (see Said, 1979; Mills, 1997; Allen, 2002). In order to discuss race in its specific and historical form, this modern sense of racialization is what my students and I first try to understand. Any talk of visions of race must initially discuss its propensity for divisions. That is, whites created race in order to divide the world, to carve it up into enlightened and endarkened continents, and to delineate the white subject from the black object of history.

That race divides the U.S. nation as well as others around the world certainly can be proven. After all, race was a white European concept created for the benefit of whites and burden of non-whites. However, this insight provides little guidance into the workings of race relations or how it worked out that whites have benefited from racism in an absolute way. That is, if race divides the world, how did whites come out as the subjects of its specious history? Marxist struggle against capital should complement any anti-racist work, but we must also be reflective about its inadequacy for explaining why—outside of Japanese exceptionalism—Euro and American whites have exploited the international labor force, frequently made up of third world non-white people. It is easy to see that the race-divides-the-nation thesis is more of an evasion and mystification of white privilege rather than an honest analysis of it, because "We cannot prepare realistically for our future without honestly assessing our past (Bell,

1992, p. 11). White racial knowledge fails to ask why history worked out the way it did, what actions white Europeans took to secure their domination, or the hegemonic assumptions about the goodness of whiteness in everyday discourse. Race invests skin color with meaning and erects institutions around it to modernize its processes and establishes a hierarchy based on skin color, or what Bonilla-Silva (2004) calls "pigmentocracy" (p. 226). In order to transcend current race relations, which is a concrete possibility, we must first go *through* race in order to have any hopes of going *beyond* it.

Race and the War on Schools in an Era of Accountability

As I have suggested, the study of whiteness in education is receiving increased attention, particularly as it relates to color-blind perspectives in schools. In this chapter, I argue that the No Child Left Behind Act is an example of color-blindness par excellence. NCLB's hidden referent of whiteness makes a casual pass at racial explanation that sidesteps race as a causal explanation for educational disparities. In this sense, NCLB is an "act of whiteness" and perpetuates the innocence of whiteness as a system of privilege. It is a form of whiteness as policy. Its white common sense deems racial disparities as unfortunate outcomes of group competition, uneven social development, or worse, as stubborn cultural explanations of the inferiority of people of color. I argue for a color-conscious perspective that problematizes the otherwise race-neutral discourse of NCLB.

As discussed in Chapter 5, much has been written about the nature of "white privilege" in the recent uptake of whiteness studies, a fledgling discourse that is only two decades old. These concerns have been articulated in studies of everyday forms of taken-for-granted privileges (McIntosh, 1992; Bush, 2005), whiteness as performance (Giroux, 1997), and even "whiteness as terror" (hooks, 1997). It is only lately that the discourse on white privilege (or more specifically, "white supremacy") has been applied to the realm of formal educational policy (see Gillborn, 2005). Unlike the previous figuration of "white supremacy" as the caricature of Klan members and segregationists, several scholars have launched a discourse that generalizes it as a racialized social system that upholds, reifies, and reinforces the superiority of whites (Gillborn, 2005; Bonilla-Silva, 2001; Mills, 1997). This comes at a time when the signifier "racist" begins to lose its edge, indeed its meaning. In this day and age everyone, every group is now deemed to be an equal opportunity racist and the concept withers away in the color-blind era of U.S. race relations. Or worse, racism becomes an individual problem located in personal psyche.

Despite this color-blind tendency in U.S. society, studies of whiteness have provided insights into the informal aspects of white privilege, or the everyday cognates of a more general white structural advantage. In this chapter, I hope to begin a discussion on the formal aspects of white privilege by analyzing the No Child Left Behind Act as an "act of whiteness." The educational literature is replete with critiques of NCLB as it affects children of color, poor students, or immigrants (Darling-Hammond, 2004; Novak and Fuller, 2003; Cochran-Smith, 2005). Less attention has been paid to the way it creates U.S. nationhood through the educational construction of whiteness. In other words, how does NCLB construct and imagine the white nationhood? At length, I will discuss the historical and racial context out of which NCLB arises. This contextualization is necessary in order to historicize race in the context of its specific social conditions.

When nationalism is discussed in the literature, it usually refers to people of color or marginalized ethnic groups. There is good reason for this move because nationalism has been a staple social movement of hitherto oppressed peoples, such as African Americans, Chicanos, or Native Americans (see Césaire, 2000; Bush, 2000; Robinson, 1983; Churchill, 1998). But as Lipsitz (1998) has argued compellingly, such strong and identity-based movements also find their way into dominant groups, in this case white communities, with the U.S. nation being no exception. That is, the creation of a white nation has arguably been one of the strongest forms of identity politics, both real and imagined. On one hand, a white nation is imagined every time a white subject argues for a return to the great past of American heritage or when the nativist response to immigration threatens to close the U.S. border with Mexico, as showcased by the Minute Men, an armed group in the state of Arizona. On the other hand, it is also real when formal policies establish the white nation and protect its boundaries, much like the way people fence their property (Harris, 1995), limiting which groups are perceived as "white." Educational policy assists in creating the nation, especially when it stems from federal legislation, such as NCLB. And because the USA is a white-dominated country, NCLB represents a node in nation creation that is intimate with the educational construction of a white polity. Thus, the educational literature benefits from an analysis of NCLB not only as a national policy, but an *instantiation of whiteness*. Of course, we may argue that the USA *is* multicultural and there is a push for multicultural experiences in schools. This effort should not be underestimated, but it runs against a pretty formidable fence known as whiteness.

It has been argued that whiteness is a social creation, not a biological fact (Frankenburg, 1993; Ignatiev, 1995; Roediger, 1991). In this sense, white people had to be created, not born, or as Beilke, Brooks, and Welsh (2004) put it, "White identity formation is more of an enculturation process than a skin color" (p. 42). In fact, white people did not exist about 500 years ago, or before modern race, as a form of skin organization, became meaningful through colonization of Africa, Latin America, and parts of the Orient, simultaneously consolidating the Occident as a racial force. Over time, however, whiteness is recreated through the historical process of expansion or restriction, depending on the context and state of race relations. As Omi and Winant (1986) describe:

The meaning of race is defined and contested throughout society, in both collective action and personal practice. In the process, racial categories themselves are formed, transformed, destroyed and re-formed. We use the term *racial formation* to refer to the process by which social, economic and political forces determine the content and importance of racial categories, and by which they are in turn shaped by racial meanings. Crucial to this formulation is the treatment of race as a *central axis* of social relations which cannot be subsumed under or reduced to some broader category or conception (pp. 61–62; italics in original).

Like the concept of labor and the social relations to which it gives rise (Lukacs, 1971), race relations is articulated in the specificities of its historical conditions. Race may shift and morph in its relative significance to racial groups, but its centrality in U.S. society is absolute insofar as it represents a central axis of self and social understanding.

In our time, race is partly recreated through NCLB and the mechanism of color-blindness. With respect to the meaning of whiteness, it is under constant negotiation and is part of the national and global struggle over who is or is not white at any give time, of who is allowed into what Cheryl Harris calls "whiteness as property." We have already seen arguments of how the Irish and Jews became white (Ignatiev, 1995; Brodkin, 1999), or Asians as "honorary whites" and in some cases having claims to Aryan status (Bonilla-Silva, 2004; Mazumdar, 1989). As part of what Omi and Winant call a racial formation, *white formation* does not have a transcendental essence but is malleable according to social conditions and the state of white hegemony. In other words, whiteness is able to accommodate, or make certain compromises, in order to maintain its ideological hegemony. Ignatiev's documentation of the Irish racial ascendancy toward whiteness, its transformation from green to white, is a poignant example. Today Arabs (considered by the U.S. Census as whites) are witnessing a transformation of their identity in *post-9/11 whiteness*. The Arabs' key to the white house is slowly being taken away. This does not suggest that Arabs necessarily and currently think of themselves as white, but that their proximity to whiteness is becoming less apparent, increasingly troubled, and more complicated.

In education, the very presence of multiculturalism is evidence of a reaction to a white normativity in school curricula, administrative structures, and classroom interactions. Since the 1970s, multiculturalism has challenged the centrality of whiteness or Euronormativity and Europocentrism (Said, 1979), fracturing its hold on basic education (Banks, 2006). DiAngelo (2006) puts it right when she describes whiteness as both empty and full: "Whiteness is both 'empty,' in that it is normalized and thus typically unmarked, and content laden, or 'full,' in that it generates norms and reference points" (p. 1984). Said another way, whiteness is nowhere since it is unmarked and everywhere since it is the standard whereby other groups are judged. Likewise, NCLB contains within it the absent marker of whiteness that defines the Standards Movement. To Ignatiev's (1997) chagrin, NCLB does not seek to abolish whiteness, but strengthens and solidifies it. When educators face punishments resulting from insufficient yearly progress, they are policed by an unspoken whiteness (as well as a certain bourgeois worldview, but I shall focus on race). Many affected schools and districts boast high numbers of students of color. When the white referent of NCLB is not discussed, these communities receive the impression that they are failing non-racialized academic standards. The upshot is that the fault is entirely theirs, a cornerstone of color-blind discourse that conveniently forgets about structural reasons for school failure. On the other hand, when largely white middle class schools and districts meet or exceed their target, they receive a similar but beneficial message: that their merit is entirely theirs. As a result, whiteness is reified through NCLB behind the façade of a non-racialized process of nation creation. The educational construction of whiteness goes unnoticed as an unremarkable aspect of NCLB. This chapter hopes to make this process more visible.

Our Color-Blind Era, Our Color-Mute Discourse, Our Color-Deaf Sensibility

The Civil War ended the 250-year-old and peculiar institution of slavery. However, the Emancipation Proclamation was not a measure designed to end racism once and for all, but to end a *particular form* of it called slavery. For we know too well that racism continued into the post-bondage era, this time morphing into Jim Crow institutions. After emancipation African Americans again found themselves swimming upstream during Reconstruction, living apparently "separate but equal" lives with whites. The spirit of *Plessy* v. *Ferguson* became a metaphor for U.S. race relations, at the heart of which is "heterophobia," or what Memmi (2000) calls the "fear of difference." The USA witnessed a different kind of racism, one equally as overt as slavery, but taking on a different albeit sometimes "kinder" form. Blacks and whites were considered too different to co-exist and housing and schools were segregated as part of the natural order of things. We may say that the North won the war, but the South won the peace. The Union may have been preserved but the ideology of racial separation remained the law of the land.

With the rise of the Civil Rights Movement, U.S. racism again fell into an institutional crisis and ill repute. With the world watching, Americans came under scrutiny through violent images in the media. Blacks and other people of color were perceived as victims of an unfair caste system and Americans suffered a loss in legitimacy amidst the Cold War (see Bobo and Smith, 1998). Things had to change and integration became the answer. People of color and their white sympathizers paid for progress in blood and the legislation we now know as the Civil Rights Acts is commonly assumed to have remedied the group oppression that people of color suffered. This does not suggest that fair-minded Americans do not recognize that racism continues into our present day and age. However, racism today is presumed to be more individualistic, not structural, and fundamentally attitudinal and multi-directional, not just white on black. Like the Civil War, the Civil Rights Acts were not meant to end racism altogether either, but another particular form of it known as Jim Crow. Guided by the spirit of *Brown* v. *Board of Education*, post-Civil Rights USA enters a new Reconstruction, what scholars are now calling the Color-Blind Era. We may be tempted to say that "things have changed" and we would be right. But whereas during pre-Civil Rights, people of color knew who was responsible for their unfair position in life, in the post-Civil Rights Era they are told that they are their own worst enemy, that they block their own progress in a largely fair system (see Thernstrom and Thernstrom, 1999). I think it was Seymour Sarason who said, "The more things change, the more they stay the same" (cited by Fullan, 1991, p. 38).

Sociologists have traced the fundamental transformation in whites' racial attitude since the 1960s. By and large, survey data suggest that white Americans indicate a belief in integration, disapproval with prejudicial attitudes, and support principles of equality among the races (Brown *et al.*, 2003). This is not a small matter and points to the moral success of the Civil Rights Movement to alter the nation's public racial discourse. In general, white Americans publicly declare that racial preference is wrong, that color should not prevent access to goods and services. But color-blindness goes one step further. Not only should race no longer matter, it should not be a consideration to either social policy, like affirmative action, or interpersonal interactions, like interracial dating. As Ian Lopez (2006) describes:

> Contemporary colorblindness is a set of understandings—buttressed by law and the courts, and reinforcing racial patterns of white dominance— that define how people comprehend, rationalize, and act on race. As applied, however much some people genuinely believe that the best way to get beyond racism is to get beyond race, colorblindness continues to retard racial progress. It does so for a simple reason: It focuses on the surface, on the bare fact of racial classification, rather than looking down into the nature of social practices. It gets racism and racial remediation exactly backward, and insulates new forms of race baiting (p. 6).

People should be treated fairly regardless of (i.e., not taking into account) race and its legacies. It would be hard to argue with such logic. Race should not be seen, talked about, and race-talk should not be heard with too attentive of an ear because it is tantamount to victimology: see no race, speak no race, hear no race. At the end of the 1970s, this color-blind ethos was signaled by several important, influential publications, such as William Julius Wilson's (1978) book, *The Declining Significance of Race*.

A racial paradox is at work here. When surveyed, whites express attitudes about racial fairness. But when pressed with questions about what they would do about integration, such as housing (or education), whites are less forthcoming. That is, *in principle* whites believe in integration, but more than half are *not willing to act* on this principle. By 1980, around the time that Wilson's book pronounced the declining significance of race, only 40% of whites surveyed said they would support a law that stated, "a homeowner cannot refuse to sell to someone because of their race or skin color" (Brown *et al.*, 2003, p. 42). As Brown *et al.* put it, "Defining racism isn't a matter of semantics or theoretical issue ... [and] [b]y now, the prejudice approach to the study of racism has been discredited and has become almost completely obsolete" (Brown *et al.*, 2003, p. 43; see also Bonilla-Silva, 1997). In other words, defining racism as fundamentally a problem of attitude and prejudice fails to account for the material consequences of institutional racism, behaviors that produce unequal outcomes despite the transformation of racial attitudes, and the creation of policies, such as NCLB, which refuse to acknowledge the causal link between academic achievement and the racial organization of society.

In the Color-Blind Era, success (or more important, failure) is conceived as individual or cultural. If we assume that structural racism has been solved or has negligible impact, then we are responsible for our own lot, not in the sense that we have to take inventory of our bad decisions (which everyone has), but in the sense that structural obstacles to mobility, like slavery and Jim Crow, have been lifted. Regarding cultural explanations, Stephan and Abigail Thernstrom (1999) argue that blacks lack mobility because of their pathological cultural practices, such as young single-parenthood and low value on education, not because of a debilitating structure of white racism (see also McWhorter, 2001). They do not go as far as suggesting that racism is a relic of the past. After all, theirs, like NCLB, is not a vulgar brand of color-blindness but its softened and more careful version. They recognize race but misrecognize racism. That established, they play racism down in exchange for a more optimistic look at U.S. racial relations and drawing attention to the failings of people of color. Against this, we may say that students of color may have their own problems (cultural or otherwise), but they did not create the racial condition under which they fail. This does not preclude people of color from committing self-sabotage, but under white supremacy one cannot be sure that racism did not have something to do with it.

To color-blind analysts, after some forty odd years of Civil Rights legislation, we have all but erased 250 years' effect of slavery, 100 years' damage of Jim Crow, not to mention a "little matter of genocide" for Native Americans (Churchill, 1998). In fact, whites have experienced 360 years of affirmative action since the *Dred Scot* decision declared that "We the people" (read: whites) never intended to include either enslaved **or** free Blacks as citizens of the American society (Brown *et al.*, 2003). Of course, it is possible that today's color-blindness is a way of feigning color-consciousness, that is, color-blindness is really a misnomer in a color-obsessed nation.[1] But to the color-blind society, they amount to the same thing because color-blind people do not recognize it as feigning but as a reality and more significantly, *an accomplishment*. In this manner, color-blindness serves as a metaphor for our times. This ethos implicates even corrective mechanisms that arose out of the Civil Rights tradition, such as affirmative action.

Because color-blindness discourages all racial preferences as a form of unfair advantage, affirmative action is targeted as oppressive to white Americans, although there is little empirical proof to suggest that this is happening. At the anecdotal level, we hear the occasional story (almost always hypothetical) about a white person who was not admitted by Harvard because an abstract person of color stole his spot, or a worker whose employment chances were curtailed by a phantom black or brown person. But to Brown *et al.* (2003), "To assume that government policies benefited only blacks or were color-blind, as many white Americans commonly believe, is like looking at the world with one eye" (p. 27). In fact, one of the largest recipients of affirmative action has been white women (Marable, 1996; Tatum; 1997). More accurately called "ambivalent action," (Leonardo, 2003f) affirmative action is now falling out of favor, reaching the Supreme Court in a recent case involving the University of Michigan campus. Although the High Court ruled that race may be used as a consideration in social policy, the onslaught has proven successful in large and powerful states, like California, where Proposition 209 passed, effectively dismantling affirmative action. NCLB comes at the heels of this color-blind atmosphere, challenging racial disparities ironically by recognizing "a problem without a cause."

Also known as "laissez-faire racism," "symbolic racism," or "new racism," color-blindness does not just represent the fear of difference, but the *intensification of racial difference masking as its obliteration*. This is not race abolition at its best. Within this discourse, we are all humans and any attempt to use race as an analytical framework or interpretive lens for U.S. society is itself deemed racist because it is believed to be ensnared in the white supremacist notion that race is a real form of difference. That race is an invention is common to many, if not all, legitimate scholarship on race (Lott, 1999). So this assertion is not new and race-conscious scholars agree with color-blind scholars on this point. In fact, the critique serves as a straw man because it refutes an argument that no one credible is making. That said, to suggest that race is *only* a social construction ignores its real effects through the inability to engage actual, empirical states of affair (Feagin, 2006). David Gillborn puts it best when he describes race as a "black hole."[2] Figuratively, we cannot actually see race (since it is not real in the scientific sense), but we observe its ability to create a gravity field around itself, pull our self-perceptions and desires into its vortex, and sometimes warp our sense of how it actually works. In other words, race creates real effects. Race may be ideological, but it produces material consequences.

To conclude this section, we may characterize color-blindness with the following tenets.

The contours of color-blind discourse include:

1. Race and racism are declining in significance.
2. Racism is largely isolated, an exception to the rule.
3. Individualizes racism as irrational and pathological.
4. Individualizes success and failure.
5. Blames people of color for their limitations and behaviors.
6. Mainly a study of attitude and attitudinal changes, rather than actual behavior.
7. Downplays institutional relations or the racialized system.
8. Plays up racial progress.
9. Emphasizes class stratification as the explanation for racism.
10. Downplays the legacy of slavery and genocide (as long ago).

Without explaining each one of the 10 tenets, color-blindness would have us forget history (both in the sense of a past and its continuity with the present), psychologize racism without the benefit of a sociological understanding, and displace racial stratification with competing explanations, such as class analysis. A well-informed race analysis is arguably richer (no pun intended) with class analysis, but subsuming racial oppression under the general framework of class exploitation proves unconvincing to many people of color who experience the racial nature of white supremacy. In this sense, color-blindness infects otherwise radical theory and exposes its reactionary position on race structures.

NCLB: "No Color Left Behind" or "No Caucasian Left Behind?"

It is from within this historical condition of color-blindness that No Child Left Behind originated. Therefore, it is a symptom of our times. When NCLB received overwhelming support from both Democrats and Republicans in 2001, it was hailed as the most sweeping educational reform since the original Elementary and Secondary Educational Act 40 years ago. The name was adopted from the Children's Defense Fund: "Leave No Child Behind" (Welner and Weitzman, 2005). Noble in its ostensive intent, NCLB reached across the political aisle when it recognized a pattern whereby certain groups of students were not succeeding compared to their counterparts. It sought out these groups and enacted a federal mandate from a political party that usually favors state sovereignty. Although Republican history certainly shows a proclivity for states' rights, in his two terms President Bush has supported a particular deployment of federal action as part of nation creation, sparked symbolically by the Supreme Court's decision giving the nod to President Bush's first term. NCLB is the educational cognate of the Patriot Act following the terrorist attacks on the World Trade Center in 2001, through its emphasis on nationhood and Americanism. It was foreshadowed by *A Nation at Risk*, a report commissioned by the Reagan administration in the 1980s.

Consistent with the discourse of the War on Terror, if there are any failing schools in the USA, NCLB will "smoke 'em out." In contrast to previous reforms where underperforming schools were provided resources for remediation, NCLB introduces the threat of student exit from schools and bleeding of moneys from low-performing schools (Sunderman and Kim, 2005). It is the educational War on Terror that will show the rest of the globe that Americans "mean business." In fact, NCLB contains Section 9528, a provision that obligates schools to provide access to military recruiters or risk losing funding (Furumoto, 2005). One might ask what the military has to do with education. As part of nation building, social institutions (what Althusser called Ideological State Apparatuses), such as schools, have always been part of the military project, of inculcating militaristic values and their endorsement. With the help of NCLB, the Pentagon would like to double Latino presence in the armed forces to 22%, which would increase the current 60% of soldiers of color in a nation represented by roughly 70% whites, a veritable dark wall of protection for whiteness. As the educational Patriot Act, NCLB sends a message to young children regarding what it means to act like a patriot: accept the rightness of whiteness.

The whiteness of NCLB is the hidden referent of the federal act. It is the guiding ideology that frames how school failure will be explained and how it should be remedied. This analysis does not suggest that people of color who support NCLB are somehow "acting white" or that NCLB is "for white people." Rather, NCLB is articulated with whiteness within the conjuncture known as the Color-Blind Era. As Melissa Da Silva (2005) puts it, "appealing to a white-normed commonsense highlight[s] the real danger of NCLB, that is, all the ways in which it reinforces and contributes to color-blind racism . . . the preservation of white privilege—that is, the rational, material interests . . . of American whites" (http://www.educationnews.org/how-is-nclb-a-mechanism-of-the-a.htm). NCLB overtly targets improving four subgroups of student performance: minority children, students with disabilities, poor children, and English language learners. Regarding race, it would be tempting to dub NCLB as "No Color Left Behind." In principle, it is laudable to hold schools to higher standards with a promise of academic proficiency in at least the three Rs. It is about time that someone insisted on an accountability system with an attitude. For the degradation of students of color has lasted long enough and NCLB represents the chutzpah that educational reformers have been waiting for. However, consistent with a racial formation analysis, with NCLB it seems that "the color line has not been erased so much as it has been redrawn" (Freeman, 2005, p. 191). Insofar as NCLB is guided by an ideology of whiteness, it depends on the continuation of racial differences as part of a logical, rather than social, outcome. In other words, ostensibly giving public schools a chance to show progress, NCLB gives whiteness the license to declare students of color failures under a presumed-to-be fair system.

On *prima facie*, NCLB seems to be driven by a racial understanding. But recognizing a problem does not equate with locating the source of that problem. In other words, NCLB acknowledges the symptoms, but not the causes of the achievement problem affecting children of color. It frames race as incidental ("they happen to be whites or Blacks, etc."), rather than causal ("because they are whites or Blacks, etc."), to student disparities in achievement. Deserving to be quoted at length, Welner and Weitzman (2005) declare:

> Americans appreciate the notion of accountability, at least in theory. Students should be responsible for their own learning. Teachers should be responsible for teaching. Principals and school districts should provide teachers and students the resources needed for success. If any of these people do not carry out their responsibilities, there should be repercussions. When students underperform, they should be failed and their teachers and school administrators should be sanctioned or fired. But confronted with the reality of the crisis conditions in many American schools, these simplistic responses amount to little more than empty blustering. More to the point, they amount to a cry that something— some unspecified thing—needs to be done and that teachers and educational authorities know what that thing is and will do it if only a big enough sword is held over their heads (p. 246).

NCLB does not make visible the structural obstacles that children of color and their families face, such as health disparities, labor market discrimination, and the like, processes that a class analysis alone cannot unmask (Brown *et al.*, 2003). This is vintage whiteness. In fact, NCLB hides these dynamics even more efficiently, tucked away in the language of tough love and harsh sanctions. Employment discrimination disappears in the abstract individualism of NCLB, where the threat of laissez-faire market forces becomes the final stop for persistently failing schools that will finally succumb to privatization under the voucher system. Some analysts have pointed out that NCLB is an attack on public schools, showcasing their hopelessness and moribund status (Darling-Hammond, 2004). This is what Kohn (2004) calls NCLB's "clever gambit" that forces educators and families either to be against public schools or accept mediocrity. This does not suggest that if NCLB were to acknowledge structural, racial inequalities, it would succeed in eliminating them, thereby saving public schools. But their absence signals its ultimate and perhaps predictable failure— its "conciliatory nature" (Freeman, 2005, p. 196)—like the fate of many reforms squeamish about race before it. The intractability of systemic school reform should not be underestimated and we should not pretend that it will take less than a Herculean effort, but some of the causes of school failure are not a mystery either. A nation that supports an undeclared apartheid through color-blind policies produces foreseeable results. It is difficult to be surprised when such policies do not make a dent in narrowing the achievement gap.

It would be quite hopeful to expect major federal or even less ambitious educational policies to address these structurally determining factors. But such expectations would be a sign of either naïveté or blind optimism. That said, from an analyst's point of view, NCLB's inability to locate educational disparities within larger relations of power does not just betray its color-blind ideology, but its *reinforcement of whiteness*. Ultimately, it subverts its own claims to "fix the problem" because it confuses symptoms for substance, implicating it in a certain performative contradiction. It is unable to deliver its own promise even as it annunciates it. All four subgroups targeted by NCLB implicate children of color. It is a well-known fact (or a dirty little secret) that African Americans, particularly boys, are diagnosed with difficulties overrepresenting them in special education; English language learning impacts more non-whites; and NCLB's targeting of minority children speaks for itself. The fourth category of children who live in poverty includes white children but their whiteness is not responsible for their poverty, but rather their class status or their position in the relations of production.

As previously mentioned, white working class people embody the contradictions of both race and class, but NCLB does not leave them behind because they are whites, but because they are poor. One of these contradictions is showcased by poor whites' capacity to cope with their poverty due to the consolation provided by their membership in the white race. Living an exploitative, material life, poor whites often displace their critique of the bourgeoisie with animosity towards poor minorities in particular, and people of color in general. This leads Roediger (1994) to suggest that poor whites' "correct" analysis of their impoverished condition is bound up with a racial analysis; that is, their economic liberation is at once their racial emancipation. That said, and without minimizing the exploitation that poor or working class whites experience, their whiteness alleviates some of their suffering through what Du Bois (1998/1935) called whites' "public and psychological wages" (see also Roediger, 1991). In other words, poor whites are not poor *because* they are whites, but *despite* this. It would be a bit like arguing that if Stephen Hawking were to become Prime Minister of United Kingdom, it is due to his physical disabilities. Rather, Hawking would have to compensate for his physical disadvantages, such as being the brightest mind on the planet. He would earn the title despite his challenges.

Poor whites have racial advantages despite their poverty. White bodies register this contradiction and it is not possible to separate out their white identity from their class experience. Poor or working class whites *feel* their exploitation as concrete white subjects. They cannot parse out the portion of their identity that is responsible for their suffering, and that for their privilege. That said, analysis is poor without a sense of causality. Or as Brown *et al.* (2003) remark,

"White Americans may face difficulties in life . . . but race is not one of them" (p. 34). Structurally speaking, policy analysis must be able to trace the origins of benefits and disadvantages. Without a discourse of causality, educators confuse epiphenomena with substance, correlations with causation.

Regarding people of color, structural racism usually takes on an economic form or has economic ramifications through employment discrimination and the racial division of labor. In contrast to whites, many people of color under white supremacy are poor because they are racialized minorities, not despite this. We may repeat the same reasoning for whites with disabilities, whose whiteness is not the source of their problem unlike students of color with disabilities, whose racial identity influences their overrepresentation in special education programs. Students of color diagnosed with disabilitites face at least two strikes against them. If Novak and Fuller (2003) are correct in suggesting that NCLB comes with a "diversity penalty" by punishing schools with higher populations of students of color, then the opposite must also be true insofar as NCLB comes with a *whiteness reward* for mostly white schools. Although this language may appear like the "oppression sweepstakes" discourse, it is an attempt to disaggregate causality from correlations between oppression and one's identity. Despite my sympathies with Marxism, the root of racial disparity is not *economic in nature* since an analysis of the inner workings of capitalism alone cannot explain it. Rather, racial oppression takes an economic form without necessarily being economic in nature. Because the hidden referent of NCLB is whiteness and its ideology is color-blind, it is tempting to dub it "No Caucasian Left Behind."

NCLB's "pull yourselves up by your own school straps" mentality betrays a certain lack of appreciation for the racial conditions in which schools exist. For example, it pretends that the achievement gap is ultimately a problem of both teaching and the educational state apparatus, something that could be addressed by putting pressure on teachers to "do their job." This is why NCLB defines funding for the Act in a manner that only covers testing costs, since teaching grade and subject proficiency is already a teacher's job. It does not acknowledge the resources required to provide struggling students the opportunity to excel. Although it is common that authorized funds do not match appropriate funds, NCLB's appropriation for Title I, Part A for the first four years (2002–2005) of its enactment shows a $21.5 billion shortfall (or 31% missing) (Welner and Weitzman, 2005). This is tantamount to providing funds to test children but not to teach them, according to Senator Kennedy. Or as Darling-Hammond (2004) observes, NCLB "ignores the important inputs of resources that enable school quality, [which] mistakes measuring schools for fixing them" (pp. 8–9). Although President Bush is right to criticize the "soft bigotry of low expectations," this funding shortfall creates what Welner and Weitzman call the "soft bigotry of low expenditures" (p. 242). According to one conservative estimate, total national spending on education would need to increase by $137.8 billion, more than 11 times the current Title I funding. Even if schools continue the upward trend in progress evidenced in the 1990s, one analyst calculates that schools would take more than 100 years to reach the NCLB's target (see Darling-Hammond, 2004). Even this figure is conservative, if reforms fail to address the structures of racism. It might be tempting to declare NCLB a naïve attempt to reform public schools. Nothing could be farther from the truth. It is a well-informed and brilliant strategy of color-blind proportions. As it stands, NCLB's color-blindness ensures that school reform will proceed at the snail's pace of whiteness.

The Future of Race, Whiteness, and Education

In exchange for a color-blind discourse, this chapter and book have argued for a color-conscious perspective. NCLB enters its second phase of reauthorization and it becomes even more imperative that critical discussions around its color-blindness occur among educators. Bonilla-Silva (2005) outlines color-conscious analysis and its contours include the following list:

1. Racial phenomena are regarded as the "normal outcome" of the racial structure of a society.
2. The changing nature of what analysts label "racism" is explained as the normal outcome of racial contestation in a racialized social system.
3. The framework of racialization allows analysts to explain overt as well as covert racial behavior.
4. Racially motivated behavior, whether or not the actors are conscious of it, is regarded as "rational"—that is, as based on the races' different interests.
5. The reproduction of racial phenomena in contemporary societies is explained in this framework not by reference to a long-distant past but in relation to its contemporary structure.
6. A racialization framework accounts for the ways in which racial/ethnic stereotypes emerge, are transformed, and disappear (pp. 21–22).

Color-consciousness begins from the assumption that race matters, from womb to tomb. Racialism is a natural part of a racial formation, something into which children grow. In the USA it is not deviant to think and act in a racial manner; rather, feigning color-blindness is deviant (which is different from "normalized"). In other words, it takes a lot of energy and effort to perpetuate color-blindness because it is unnatural. In a context of racial contestation, racial behaviors are rational insofar as they represent a racial subject's aware-ness of racial antagonisms and acts to secure or take away power. Seen this way, a racist person is not merely uninformed, ignorant, or misguided. That is, he is not irrational but behaves consistently with his racial interests (which is not the same as being guided by "reason"). Finally, racial formations, as

Omi and Winant never tire of reminding us, shift and have no transcendental essence. They reflect the racial understandings of their time.

Notwithstanding the insights from whiteness scholars, an important and still relatively underresearched topic of race studies is whiteness, particularly as this relates to educational policy. What is whiteness and what does it want from us? Whiteness is a skin collective that cannot be reduced to its members. Blacks, Latinos, and Asians participate in whiteness, although it benefits whites in absolute terms. This means that, as Ignatiev and Roediger suggest, at least in theory, if not in practice, we must disaggregate whiteness (a racial ideology) from white people (racialized individuals). This is a position that parts from Gary Howard's (1999) claim that white people and whiteness are unavoidably implicated in each other. This binding between whiteness and white people is reasonable because they are frequent partners in crime. But conceptually, it becomes a form of reduction, of reducing white identity to ideology. In other words, I am suggesting that whites do have a choice regarding whiteness and may opt to commit "race treason," or what Ignatiev and Garvey (1996b) call "the ultimate act of humanity" (p. 10).

When we define the ideology of whiteness as hopelessly bound up with what it means to be white, then whites are trapped into a particular way of making sense of their racial experience and as James Baldwin once remarked, "there is no hope for [them]" (cited in Roediger, 1994, p. 13). Along similar lines, as long as educational reform is driven by a white logic, there is no hope for schools, which does not vitiate against local or smaller-scale reforms. But it points out that nothing short of a radical shift in our perspective on race will produce what educators fondly talk about as "race equality." It will remain at the level of polite dinner table conversation. Yet one question remains: What does it mean to abolish whiteness and how does it occur?

Empirically, transforming whiteness lacks any concrete example. When whites congeal into a skin collective (and people of color may join them), the results have been predictable. History shows that Irish workers picked race over class by edging out Black workers, Californians voted against affirmative action (a staple of Civil Rights legislation), and suburbanization created the hypersegregation of blacks in ghettos. When white ideology (i.e., whiteness) is centered, the margins suffer. *There is no example to the contrary.* To the abolitionist, rearticulating or transforming whiteness appears more like a wish fulfillment. How does one, for example, rearticulate fascism to be something other than we know it? Contrary to rearticulation, it does not imagine a new form of, but represents the possessive investment in, whiteness (Lipsitz, 1998). It is stuck in the quicksand of annunciation, as if whiteness could be wished away through a discourse of white positivity that is nowhere to be found. That said, as I argued in Chapter 6, rearticulation may represent the road to whiteness without it being its destination. Whiteness has existed for one simple reason: racial stratification. On the other hand, white Americans exist at the intersection of discourses that struggle for supremacy over their subjectivity. They exist in multiple worlds and have had to make decisions about traversing the racial landscape that is the United States. In history, whites may be and have been transformed.

It has been suggested that abolishing whiteness does not equate with abolishing white people. In other words, ridding society of whiteness (an ideology and material structure) does not mean the disappearance of white people, let alone committing genocide against them (McLaren, 1995; McLaren, 1997). Upon further reflection, the abolition of whiteness comes with the eventual vanishing of white people. The white race was an invention; therefore, white people had to be "created." Monique Wittig (1993) once argued that "one is not born a woman." By this, she means that "woman" is an idealized creation, a subject onto whom a patriarchal society grafts expectations and roles, such as "mother." In this sense, "woman" is not real in the ontological sense, whereas "women" is a sex-class and provides a basis for group identity and solidarity. The dissolution of a patriarchal society may come with the eventual disappearance of certain categories. Indeed, this may signal the end of gender as an organizing principle. In racial terms, dissolving whiteness, both in the ideological and institutional sense, means that the category white would no longer be useful. The same "white" bodies (in the physical sense) will exist but a society would not signify them as white. In short, abolishing whiteness would mean abolishing the concept of white people. White people would no longer exist and whither away.

The neo-abolitionist discourse comes closest to this position and we may go a long way with them. It is one of the most provocative white-led race discourses to come along since the original abolitionism. However, in arguing for the disappearance of whiteness, neo-abolitionism makes the mistake in suggesting that races do not currently exist. This leads Ignatiev to reject the invocation of races, white or otherwise. It is tempting, even understandable, to argue that "Given their dubious ontological and moral pedigree, it [is] difficult to show the desirability of racial identities" (Ingram, 2005, p. 256). Ignatiev encourages whites to repudiate their whiteness, sever their loyalty to the white race, and denounce their membership in the group. In other words, to Ignatiev we cannot make disappear a people that does not exist in the first place.

Ignatiev appears to conflate the concepts of "real" and "existence." Although race may not be real (particularly in the scientific sense), it exists in real terms, such as a racial economy and its institutions. As Apple (2003) notes, "Indeed, it would be misleading to talk of race as an 'it.' 'It' is not a thing, a reified object that can be measured as if it were a simple biological entity. Race is a *construction*, a set of fully social relationships" (p. 109; italics in original). Furthermore, racial groups, policies, and histories exist. Without this admission, neo-abolitionism represents less the approach to abolishing whiteness and more its lifeline and current *modus operandi*: now you see it, now you don't. It is the hallmark of color-blindness to suggest that races do not exist, something that many whites would likely be comfortable annunciating. It is hardly subversive for whites to announce that they are not white. This is already their inclination. The opposite is more difficult and resisted: white racial ownership.

No Child Left Behind does not signal the disappearance of whiteness, but its solidification. Its color-blindness ensures the continuation of racial structures, not their abolition. Because it is not guided by a race-conscious appreciation of U.S. society, it does not discredit whiteness but ultimately people of color. When the year 2014 rolls around and the achievement gap has not been significantly narrowed, the nation's eyes will be on students and families of color. They, not whiteness or white people, will be indicted. By and large, they already know this. When U.S. democracy falters in matters regarding race, color-blindness locates the problem in people of color as alibis for a condition they did not create. After all, NCLB gave public schools and people of color an opportunity to show their mettle. In the eyes of whiteness, what more do we need? Read as a racial narrative, NCLB is whiteness turned into policy.

Race, Class, and Imagining the Urban

ZEUS LEONARDO AND MARGARET HUNTER

In the social sciences, there is no paucity of studies about the urban as a "real" place. To take a few examples, in Massey and Denton's (1993) *American Apartheid*, the ghetto receives plenty of attention, as a historical process whereby blacks suffer from whites' deliberate construction of housing segregation at the turn of the twentieth century. In Anyon's (1997) own analysis of the ghetto, she traces its origins in the political economy and the school systems it produces. Massey and Denton, and Anyon's sociological accounts have helped scholars and educators understand the "urban" (particularly the ghetto[1]) as a concrete place, whose racial and economic formation is material. In this chapter, we discuss how "urban reality" is as much an *imagined*, in addition to a real, place (Berger and Luckmann, 1966). That is, the urban is socially and discursively constructed as a place, which is part of the dialectical creation of the urban as both a real and imagined space. The urban is real insofar as it is demarcated by zones, neighborhoods, and policies. However, it is imagined to the extent that it is replete with meaning, much of which contains contradictions as to exactly what the urban signifies. For instance, there are urban communities that are "positively" urban like the "Upper East Side" side of Manhattan, New York, but not Harlem or the South Bronx; Santa Monica and West Hollywood, California but not Compton or Echo Park. In other words, in light of power relations, urban may signify the hallmark of civilization and the advances it offers, or a burden and problem of progress.

Introduction to the Dialectics of the Urban

The urban setting is a dialectical example of the process of modernization. For some people, it represents an outlet for entertainment and a venue for a sophisticated life, whereas for others the urban seems like an inescapable cul-de-sac of poverty and daily degradation. By examining the mediatized and dominant ways of representing the urban, we arrive at the "social imagineers" (Giroux, 1999) of the urban as both a blessing and a burden. However, this chapter is not an urban planning paper, but a sociological analysis of daily life as it concerns the urban as an imagined and educative place. Thus, it hinges less on formal processes, like housing policies, and more on the informal process of meaning-making, of signifying the urban through a chain of images and discourses, which are themselves constitutive of the education one finds in urban settings. It is not a study of ideology as divorced from the material process (Leonardo, 2003b). Rather, it is a search for a *proper relation* between ideology and material life, two processes that are dialectically linked instead of opposed. Last, it does not propose a spatial theory of the urban context, but a theory of the *urban imagination*.

The discussion shares some affinities with Robin Kelley's (1998) treatment of the social science wars over representing the ghetto through structural or cultural theories, both of which are tethered by the construction of the ghetto as home to a monolithic and debased underclass culture. Kelley favors a political engagement of the aesthetics of the ghetto, arguing that its music and daily lifestyles are a source of pleasure for its participants. To Kelley, the cultural wars have taken "playing dozens," or hurling insults as a form of entertainment, to a whole new level that forgets its playfulness and only deploys insults at the urban and the people who live in it. We go a long way with Kelley but part from him in our emphasis on the structural, rather than aesthetical, aspects of the urban as these find their expression through contradictory meanings. This method has several advantages, including a nuanced look at racialized, commodified, and gendered meanings attached to the urban in popular and youth culture, and the social relations that both create and are created from such meanings.

As an imagined space, the urban is constructed through multiple and often contradicting meanings. These meanings are sites of contestation as to what the urban signifies in people's imagination. Consequently, the imagined aspect of the urban setting affects urban education because it socially and culturally constructs the people who live in it as well as their needs. Urban dwellers and their "nature" are not a given and must be mediated through systems of meaning, competing discourses, and ideologies. We find that the urban has been constructed in three powerful ways: as a sophisticated space, an authentic place of identity, and a disorganized "jungle." In order to avoid presenting the urban through a binary as essentially either a "positive" or "negative" place, we take a critical, dialectical position on the social meanings that constitute the urban for their traces of power relations, specifically with respect to race and class structures. In short, the four following sections problematize and critically examine the everyday meanings of the urban. In the first section, "The Sophisticated Urban Space," we analyze the representation of the urban as a sophisticated space where modernism expresses its advances in civil society through art and culture. In this case, being urban is a sign of being modern, of civilization itself. It is a reminder of what Matthew Arnold once called the best that Culture in all its grandeur has to offer. In the second section, "Urban Space and the Politics of

Authenticity," we argue that urban (often ghetto) spaces are constructed as authentic places of identity for people of color. Both whites *and* people of color construct the "essential" or "real" person of color as urban, usually born from the concrete activities and histories of the urban but also a form of style or the self-(re)presentation of minority youth one often finds in inner city schools.

In the third section, simply titled "The Urban Jungle," we analyze the popular cultural perception of the ghetto as a pathological place marked by a profound disorganization, criminal character, and moral malaise. In this most popular and durable representation of the ghetto, images of the underclass shine through the lens of the culture of poverty argument first launched by Oscar Lewis (1968), reincarnated by William Julius Wilson (1987), and appropriated by the educational system to address the "urban problem," which goes by the common label of the "achievement gap." This pejorative sounding section regarding the urban differs from the previous two sections that cast the urban as "positive." Last, in "Social and Policy Implications for Education: Re-imagining the Urban," we make initial connections between the urban imagination and educational policies targeting urban settings. We argue that daily constructions of the urban (particularly the poor or pejorative version) are consequential to the way educators imagine the kind of schooling appropriate for urban students. We end the chapter by re-imagining the urban as a place of struggle over the very meaning of race and class in the context of the United States.

The Sophisticated Urban Space

As part of modernization, the urban represents the advances achieved through technology (e.g., computer engineering and media), the complexity of metropolitan living (e.g., contrapuntal lifestyles and cultural hybridization), and confrontation with difference (e.g., immigration and ethno-racial mixing). In fact, to be "urbane" is literally defined as a positive thing, as in "to be sophisticated" or "refined." Since the Industrial Revolution, the urban setting has been constructed as a place where the future meets the city, an idea that Voltaire was fond of and Rousseau despised. The urban represents the forward progress of civilization both in terms of material production for Karl Marx and cultural manners for Matthew Arnold. It was the way out of the constrictions of medieval social systems towards the opening up of the social universe as well as cultural universals. In short, *homo urbano* was the next development away from provincialism, which is a stone's throw from primitivism. On this level, the urban defines the new social subject who is part of global development guided by the new civil society and the state institutions that Hegel once valorized. In short, being urban is a positive thing to be.

However, when we consider that urbanization occurs in the context of power relations, contradictions begin to surface. For example with respect to diversity, being urban usually connotes supporting the "right amount" of ethnic and racial difference, but not too much. Often tokenism stands in for real integration in order to preserve a certain image of the urban as a *controlled place of difference.* Thus, during the Great Migration in the USA the exodus of blacks from the South to Northern urban centers prompted whites to contain them in ghettos, making integration all but a fantasy rather than a reality. In this instance, urban carried a double-edged meaning for blacks who searched for better job opportunities only to find white labor resistance to their integration (Roediger, 1991; Ignatiev, 1995). Urban America became an opportunity structure for ethnic whites, like the Irish, escaping religious and cultural persecution on their own land. By choosing to be members of the white racial imaginary, oppressed ethnic Europeans found their social promotion in the urban setting, edging out blacks. In the latter's perspective, civil society was everything but civil.

In schools today, controlling for difference is sometimes exemplified in American colleges and universities' desire to portray themselves as "diverse," even if they aren't, of using the term "urban" without the burden. In fact, this deception was exposed when the University of Wisconsin digitally inserted a black male into one of its marketing photos so that the university could project a particular image of itself for the public; more important, it enabled the university to create the image it wanted for its own self-understanding. In short, some universities and teacher education programs use the signifier "urban" to describe themselves in a way that seems diverse (and therefore sophisticated), without having to bear the burden of difference. In this case, appropriating diversity or urbanism is a way of marketing a school or program as "cutting edge," as dealing with *pluribus* while only having to live with *unum.*

Of course, the point is less about policing these universities and creating alibis out of particular campuses, and more about analyzing how the concept of "urban" is being constructed in order to deploy a particular image—better yet, deploying power for particular ends. In other words, the analysis hinges less on casting aspersions about a school's desire for diversity and more on the contradictory meanings that result when it is invoked. Our point is that the increasing value of the signifier "urban" in education suggests that as *the* representation of diversity, urban people (read: students of color) are being recast in a "positive" light. Directly related to the meaning of urban, racial diversity is conscripted into a logic that co-opts it as a marker of cosmopolitanism, but with neither the reality nor the burden. Educators who deal with the urban are constructed as sophisticated, but the urban students and families themselves are not.

Currently, American K-12 urban schooling promotes the importance of diversity, which is said to be good for education in general. In its authentic sense, diverse classrooms provide a setting where people from different backgrounds can debate an issue from various perspectives and in the process learn about their own uniqueness (Banks, 2002). This seemed to be the logic behind the University of Michigan Affirmative Action Supreme Court decision that supported racial considerations in admission processes as well as the rationale behind maintaining affirmative action in education in general. Rather than using the now problematic image of the melting pot, urban settings have become the *meeting point* of civilization. It holds the promise of unity *and* diversity. This does not come without challenges but it promotes the promise of intergenerational, interracial, and international relations that the new global citizenship offers in the urban setting.

Because of the popular misconception that multiculturalism is a positive tool *for* students of color (see Glazer, 1997) or worse, as dividing the nation (Schlesinger, 1998), in urban settings the signifier "diverse" becomes a synonym for "students of color." It happens frequently enough that teachers describe their school with a mostly black or Latino student population as "diverse." Often, they sincerely value such "diversity." Of course, a predominantly black or brown school is not diverse, but its precise opposite, the hallmark of *de facto* segregated education. In this case, the meaning of urban becomes grafted onto bodies of color, making diversity, urban, and people of color coterminous with each other. Urban and multicultural schooling transform into an education *for* students of color; rarely do teachers describe an equally white suburban school as "diverse" or that multiculturalism or race-based pedagogies may enrich white students' educational and social experience. Whites seldom regard multicultural education as good *for* them, as a way to broaden their sense of civil society and expand their notion of humanity, that is, unless being "multicultural" makes them appear open, tolerant, and sophisticated. In contrast, many multiculturalists have argued that valuing diversity entails basic education for all students, including whites (Banks, 2005; Nieto, 2003a; Sleeter, 1995b). When critical, it is a form of transformative education that allows both whites and students of color to know more deeply their own histories as inflected by other groups' struggles. This is urban sophistication in the inclusive sense, rather than the property of some and a problem for others.

As part of being sophisticated, urban dwellers are often imagined as cosmopolitan, open-minded and perhaps most important, progressive. This was evidenced precisely in the 2004 U.S. presidential election when many New Yorkers and Los Angelenos (both from coastal Democratic-controlled states) blamed Bush's victory on the Republican-controlled states in the middle of the country. This is reminiscent of the national problems of racism typically blamed on Midwesterners or Southerners, who pose as alibis for the country's general and pervasive level of racism. In fact, coastal (including urban) California has been at the forefront of the recent onslaught of racist policies enacted against immigrants of color, such as Proposition 187 and 227, the former decreasing undocumented families' medical and educational services and the latter attacking the legitimacy of bilingualism in schools and public places (which in California means Spanish). Despite this onslaught to discredit public schools, they are among the last institutions to leave the urban setting, watching the steady exodus of businesses and hospitals flee towards capital and more profitable spaces (Noguera, 1996). In other words, U.S. urban schools bear the burden of progress, of educating people's children in the face of increased pressures for privatization.

On the same note, the high-profile police brutality cases against people of color have also been documented in urban Los Angeles and New York. We are not refuting the difference between Democratic and Republican strongholds. California and New York have two of the largest urban cities in the country and are obviously Democratic, especially when compared to other states. Although major urban settings may be racially problematic, people of color have felt a sense of protection by virtue of living in them because they recognize that difference is a fact of everyday life in these settings. In other words, people of color see their faces reflected in everyday life, even when these images are problematic. They are present and rarely silent. That said, the discourse during the 2004 presidential election forsakes a more accurate understanding of white supremacy that goes beyond the rural-imagined Klan and Neo-Nazis, and implicates even liberal urban whites. That is, white supremacy is more about the centrality of white advantage from which urban whites do not escape and often actively deploy. Each form of racism expresses its specific logic, traditional racism in rural settings and a more "sophisticated" color-blind racism or tokenism in urban centers.

The urban has become a place for the white enjoyment of arts, music, and dining. In many cities, middle class whites may drive their Chevy Suburbans into poor urban areas to valet park and attend the opera, symphony, or concerts but never have an "experience of color" despite being in a poor or black/brown area. For example, they may dislike Mexicans, resent them for "browning" California, and vote for Proposition 187, but they are avid lovers of their local Mexican restaurant and speak the occasional Spanish food phrase. Angelenos may feel comfortable with Mexicans who provide the bulk of cheap labor in the Southland, but curtail Mexican families' access to social services and basic education. These dynamics are exacerbated in multiracial urban cities limiting access to high-status knowledge and advanced courses in subjects like math and science (Oakes, Joseph, and Muir, 2004).

In this sense, the meaning of urban becomes a site of consumption. Being urban is consumed for a given amount of time, enjoyed, and then forgotten until the next excursion. The urban resembles the colonies frequented by the colonists who never feel out of place, never not in charge (Memmi, 1965). Like the colonist who is numerically outnumbered in occupied areas, white and middle class people in the urban playground do not feel conspicuous for long. Using the colonial framework, the urban becomes an internal colony (Blauner, 1972; see also, Ladson-Billings, 1998), a cultural and material condition that links cities as diverse as Soweto and the South Bronx. These spaces are complete with a colonial-like educational system that treats the urban "natives" as something to be assimilated, civilized, and converted. Real urban dwellers (not to be confused with the stylized version of *homo urbano*) may not be constructed as sophisticated, but through proper education, it is believed they can become modernized.

The urban is a heart of darkness for the internal colonist who enjoys it like Walter Benjamin's flaneur, or dandy-about-town. In the popular show, "Sex and the City," the white and well-to-do main cast lives the glamorous urban life that is Manhattan. As petite sophisticates, these four flaneuses treat the audience to adventure after adventure in their endless pit of a high-brow, but seductive lifestyle. Dressed to the hilt and as cosmopolitan as their drink, the protagonists are a perfect display of the urban sexual splendor at which even Freud may have blushed. Somehow, the show would not have been as powerful were it named "Sex and the Rural Town," taking place in small town USA and premised on the sexual adventures of two farmers' daughters, although this did not prevent Paris Hilton and Nicole Richie from trying. "Sex and the City" works precisely because of its urban allure, where exploits are part of the new feminism after the sexual revolution. It does a marvelous job at showcasing the urban crunch of time and space where meaningful relationships are equally as fleeting yet fulfilling. It shows the level of emotional sophistication necessary when one-night stands are reduced to 30 minutes. In the show, the sociology of sex hinges on the characters' ability to emerge from the urban landscape emotionally vulnerable but rarely disheveled in their appearance. This is the urban-as-playground at its best and it takes an emotionally savvy, sophisticated viewer to appreciate its excesses.

Arguably, New Orleans once posed as the southern urban playground. That is, until Hurricane Katrina hit. Previously, it was the site of a carnivalesque celebration of difference during Mardi Gras, where an intersubjective *heteroglossia* would have made someone like Bakhtin feel right at home. After Katrina, the urban carnival was abandoned and what was once a city by the sea became a city under it. In the dialectics of the urban, New Orleans could not have experienced a more stark reversal. Amidst fields of black evacuees, the city was not only deemed a national disaster area, but abandoned by what many consider a neglectful president whose reaction was faster during the Asian tsunami that struck halfway across the globe in Thailand. The disasters in New Orleans revealed the urban once again as a problem for the poor and black. The event holds pedagogical lessons for students as they understand the burdens of being urban.

First, with the help of the Associated Press students learn that white victims "find" food and drinks, whereas blacks "loot" stores.[2] Second, when the survivors trekked from New Orleans to Houston, Texas for shelter and aid, former first lady Barbara Bush commented that the relief efforts may create another problem insofar as the victims would want to remain in Houston due to the city's hospitality. Inadvertently, students learn that displaced poor people cannot tell the difference between the comforts of their own home and the utter lack of decent conditions in the Texan holding centers, notwithstanding the diligent assistance from relief volunteers. Instead of seizing the opportunity to examine the social institutions that turned a natural disaster into a social one, Barbara Bush expressed her fears that the evacuees in Houston would overstay their time in Texas due to the city's overwhelming hospitality. In short, she fears that the evacuees would turn the city of Houston into the wrong kind of urban, filled with poor blacks who need help. Mrs. Bush unwittingly became a symbol for what Joyce King (2004a) calls "an uncritical habit of mind," a certain "dysconsciousness" that prevents people from seeing the social order of things. Third, despite the ostensibly racial nature of the slow response, black folks are again being told that, harking back to the Rodney King videos, they are not seeing what they think they see with their own eyes: that is, the response apparently was not racial here. In this instance, urban means black and poor, and in the context of post-Civil Rights race discourse both are part of the life choices one makes. The whole saga prompted Reverend Jesse Jackson to proclaim that Americans have a high threshold for black people's suffering. It prodded the hip-hop artist Kanye West to declare that President Bush does not care about black people. Luckily with this last point, and appropriating from Spivak (1988), students also learn that the urban subaltern can speak, that they are able to "decipher knowledge" in King's (2004b) sense (following Foucault) of the ability to critique regimes of knowledge and alter consciousness in search of an alternative explanation for social events.

Urban Space and the Politics of Authenticity

Although whites tend to imagine urban spaces as either sophisticated playgrounds or dirty, violent ghettos, some people of color offer another way of imagining the ghetto, as a home of authentic cultural practices. For many people of color, particularly Latinos, African Americans, and some Asians, urban spaces are home; that is where they grew up or live, where they return to visit family if they moved away, where they go for ethnic-specific groceries or for their own ethnic restaurants, where they get their hair done, or anything else. Because urban areas are home to so many people of color, both literally and figuratively, there is an abundance of images of urban areas as romantic, nurturing, accepting havens from a cold outside (read: suburban) world.

Many black movies and television shows portray poor urban neighborhoods as homey, familiar, nurturing environments, despite some of their dysfunctions or idiosyncrasies. These counter-narratives suggest that despite the poverty and occasional violence or street crime, urban neighborhoods provide a home to those who live there. These images are created in contrast to mainstream, white views of poor urban neighborhoods as dangerous, violent, mean, and uncaring (Guerrero, 1993). Whites also essentialize the ghetto as the place of "real" blacks, Latinos, and Asian Americans largely because the mainstay of their interaction with racial minorities comes in the form of media consumption, of watching television shows and music videos about them, and listening to rap or hip-hop songs. As the "reality" television show, "Black. White." points out very well, an archetype of the white urban imagination is that *blacks are a rap video*, complete with the accompanying expectations that they should behave in such a manner. Without concrete, therefore varied, interactions with people of color, whites project their ideal image of blacks, Latinos, and Asians as essentially and one-dimensionally urban and espouse few counter, non-stereotypical images of them. In schools, this means that a largely white, female teacher population is ill-equipped to deal with urban students and their realities.

In addition to being portrayed as a loving environment, poor urban neighborhoods are also imagined by some as the site of authentic cultural practices. The series of movies that include "Barbershop" and "Beauty Shop," for instance, centers on the black hair salon or black barbershop. Both of these locations are uniquely black and house not only cultural interactions about hair, but ways of talking, interacting, and relating to one another and the surrounding community in uniquely black cultural ways. This series of movies and other contemporary black movies answer the existential question, "What does it mean to be black?" in problematic, yet predictable ways. For many African Americans and other ethnic groups, authentic identity originates in poor, segregated neighborhoods. Real blacks reside there and they act, talk, and behave in legitimately black ways. When they do not follow these prescriptions, their authenticity is questioned. This is ultimately what Fordham (1988, 1996) finds in her studies on "racelessness," where blacks who achieve in schools are perceived as "acting white" (read: not urban, not authentic).

Authentic cultural practices are thought to abound in urban neighborhoods. For many Latinos, the ability to speak Spanish is crucial in urban areas where more recent immigrants are likely to be living (Lopez, 1997). Many people imagine that the food served in Mexican restaurants in East Los Angeles is more authentic than that sold in whiter parts of the city or the suburbs. Likewise, many Asians must travel to their own urban ethnic enclaves—sometimes also poor—to buy the grocery items that they need to cook the meals specific to their culture. This reality reinforces the notion that authentic language practices and food reside in urban spaces. Like blacks, Latino students also face the challenges of essentialism when they do not speak Spanish and are branded as inauthentic, marginalized from the community, yet are not accepted because of a more general xenophobia in mainstream white culture (see Suarez-Orozco, Suarez-Orozco, and Doucet, 2004). It creates a condition that Valenzuela (1999) calls "subtractive schooling," which is another way of saying that education for Latino youth does not only fail to add to their school experience but actually takes away from their cultural way of being. Of course, it is possible that the brand of inauthenticity leveled against students of color involved with their own communities, is a coping mechanism cultivated by people of color who feel disempowered or are shut out from the culture of power. In order to assuage their own sense of marginalization, it is a power play they can hold over the heads of minority students who ascend to middle class status. For successful students, their claims to authenticity may reflect their internal struggles about achievement and maintaining a close tie with their communities. As part of Du Bois' (1984) "talented tenth" and Steele's (2004) "domain identified," this ascending group of students face challenges within and without the group, not authentic enough for their own social group, not white enough for the mainstream.

Both people of color and whites tend to imagine urban spaces as more authentically "ethnic" or "racial" than suburban or rural spaces. Because we view urban spaces as more authentic (e.g., more truly black, more Latino), being "from the 'hood" takes on a particular status and meaning for many students of color. Being from the 'hood is seen as a positive and "real" experience of blackness or brownness. In other words, it requires both race and class authenticity. For example, to be truly black, the common perception is that one must be or have been from a poor, black neighborhood (Johnson, 2003). Many whites and people of color believe that exposure to the hardships of black or Latino life is a prerequisite for an authentic ethno-racial identity. In mass culture, this dynamic can be seen in the figures of Kobe Bryant and Alan Iverson. Bryant, a basketball player who comes from an upper middle class upbringing, is said to lack "street cred(ibility)" (Rovell, 2005). He lacks a certain authenticity with both his black and white fan base, many of whom are interpellated by an essentialist discourse on urbanness and blackness. It is not hard to imagine that the criticism constructs Bryant as not of the 'hood, something also leveled at another player, Grant Hill, who did not grow up in the 'hood. However, the same cannot be said for Iverson, whose "bad boy" image and tough childhood earn him the brand of authenticity and credibility without much effort. Iverson's black Horatio Alger storyline is not only urban but thoroughly American. His case shows that it is also not enough simply to be from the 'hood. One must be in regular contact with the 'hood in order to avoid being seen by both people of color and whites as a sell-out or as not really black (or brown or yellow in some cases). The question seems as much about "Who is urban?" as it is about "Who is black?"

The problem with imagining authenticity this way is that it locates "real blackness" or "real Chicanismo" in a particular set of experiences and social locations that are not part of U.S. public school culture. Schools are then defined as white places and "real" people of color become interlopers in their own neighborhood schools (Ogbu, 1995; Fordham, 1988). This is true to some extent. U.S. public schools value and inculcate white cultural practices, and consequently communicate to their students that "white is right." Some schools, particularly charter schools, have made attempts to create culturally responsive curricula that value and engage the cultures of the student body (Gay, 2000). Notwithstanding the criticisms of charter schools as private schools in public sheep's clothing, this has been one strategy to bridge the cultural divide between schools and the students of color from segregated urban neighborhoods and the educational system that alienates them from their home cultures.

Urban neighborhoods typically represent authentic ethno-racial identities in part because much grassroots and community based organizing happens in them. Aside from the problems of urban areas, like drugs and violence, many community organizations exist there, in part to help alleviate some of those problems. For example, police brutality is a significant problem for young men of color in poor neighborhoods. Urban communities have reacted to this problem by creating grassroots organizations to raise awareness and pressure police departments to change their policies and investigate cases of police misconduct. The criminalization of youths of color happens in a euphemized form in schools where black students are punished more harshly than their white counterparts for similar offenses (Parker and Stovall, 2005). This prompts a movement that links community based organizing to schools, making them sites for education and a more comprehensive urban reform beyond, but including, the school grounds (Warren, 2005).

For many suburbanites, the community organizations that do much of the work in sustaining and improving urban communities are outside of their purview. Because so many whites and suburban residents have little or no contact with people of color or the poor (aside from their nannies and housekeepers) their knowledge of life in poor urban areas is obtained from local news and popular culture. The important role of local organizations for neighborhood peace, mentoring, affordable and fair housing, anti-gang efforts, and improved public education are largely unknown to people outside urban settings, but very familiar to those who reside there. For example, criticized for his anti-Semitism in the media, Minister Farrakhan's role in urban community building rarely makes it on the news. Turned into a media spectacle, Reverend Al Sharpton's community advocacy is eclipsed by his eccentricities. These two examples suggest that attempts at urban renewal often happen with little recognition or fanfare from people who essentialize it as authentically ethnic or racial but not as a place of community agency.

The consequences of suburban and white ignorance of these community organizations are significant. Much of the public imagines people of color in urban areas as drains on the school system, lazy, helpless, and hopeless. Even when they are viewed sympathetically, which is not often, they are seen rather as passive victims of larger social inequalities, not agents or experts in their own lives. This image of urban residents portrays them utterly without power, creativity, perseverance, or intelligence to fight back against an unfair system.

As a result, public policies that regulate the urban poor typically treat them as passive and childlike. This image in part comes from the public's general ignorance about the substantial community organizing that happens in urban neighborhoods. People of color create organizations, creatively use meager resources, routinely lobby their elected representatives, and improve their communities. Even in the poorest neighborhoods, grassroots organizations exist to help alleviate the social and economic problems facing urban residents. These authentic community organizations are a key piece in the puzzle to improving life in urban neighborhoods and their schools.

The Urban "Jungle"

Aside from the many ways we have discussed it thus far, representations of urban schooling most commonly evoke images of the urban as "jungle." In this section, we discuss and problematize this representation in its larger context, including its racist overtones. In the "urban jungle" people imagine their city centers as teeming with black, brown, and yellow bodies, which are poor and dirty, criminal and dangerous. Gangs, violence, and drugs are closely tied to any image of the urban for most people. Some of this is real. Certainly most urban areas deal with disproportionate amounts of violence, particularly among young men, and a drug economy that makes victims out of buyers, sellers, and everyone in between. Our task here is not to assess the veracity of this image, but to define the implications of this particular social imagination on the schooling experiences of young people in urban areas.

Because so many people subscribe to the racist notion that urban areas are "jungles," many Americans believe that spending money on urban schooling is a "waste." Many people perceive children in urban areas as hopeless, going nowhere, unworthy, and without value or potential. In a word, they are "uneducable." Consequently, allocating money to urban schools is routinely a fierce political battle. In *White Racism,* Feagin and Vera's (1995) theory of racism as societal waste sheds light on this issue. They suggest that instead of thinking of resources spent on people of color as a "waste" we ought to realize that allowing all the potential and talent of people of color to go unused is true societal waste. Feagin and Vera argue that racism is a form of societal waste that the USA cannot afford. "What kind of things might we already have accomplished or invented had we developed all of our talent?" they ask. The problem is that many school board members, superintendents, state congressional representatives, and governors do not view racism as societal waste. Instead, in our color-blind era they are more inclined to see the victims of racism as a waste themselves, without talent, creativity, or intelligence to offer society. Perhaps even worse, many of our policymakers view children in urban areas as unworthy of the right to an education, and ultimately only useful for low wage labor or fueling the prison industrial complex (Piven and Cloward, 1993; Davis, 2003).

Central to how many policymakers view students in urban areas is how they think the kids and their families got there to begin with. Are the poor deserving or undeserving of social aid? This question is the basis for these concerns. The long-standing culture of poverty debate in social science and public policy circles highlights the way that different constructions of the problem produce starkly different policy solutions. Social science researchers have arguably done as much harm as good to poor people by studying their communities. Several analysts (D'Souza, 1996; Sowell, 1995; Murray, 1995) construct behavior in ghettos and *barrios* as out of control, and that the people living there are pathological and culturally deviant from the mainstream. Even scholars who acknowledge the effect of institutional discrimination often fall prey to cultural explanations for ghetto persistence (Wilson, 1987; Anderson, 1990; Massey and Denton, 1993). Some of these researchers have argued that there is an "underclass culture" that encourages laziness, joblessness (read: welfare dependence), victimhood, lack of personal responsibility (thus the 1996 Welfare Reform Act), instant gratification (read: illegal activities), irresponsible sexual behavior, and a lack of family values (Murray, 1995). Some pundits, like D'Souza (1996), even go as far as arguing that it is the deviant culture of urban people that is the root of the structural problems social scientists have measured (unemployment, income gap, education gap, family structure, incarceration rates, etc.). Sometimes, this charge occurs from inside communities of color, as in the case of Bill Cosby's speech in front of the NAACP's celebration of *Brown* v. *Board*'s 50th Anniversary, where he criticizes the parenting practices of poor and working class black families. We will have more to say about this event in the last section below.

The scholars and policy analysts who believe that the problem is largely cultural are likely to suggest "assimilation" efforts aimed at re-socializing the urban poor into the so-called mainstream. This means tying welfare benefits to "good behavior," like getting married, as was done in 1994 in Wisconsin where the welfare reform program was often referred to as "Bridefare" (Neubeck and Cazenave, 2001). Another strategy from the culture side of the debate is aimed at re-socializing mothers into workers. Mothers are rewarded for their "good behavior" of working outside the home by receiving welfare benefits, now denied to those who do not leave their children in order to enter the workforce. This national policy, the 1996 Personal Responsibility and Work Opportunity Reconciliation Act, drastically reduced welfare benefits and required all people to work (even mothers of small children) in order to create a "culture of work." This strategy has been punitive and paternalistic: change your ways or lose out on the resources of the country. It is also important to note how the family value of mothering is inverted for poor women and women of color. There is a strong cultural imperative, especially from conservative policymakers, for mothers to stay at home with their children. When poor women do this, however, they are seen as lazy, pathological, undermining a culture of work, and therefore ultimately harming their own children (Reese, 2005).

Others disagree with the cultural analysis and favor a focus on structural explanations of ghetto and *barrio* conditions. Instead, to explain the educational and social disparity this set of scholars uses the language of institutional discrimination, inadequate educational opportunities, economic restructuring, a reduction of real wages for the poorest workers, inadequate medical care, and racial segregation (Katz, 1990; Gans, 1996; Feagin, 2001; Bonilla-Silva, 2003; Brown *et al.*, 2003). The culture vs. structure debate is still important because the two different understandings of the problem lead to two starkly different assessments of whether the poor are deserving or undeserving, and what types of policies should be enacted to solve the problem. In this analysis, student readiness and home culture are not so much the determining factors as much as how the breakdown of neighborhood works against stable lives for young people, economic poverty means that basic material comforts are missing, and structural racism becomes a daily assault that students of color (particularly poor) must navigate and avoid despair while doing so. There are still a significant number of scholars and analysts who believe the problem of persistent poverty is largely institutional. They suggest structural solutions, such as improving public schools in poor neighborhoods, strengthening unions, requiring businesses to pay a living wage, reducing police brutality and abuse, enforcing anti-discrimination laws, and developing businesses and jobs in inner-city areas (Kozol, 1991; Wilson, 1997; Nelson, 2001; Katz, 2002).

The culture of poverty debate has always centered primarily on people of color who are already U.S. citizens. The debates are typically about African American communities and sometimes about large Latino communities like Puerto Ricans in New York or Mexican Americans in Los Angeles. However, there is another very important and dominant image of urban neighborhoods—as foreign. Many people imagine urban areas as dirty, smelly, crowded immigrant enclaves where few people speak English and residents are hostile to whites or outsiders. In this scenario, many view urban neighborhoods as dominated by an informal or black market economy, third-world-like in their conditions of poverty, and a haven for those who "refuse to assimilate" to American ways. This image is particularly true in cities that host large numbers of migrants in the United States such as Los Angeles, Miami, Houston, and New York. Immigrant neighborhoods, often labeled in the diminutive of their residents' place of origin, such as Little Saigon, Little Havana, and Koreatown, represent for many people the heart of the problem with today's immigration: cultural pluralism. Catering to these "foreigners" by multiculturalizing the school curriculum, providing strong versions of bilingualism, or diversifying the teaching staff become part of the larger problem. The solution put forth is to create an educational version of the Patriot Act in order to reclaim the U.S. nationalism lost in the wake of "minority rights" that led to the softening of American global domination.

Aside from the most common complaints about today's immigrants ("They take our jobs" and "They come for the welfare money") many people complain that today's immigrants refuse to assimilate to American (read: Anglo) ways and are therefore hostile to American culture. Urban immigrant neighborhoods highlight this alarmist concern over national language, food, religion, and increased separatism because they are typically spaces where business is done in languages other than English, the products and foods available are unfamiliar to most people outside of that ethnic group, and the signs and storefronts often reflect the languages, values, and concerns of the particular ethnic group. Many whites (and some African Americans as well) find it disconcerting to have their own language and cultural norms decentered from their dominant Western and American position. Although the diversity and number of ethnic restaurants make urban areas attractive to many people, those traits also offend many Americans who are uncomfortable when Anglo dominance is challenged.

Nativist attitudes have implications for school policy. Because many policymakers and even some teachers view urban neighborhoods as foreign and therefore problematic, schools often project negative attitudes toward their students from immigrant families. Some teachers resent immigrant parents for not being more "involved" with the school even when the school environment is hostile to non-English speakers (Valdes, 2001). Attitudes about bilingualism are also wrought with contradiction. Many people in the USA glamorize bilingualism when it is attained through study at elite European universities, but denigrate it when immigrant languages (e.g., Spanish, Chinese, or Farsi) are maintained at home (Fishman, 1966). That is, when American whites speak a language besides English, this skill is perceived as "liberal" or "sophisticated" (i.e., the right kind of urban). When Mexicans learn to speak English (a process whose difficulty should not be downplayed), but insist on maintaining their Spanish, they are imagined as resistant to American culture (i.e., the wrong kind of urban). Despite the wave of public hysteria to the contrary, noted sociologist Alejandro Portes (2002) assures the U.S. public that "immigrant children today are rapidly embracing English over their native languages. The threat is less of a Babel-like society than of a society without cultural memory—at a cost to both immigrant children and the nation" (p. 10). Ultimately, U.S. xenophobia will erode the nation's effectiveness in global interactions and undermine the success of immigrant students in U.S. schools.

Urban neighborhoods are clearly racialized spaces, but they are also gendered spaces and the experiences and images of men and women in them differ significantly. The racist cliché of the "urban jungle" is also a highly gendered one. The urban jungle is decidedly feminine when the pundits talk about teenage parenthood, welfare dependence, and the out of control sexuality of women of color (see Luttrell, 2003). However, the urban jungle can also be masculine when the topics are gangs, violence, and the drug economy. Although women and men are of course involved in all of these activities, the different issues evoke specific images of problem women or problem men, all of which affect how younger people are perceived in schools. When women from urban areas are discussed it is most typically in relation to their sexuality and bodies. Popular culture reflects this characterization of young women of color, particularly through music videos. Even a cursory examination of hip-hop videos reveals an unending parade of young women of color, hyper-sexualized and routinely degraded. Similarly and interconnected, real women in ghetto or *barrio* neighborhoods are seen as sexually out of control (they have several male partners), overly fertile (they have too many kids), irresponsible (they refuse to use birth control), and unfit mothers (they are addicted to drugs while pregnant) (Collins, 2004). All of these assaulting and controlling images of women of color in urban areas suggest that they are "bad women" and just as significant, they are unlike the "good women" who are married, white, suburban, and middle class.

When girls are pregnant in urban high schools they are often humiliated by school nursing staff and school counselors. They are often told that their futures are over and they are on the road to welfare dependence and a lifetime of hopelessness and poverty just like their mothers, aunts, or neighbors. In her book, *Pregnant Bodies Fertile Minds*, Wendy Luttrell (2002) describes the dominant discourse on teenage mothers in schools as "wrong girls." In her ethnography she chronicles the humiliating treatment the girls receive from adult school staff as well as the alternate view of themselves that many of the girls offer. Luttrell's evidence suggests that despite the pathologization of young pregnant students of color, this group of girls is able to project a counter-image of themselves as having some "good sense," of recognizing the myths that impinge on their subjectivity, not unlike Willis' (1977) lads in *Learning to Labor*, who were able to penetrate the discourses about their own working class limitations (see also MacLeod, 1987). Luttrell's book is one of a handful of works that discusses how girls respond to negative discourses and policies toward them as young mothers (see also, McDade, 1992).

Urban spaces are often seen as hyper-masculine spaces dominated with acts of machismo and one-upmanship (Anderson, 2000). This is especially true with respect to urban gangs and drug markets. Although girls and women are increasingly involved in gangs and drug sales, the public still largely views these activities as male. In the nightly news in most American cities, gang culture and life are reduced to the description of a shooting frequently followed by the disclaimer, "Authorities believe the shooting may have been gang related." This sentence can be found at the end of almost any homicide description in an urban area, usually attached to the picture of a young male of color. Certainly, many shootings in urban areas are "gang-related" in the broadest sense, but they are also related to many other more mundane things: hurt pride, self-defense, economic disputes, etc.

The American public is at once enthralled with urban gang life and appalled by it. Hollywood has produced dozens of movies about young African American, Latino, and occasionally Asian men involved in illegal activities and violent gang life (Benshoff and Griffin, 2003). Some of these movies have been more thought provoking than others. Nonetheless, despite the national love affair with urban crime drama, there is also a substantial punitive streak among much of the American public. The majority of voters support harsher and harsher prison sentences for drug activity and violent crime (Johnson, 2001). Laws such as three strikes, mandatory minimums, and longer penalties for crack cocaine and other "urban drugs" all provide evidence for the punishing tendency of suburban America on urban kids. Nowhere is this development more poignantly captured than in the 2004 documentary film, "Juvies." The film takes the viewer through the lives of troubled adolescents whose mistakes earned them jail sentences made excessive by the "enhancement" laws that some states, like California, have adopted to punish criminals who appear to have ties with gangs or were carrying guns when the crime occurred. These gang and gun enhancements basically seal an adolescent's life when they add many years on top of normal sentences. As a commentator on the film remarked, a youth population that displays violent behavior shows us the extent to which their society is plagued by a violent condition not of their own making.

Our views of young men in urban neighborhoods have already had a significant impact on our public policies. The policies of local police forces have also changed in response to the perceived threat of young urban men: more surveillance, broader ability to disperse crowds and control what public space people occupy, and the ongoing problem of racial profiling. For example, in Los Angeles, it is now illegal for people to "cruise" in their cars with music blaring from them. Our level of tolerance for loud music aside, this development is clearly racial for it is a response to the booming, bass-heavy music to which many young students of color listen in the urban setting. In contrast, the white image of a motorcycle rider atop a loud Harley-Davidson is not criminalized. In fact, one can order a Harley with a specific muffler sound in pursuit of a certain aesthetics. The immediate irony here is that the music form of hiphop (black noise) is eclipsed by bellowing mufflers as a form of art (white noise). This analysis is not meant to caste aspersions on Harley riders, but to point out the racial politics of urban life, the first criminalized, the second aestheticized.

It is also worth mentioning that all the concern about violence committed by young men of color is coupled with a near complete disinterest in the hundreds and sometimes thousands of young men of color who are killed in urban neighborhoods each year (usually by other young men of color). Most suburban residents fear for their own safety when they think of urban violence and are ignorant of the large number of lives of men of color lost in their own cities each year. This ignorance is assisted in part by the local news outlets that rarely cover homicides of poor, young men of color—that is, until it involves a white victim. By themselves the lives of young men of color are often viewed as too unimportant to be covered in the news.

The attitude of many white, suburban Americans toward urban life is full of contradictions. In a sort of modern-day minstrel show, many middle class white students perform their image of urban blackness and brownness by imitating their view of urban life through clothing, music, language, and behavior. This aping of urban culture, however, is a big money business. Rappers, clothing companies, the music industry, Hollywood, and other social imagineers have worked together to sell the ghetto in a way that is unprecedented in U.S. history. It is fashionable, in its own outsider, low-status way, to don urban clothing lines (Fubu, Enyce, Baby Phat, Apple Bottom), listen to rap or hip-hop music, and speak with the current colloquialisms of urban youth. In this sense, the urban is simultaneously performed and ridiculed. It is contemporary chic and denigrated—"don't act so ghetto"—all at once.

Urban life has been commodified and is for sale often for prices only middle class suburbanites can afford. Urban identity can be performed or "tried on" by white students or middle class people. They can dabble in the "urban" without ever losing their access to suburban space and white privilege. In short, they have the luxury of being urban without the burden. They can partake in the "jungle" without communing with its people—that is, unless we invoke the image of Tarzan, played by white actors who seem to be the only white person in the real jungles of Africa. This is not a new development, previously witnessed in the days when white entertainers from Pat Boone to Elvis appropriated and legitimated black music. What seems novel about the new fetishism is its economic intensification and its urban character. In the case of music, there was much about the previous racial appropriation that took from rural black sounds of blues. Today's appropriation is decidedly urban.

Social and Policy Implications for Education: Re-imagining the Urban

Imagining the urban is intimately connected with policies that impact urban people's lives, particularly students of color. From medication to education, the pathological depictions of the urban contribute to policy creation that predominantly endorses behavioral and cultural responses to urban conditions instead of an institutional intervention to address its deep structure. This tone is summarized in the recent furor over Bill Cosby's public comments about the crisis in poor black communities. Previously in "Fat Albert," Cosby was able to connect with the black urban community in a way that did not alienate its youth. In his NAACP speech, Cosby's criticism of the "wrong kind of blacks" (read: poor) imagines the urban as a criminal, pathological, and largely self-perpetuated poor black condition. Delivered at the NAACP's event to commemorate the 50th anniversary of *Brown* v. *Board of Education*, Cosby's "Ghettosburg Address" (http://en.wikipedia.org/wiki/Ghettosburg_Address)

has sparked not only controversy but is likely to influence public policy regarding urban education for students of color. The speech does not only represent Cosby's clarion call for poor blacks to change their "misguided ways;" it is interpreted through the public's urban imagination, one that now finds its legitimacy in a high profile black figure. Cosby's message reminds us of the class warfare within the black community itself, one half that relegates the signifier "Nigger" to racist whites, while the other appropriates "Nigga" for new urban politics.

Cosby's speech is heuristic insofar as it provides an exemplar for our general point about the social construction of urban spaces. It is not important so much for its truth-value (that is, whether or not poor blacks are responsible for their plight), but for its social consequences and implications for education policy. Although Dyson (2005) correctly points out that Cosby does not have a social researcher's training, Cosby's sheer stature is enough to capture the imagination of the American public, its "collective racial unconscious." Cosby's commentary also affects the black political landscape and community. Spike Lee showed mild support for the comedian whereas "Boondocks" comic artist, Arron McGruder, criticized Cosby for "vilifying the black youth." All three entertainers were interviewed separately by talk show host Tavis Smiley. One may level the same criticisms at Chris Rock, whose stand-up show in Washington, D.C. expressed sentiments similar to Cosby when Rock publicized his disdain for "Niggas" and love for "black people." The main difference is that whereas Cosby's speech seems to cut himself off from poor blacks (the wrong kind of urban), Rock's performances still seem to maintain a strong connection through his comic material, including his love for hip hop and rap. In other words, Cosby leads us to perceive little or no redeeming aspects to the black urban culture and experience. In his own defense, Cosby considers his speech a form of challenge to poor blacks to change their parenting ways. That said, Cosby's shaming tactics may subvert his desire to "uplift" poor blacks.

In schools, we do not have to look too far for connections. For example, when Cosby suggests that black youth should dress more appropriately, this implicates black students who may be perceived as not ready to learn based on their appearance. When Cosby shows concern for the way that black youth speak in public (whether or not we want to call this black English), he joins the discussion over language politics in schools. Not only does this pressure black students to adopt a more middle class vernacular, but what is perceived as a standard, unmarked, white way of speech. This is reminiscent of a problem with even insurgent books on integration, such as Kozol's (1991) *Savage Inequalities*, where it is assumed that black students would do well to study next to white students, that is, blacks *need* whites in order to do well in school (Foster, 1993). We do not debate the importance of necessary skills for the advancement of one's career and social legitimacy. But to suggest that blacks lack access to decent education and jobs because they speak non-standard dialect and dress with low-rise pants belies the structural origins of their oppression. In fact, so-called black wear and language are hardly black-specific anymore, as white, Asian, and Latino youth have appropriated such styles. They have become "merely urban" as hip hop becomes popular with whites, many of whom live in the suburbs. In the case of whites and Asians, compared to black youth their life chances do not seem damaged to the same extent when whites and Asians dress or talk "black." They are not imagined as criminals in the same way for wearing the same thing.

To the extent that urban youth of color promote their style as a form of resistance to whiteness (Dyson, 2005; see also Rose, 1994), they represent what Gramsci (1971) calls "good sense." These acts, while not necessarily counter-hegemonic, recognize the urban space as a place of struggle. To the extent that they dress against whiteness, black youth are cognizant of the racial strife that they did not create but live with on a daily basis. If educators listen, they discover that youth of color, while ensnared in their own contradictions, penetrate the racial and class formation, and are able to exert their own will on these processes rather than merely being reproduced by them. Instead, the common school reactions to these urban dynamics include: metal detectors, more police on campus, emptying of backpacks, random searches of lockers and bags, no hats (to avoid gang affiliation). Since most, if not all, educators believe that creating a learning culture is part of raising achievement, we must conclude that these incarcerating policies re-create prison conditions where little learning is likely to take place. Student resistance in the urban setting is often difficult to decipher. It is complicated by the effects of media, fast capitalism, and a heightened sense of identity politics. Often, urban youth grow up more quickly than their suburban counterparts because the former are faced with harsh conditions and an even harsher future prospect. The innocence that adults treasure in young people is lost more quickly in urban youth.

Urban Latino students have dealt with the transformation of the *barrio* from a literal term connoting community to a term of burden. Through English-Only movements and anti-immigrant legislation, Latino students have been imagined as the culprits of the Third-Worldization of urban places, like Los Angeles. With their national attrition rates higher than those for blacks, Latino students may become the new urban underclass. When we imagine them as "illegal immigrants" rather than displaced people in search of a decent life, and whose labor is fully welcomed by both policymakers and business owners, educators ensure that Latino children's education becomes expendable. At best, their education remains irrelevant to their worldview and cultural understanding, ignoring much of the cultural resources that urban families have to offer, otherwise known as "funds of knowledge" to Moll and Gonzalez (2004) and "ecologies of engagement" to Barton, Drake, Perez, St. Louis, and George (2004). Or, we run the risk of dumbing down their curriculum by depriving them of access to classic European texts with high status and replete with cultural capital, in exchange for a "relatable education" with examples about drugs, gangs, and other problematic constructions that are rarely put in their proper structural contexts.

As mentioned, the urban imagination also comes in gendered forms of racialization. Cosby's comments contribute to this dynamic when he criticizes black women for failing to control their children, their own sexuality, and their men. Controlling images of women in urban areas have direct implications on policies in urban schools. For instance, many girls of color in urban areas are encouraged to use birth control from an early age. Often the types of birth control that are suggested are invasive and hard to reverse such as Depo Provera and Norplant. Young urban women's sexuality is seen as problematic and needing to be controlled in contrast to suburban female sexuality, which is often viewed as something to be protected and saved. The sexuality of girls of color is a problem; the sexuality of middle class white girls is a virtue.

In light of the high stakes testing that No Child Left Behind has put in place in U.S. schools, urban schools again take center stage in the elusive search to bridge the "achievement gap." Under this legislation, teachers and administrators are in a mad dash to show Adequate Yearly Progress or face sanctions, including the reconstitution of its teaching and administrative staff or takeover by a private educational company. Commendable for its public decree that failing schools shall not be tolerated any longer, NCLB won the support of both Democrats and Republicans on Capitol Hill. In addition, it targets precisely the student subgroups that need the most assistance: students with disabilities, English language learners, poor students, and racial minorities. In particular, urban schools show that several of the subgroups, like English language learners, children of color, and poor students, meet to paint a complex picture of *who* is being left behind, but equally as important, *where* they are. In addition, since it is a well-known fact that students of color are classified with disabilities at higher rates than their white counterparts, NCLB's impact in urban settings is all-encompassing. Already suffering from lack of resources, faster teacher burnouts, and higher levels of violence, urban schools are imagined as the testing ground for a school reform that offers little extra funding. In fact, NCLB falls short of providing more funds to struggling urban schools in light of the unequal needs they face because its creators declare that getting students to proficient levels in reading and math is already the school's job.

High on threats and low on assistance, NCLB dooms public urban schools to fail targets that are virtually impossible to meet (Darling-Hammond, 2004). The Act lays down the gauntlet for schools to improve in as little time as two years or lose control of their funding, face student exodus, or eventual reconstitution of their staff. NCLB receives criticism not so much for its noble dream of leaving no child behind, but for its ability to leave behind the social origins and conditions that plague American urban schools, such as racism, economic inequality, and institutional discrimination (see Cochran-Smith, 2005). Urban schools suffer a lion's share of NCLB's burden and blame if all students do not reach 100 percent competency by 2014, an unreasonable expectation in light of the fact that no state or country currently boasts those achievements (Linn, 2003).

NCLB's measure of Adequate Yearly Progress will confirm the popular image of inner-city schools as a problem, or the negative pole in the dialectics of the urban. It comes with a "diversity penalty" for urban schools that serve multiple social groups and are required to report satisfactory progress on more indicators than homogeneous schools (Novak and Fuller, 2003). Urban immigration, media spectacles, threats of terrorism, violence, and higher costs of living converge to create a learning condition that NCLB's focus on higher test scores is woefully unable to crack, a move which "mistakes measuring schools for fixing them" (Darling-Hammond, 2004, p. 9). Higher test scores, while showing one kind of improvement, fail to account for the relevance of the learning taking place in urban classrooms, favoring a language of outputs (e.g., test scores) over inputs (e.g., instructional support).

Re-imagining urban schooling takes a concerted effort to recast its conditions neither as a gift of progress nor its underbelly for some unfortunate people. It requires a radical shift in urban planning, economic base, and schooling infrastructure. But consistent with this chapter's thesis, it also necessitates an equally radical questioning of the way educators and concerned people currently imagine the urban from a place of decline to a place of possibilities. Part of this recasting of the urban means that businesses may work more closely with communities in addressing the waste of both human potential and talent, which would add to the viability of the nation, let alone the creation of a democracy (Henig *et al.*, 1999). Although it would be difficult to re-imagine businesses separate from their profit motives in the context of late capitalism, there is a difference between for-profit educational ventures like the Edison Project and the kinds of neighborhood compacts that Henig *et al.* found in places like Washington D.C. and other urban cities around the USA. Likewise, Henig *et al.* suggest that urban leadership would not only help urban communities and schools through increased funding, but also through increased civic capacity to speak politically about issues that affect their lives. It no doubt requires a critical amount of coordination between students, teachers, administrators, parents, scholars, businesses, politicians, and NGOs, but we should expect nothing less in re-imagining the urban, if by that we do not mean the idle notion of mind activity. Rather, if by re-imagining we mean a dynamic and engaged cultural process, then it is more a material act at its base and less a tinkering with ideas about the urban absent of institutional change.

In this chapter, we have argued that imagining the urban is an intimate part of making urban schools. It is an imagined reality that Americans construct even as we make daily sense of it. Re-imagining the urban in this context means that school reform must account for the complexity of teaching in an urban setting where the specific forces of civilization meet, such as the political economy, racialization, and gendered meanings. This re-imagining has taken some root in the "new urbanism" movement of housing and lifestyle that is dense but planned, with a mixed use of housing and commercial space, mixed income, and smaller utility spaces. This is the urban as anti-suburbia. This is also a response to the urban as "unlivable." The dialectics of the urban may still be resolved into a higher logic that makes its promises and burdens a shared venture between whites and people of color, between the rich and poor. Re-imagining the urban does not only take a certain courage to change, but a commitment to education in the concrete, rather than sentimental, sense.

10
The Souls of White Folk

Up to now, I have argued for a critical engagement of race, whiteness, and education but have kept the scope within the implicit assumption of the nation state. As globalization becomes an intellectual as well as political project, this chapter argues that critical education benefits from an intersectional understanding of race, whiteness and globalization discourse. At the turn of the 1900s, W.E.B. Du Bois argued that the problem of the color line is the twentieth century's main challenge. Following Du Bois, I suggest that the problem of the twenty-first century is the *global color line*. As capitalism stretches across nations, its partnership with race relations also evolves into a formidable force. Appropriating concepts from globalization, this chapter outlines a global approach to race, and in particular whiteness, in order to argue that the problem of white racial domination transcends the nation state. Borrowing concepts from globalization discourse, such as multinationalism, fragmentation, and flexibility, a critical pedagogy of whiteness promotes an expanded notion of race that includes global anti-racist struggles. Finally, the chapter concludes the book by suggesting that educators consider seriously the insights of the neo-abolitionist movement.

Globalization literature is filling up bookshelves in bookstores and libraries. One can buy Mander and Goldsmith's (1996) activist-oriented collection of essays on the global economy, a critical geographer's response to the current economic restructuring in David Harvey's (1989) *The Condition of Post-modernity*, and Jaggar and Rothenberg's (1993) popular *Feminist Frameworks* includes a global feminist perspective in its third edition. Of course, who can forget Marshall McLuhan's coining of the phrase, "global village," to describe fast technology's capacity to link the backroads of rural China to the potholes of New York. One can expect that the arrival of *Globalization for Dummies* should be right around the corner.[1] In education, there is a burgeoning engagement with the shifting purpose of schools in a world economy. In 2000, *Educational Theory* devoted an entire volume to globalization. School reform has taken on a global face in Hargreaves, Lieberman, Fullan, and Hopkins's (1998) *International Handbook of Educational Change* and Peter McLaren (2000) reinvigorates the pedagogical lessons of "el Che" in international socialist struggles against capital.

However, as I argue in this chapter, there has not been a pronounced attempt to integrate globalization discourse with whiteness studies. Wells, Carnochan, Slayton, Allen, and Vasudeva's (1998) excellent introduction to the different social and educational theories on globalization documents the dominant concern with the economy in globalization literature. Ricky Lee Allen (2002), following the example of Immanuel Wallerstein, has launched a critique of the white educational left for announcing globalism through a curious neglect of the past hundreds of years of global colonialism by largely European forces, a process that is neither novel nor come lately. This chapter takes a different tack on the relationship between globalization and whiteness. Just as Blackmore (2000) finds it problematic that gender issues are not incorporated into the discourse of educational reform and globalization, race, and in particular whiteness, must also be situated in the global context. In short, I argue that, like the economy, whiteness as a privileged signifier has become global.

We are witnessing the globalization of capital through new strategies. Flexible accumulation, contract and part-time work, smaller batches of production, and exportation of labor to third world nations represent some of capital's late *modus operandi*. Multinational corporations encourage "friendly" trade relations for the mutual benefit of the global bourgeoisie. Such a diversification of the capitalist venture produces, much to Lukacs' (1971) chagrin, the fragmentation of consciousness, or the inability to grasp the totality of experience. This condition leads to the false impression that the "class situation" within a given nation is improving because much of the manufacturing and hard labor remains out of sight and out of mind. Meanwhile, the *maquiladora* factory workers of Mexico and rural women in the Philippines suffer the daily exploitation that harks back to the brutal labor conditions of earlier industrial capitalism. As the world economy evolves, we witness the incredible flexibility of capitalism to respond to crises and recessions. Yet its imperative is no different than it was when Marx first started writing about it. Capitalism bears a certain permanent trait but not the one that its proponents prefer to promulgate. Rather, as Blackmore (2000) reminds us, "Markets are based upon inequality, envy, greed, desire, and choice . . . Exchange relations are valued by market, while nonexchange relations (voluntary school work, domestic labor, and emotion work) in the 'private' are ignored" (p. 478). As the material conditions change, so does capitalism. Its sophistication is marked by its ability to flex according to, accommodate, and exploit current global conditions. Yet it is unchanging in its essential feature of the extraction of surplus value and the mystification of the process that makes this possible. Critical scholars have organized around explaining the latest mutations of capitalism in a global context. Because we know that capital is intimate with race, a close relationship exists between economic exploitation and racial oppression.

Since the publication of David Roediger's (1991) book, *The Wages of Whiteness*, there has also been a parallel development in the engagement of whiteness studies (Lipsitz, 1998; Delgado and Stefancic, 1997; Allen, 1997, 1994; Frankenberg, 1997, 1993; Ignatiev, 1995; McIntosh, 1992). As I have argued so far, whiteness is now regarded as a critical point of departure in a pedagogy of demystification. Kincheloe, Steinberg, Rodriguez, and Chennault's (1997) critically acclaimed collection, *White Reign*, advocates an assault on white privilege by exposing whiteness as a socially constructed signifier and rearticulating it through a "critical pedagogy of whiteness" (Kincheloe and Steinberg, 1997, p. 12; see also McLaren, 1995, 1997; Giroux, 1997; Fine, Weiss, Powell, Wong, 1997). Whiteness studies has achieved such momentum and currency, the ever popular journal, *Educational Researcher*, devoted substantial attention to it in the December 2000 issue consisting of critical responses to Rosa Hernandez Sheets' (2000) book reviews of the "white movement in multicultural education" (Howard, 2000; Dilg, 2000; McIntyre, 2000). Clearly, the issues of globalization and whiteness are critical components of a pedagogy attempting to understand the oppressive structures that distort clear knowledge. These structural features filter into micro-interactions between students and teachers. This chapter offers a neo-abolitionist global pedagogy by linking whiteness with globalization processes.

Neo-abolitionist pedagogy suggests that teachers and students work together to name, reflect on, and dismantle discourses of whiteness. It means disrupting white discourses and unsettling their codes. The complementary goal is to trouble race, or pose the possibilities in post-race analysis, without suggesting to students of color that their racial experiences are not valid or "real." It necessitates a problematization of race at the conceptual level because there is a difference between suggesting that the concept of race is not real and affirming students' racialized and lived experiences as "real." Students of color benefit from an education that analyzes the implications of whiteness because they have to understand the daily vicissitudes of white discourses and be able to deal with them, which mitigates some of the power of whiteness. That is, in order to confront whiteness, they have to be familiar with it. In the process, they also realize that their "colorness" is relational to whiteness' claims of color-blindness and both are burst asunder in the process. Thus, the goal is for students of color to engage whiteness while simultaneously working to dismantle it. White students benefit from neo-abolitionism because they come to terms with the daily fears associated with the upkeep of whiteness. Insofar as whiteness is a performance (Giroux, 1997), white students possess a vulnerable persona always an inch away from being exposed as bogus. Their daily white performance is dependent on the assertion of a false world built on rickety premises.

Before we embark on a study of whiteness, two concepts must be clarified: whiteness and white people. "Whiteness" is a racial discourse, whereas the category "white people" represents a socially constructed identity, usually based on skin color. For practical purposes, we are born with certain bodies that are inscripted with social meaning (Leonardo, 2000b). Most people do not radically alter their physical identity throughout their lifetime. Michael Jackson may be the exception to this rule, but no American doubts he is a black man. However, that a white student acts on the world does not suggest she accomplishes this from the perspective of a white racial paradigm; in fact, she could be articulating her life choices through non-white discourses or strategies of anti-whiteness. To the extent that a man can be feminist, whites can be anti-white. Likewise, a student of color (an identity) could live out her life through whiteness (Hunter and Nettles, 1999). Thus, it can be said that whiteness is also a racial perspective or a worldview. Furthermore, whiteness is supported by material practices and institutions. That said, white people are often the subjects of whiteness because it benefits and privileges them. As a collection of everyday strategies, whiteness is characterized by the unwillingness to name the contours of racism, the avoidance of identifying with a racial experience or group, the minimization of racist legacy, and other similar evasions (Frankenberg, 1993). White people have accomplished many great things; the issue is whether or not they have asserted whiteness in the process. Many white subjects have fought and still fight on the side of racial justice. To the extent that they perform this act, they dis-identify with whiteness. By contrast, historically the assertion of a white racial identity has had a violent career. Roediger (1994) grasps these distinctions when he claims that whiteness is not just oppressive and false, it is "*nothing but* oppressive and false" (p. 13; italics in original). That is, whenever whiteness, as an imagined racial collective, inserts itself into history, material and discursive violence accompanies it. Or to mimic Stephanie Spina (2000), we must come to terms with the whiteness of violence and the violence of whiteness.

In this sense, whiteness is not a culture but a social concept. This does not suggest that white people have no culture. White people practice everyday culture when they consume Coke, fries, and a Big Mac. Non-white people all over the world also have access to McDonalds but this is not indigenous to their culture. Whites also partake in formal cultural events, such as Protestant weddings. These practices are functional and are not harmful by themselves; they are part of what we call white ethnic culture. As a racial category, whiteness is different from white culture but connected to it through historical association. Aspects of white culture assume superiority over others and it is this historical record that must not fade from our memory (see Spring, 2000). However, whereas some facets of white ethnic culture are benign or even liberatory, such as critical traditions of the enlightenment, whiteness is nothing but false and oppressive. Although not exclusively, whiteness has historically stratified and partitioned the world according to skin color (see Hunter, 1998), or the modern sense of race as the politics of pigmentation. The assertion of the white race is intimate with slavery, segregation, and discrimination. On the other hand, white cultures abound in the form of various white ethnic practices. Whiteness is the attempt to homogenize diverse white ethnics into a single category (much like it attempts with people of color) for purposes of racial domination.

Multinational Whiteness: The Hegemony of White Images

As whiteness becomes globalized, white domination begins to transcend national boundaries. Without suggesting the end of nations or their decreased significance for racial theory, multinational whiteness has developed into a formidable global force in its attempt to control and transform into its own image almost every nook and cranny of the earth. W.E.B. Du Bois (1989) once commented that American Negroes attempting to escape white racism will fail to find a place on earth untouched by the long arms of European colonization.[2] At the turn of the twentieth century, the Philippines, Hawaii, and West Indies were added to global colonization by white Europeans and Americans. Thus the point was not to flee the American social landscape, but to change it. From the video, "Color of Fear", Victor supports this view when he lashes out against David for his naive suggestion that everyman should carve out his place in society and stand on his own ground (Wah, 1994).[3] Victor reminds us that whites have stood on someone else's ground for centuries. A pedagogical critique of whiteness must transcend its national articulations and link knowledge of whiteness to global processes of (neo)colonization whereby apparently separate white nations share common histories of domination over non-white peoples. This is an important educational lesson because students learn that the white diaspora has, to a large extent, created a global condition after its own image, a condition that whites are generally ill-equipped to understand. Or as Ricky Lee Allen (2002), this time following Charles Mills, says, "We whites may have created the world in our own image, but we completely misunderstand the world that we have created" (p. 482).

Both white and non-white students understand that a multinational critique of whiteness transcends limitations found in discourses that deal with race exclusively at the national level. For example, when discussing the effects of racism within any given nation, the common refrain of "Well, why don't _____ just go back to their country if they're not happy here? (fill the blank with an ethnic or racial group)" exposes several faulty assumptions. One, it assumes that students who voice opposition to white racism do not belong in the nation they seek to improve by ridding it of racism. Two, it frames the issue of racism as the problem or realm of non-whites who are dissatisfied with their lot in life rather than a concern for the humanity of all people, including whites. Three, as Du Bois has already articulated, whiteness is a global phenomenon and there is very little space on the globe unaffected or unpartitioned by white power. Fourth, it assumes white ownership of racialized territories; whites rarely tell other whites to "go back to Europe." Freire (1993) agrees when he says, "The oppressor consciousness tends to transform everything surrounding it into an object of its domination. The earth, property, production, the creations of people, people themselves, time—everything is reduced to the status of objects at its disposal" (p. 58).

Today, the European Community is more than an economic strategy to consolidate money currency or friendly trade relations between European nations. Since we know that economic development is also coterminous with the evolution of whiteness, the EC represents late capitalism's partnership with multinational whiteness. With the technological revolution, *late white movements* are able to connect via websites and the internet, just as easily as the Zapatistas were able to utilize email technology for their own revolution in Chiapas, Mexico.[4] The UK joins the EC, Asians create the Asian Pacific Economic Community (APEC), and an international indigenous people's movement, mark the reconfiguration of global politics (Porter and Vidovich, 2000). A critical pedagogy of whiteness must cut whiteness across national boundaries. In doing so, dialectical forms of pedagogy provide students with a discourse emphasizing what Mills (1997) calls a "transnational white polity" (p. 29) as well as transnational resistance to the Racial Contract. Critical forms of education must come to grips with global white supremacy in order for students to understand that race is both a product and producer of differences in a Herrenvolk ethics of justice for "just us" (whites) (Mills, 1997, p. 110). Of course, it should be made clear that this is a vocation that requires collaboration between whites as race traitors (Ignatiev and Garvey, 1996c), or whites who dis-identify with whiteness, and non-white resistors. In an increasingly multinational condition where we can talk about the global assembly line, what often fades to black is the global color line.

Whiteness is guilty of a certain "hidalguismo," or son of God status, in its quest to exert its brand of civilization on non-white nations. As Nilda Rimonte (1997) explains, "Hidalguismo is the obsessive pursuit of status and honor, the alpha and omega of the hidalgo's life" (p. 42). Whiteness stamps its claims to superiority, both morally and aesthetically speaking, on its infantilized Other by claiming to speak for people who apparently speak in gibberish. It aims to comprehend a people better than it comprehends itself. For example, California's Proposition 227, which challenged bilingual programs, consolidates English as the only language of instruction in schools. Although parents can request a waiver to continue their children's participation in bilingual programs, Proposition 227 struck a blow to the legitimacy of bilingual education. In the USA, the common white supremacist argument goes something like this: In Mexico, immigrant students are asked to speak Spanish. Why can't the USA ask the same and demand that students speak English? We can answer such charges in several ways.

First, the fact that bilingual education is a difficult program to implement is confused with immigrants' lack of desire to speak English. Mexicans, Asians, and other students from non-English speaking nations are (re)constructed as resistant to speaking English rather than acknowledging the formidable challenge to attaining a second language. Second, that Mexico may desire a monolingual educational system (if this is empirically the case) does not suggest that this is the ethically preferred vision for schools in general. Notice that monolingual instruction is naturalized by appealing to an external example, as if the way another nation conducts its education justifies one's own. Gramsci's concept of hegemony explains this instance as a subject's ability to confuse common sense with good sense. Third, the argument obscures the global privilege of English as the international language of business. Mexico (as well as other non-English speaking societies) may promote their own language, but they would surely welcome a student's ability to speak English since this would put the country in a better economic position in the global market. Learning English in a non-English speaking nation is not comparable to learning Spanish in California. Hidalguismo blinds whiteness to its own position in the world by projecting its specific rationalizations onto the general population.

Another mainstream discourse that obscures the multinational nature of whiteness is the attempt to construct white supremacist groups as "outside" of mainstream society. At best, the liberal discourse acknowledges white crimes against humanity as an ugly part of our past. In this pedagogy of amnesia, students are encouraged to think of the "founding fathers" as benign, national heroes who were products of their social milieu. Indeed, Thomas Jefferson and Abraham Lincoln, just to name a few, lived in a time when slavery was legal. However, that Jefferson owned slaves and Lincoln rejected racial integration or equality (see McLaren, 1997) seem to be peripheral to their development as leaders of the nation. That is, their participation in racist practices occupies the fringes of our historical memory in as much as neo-fascist organizations are constructed as fringe groups in society. This does not negate the fact that Jefferson and Lincoln were also responsible for creating certain liberatory institutions (or helping destroy them, as in the case of slavery). That said, to speak of them as caught up in the logic of the times disregards the fact that at any given historical juncture, there are white traitors who speak up against racial oppression. In other words, it is not the case that white subjects have no choice about the matter of racism.

Participation is very much within the realm of choice and whites have been able to speak against the dehumanizing structures of racism even against their own immediate interests. The example of Sartre (1963) should remove doubts about positive white participation in decolonial struggles. Barthes' semiology proffers people a "methodology of the oppressed" in their attempts to understand, as Fanon also suggested, the way that colonial relations become sedimented at the level of meaning and signification (Sandoval, 1997). Memmi's (2000) unrelenting critique of racism in Tunisia and other national contexts shows us how he understood, as well as or better than any third world subject, the crippling and dehumanizing effects of "heterophobia," or fear of difference (p. 43). In many ways, Sartre, Barthes, and Memmi's project parallels Freire's

(1993) pedagogy of the oppressed. As a white Brazilian, Freire understood the centrality of struggles against racism as the existential analog of class exploitation (see McLaren and Leonardo, 1996). Whiteness is less of an essence and more of a choice.

Conceptually, constructing white supremacist organizations as "fringe" groups is problematic. Students learn inadvertently that multinational racism sits at the margins of society, whereas racial democracy exists at the center. Therefore, neo-fascist groups are not considered a significant threat and can be dismissed as irrational whites. As Mills (1997) notes, this kind of logic makes an exception out of racism, an aberration of white supremacy, and a deviation from the norm in Western development. A counter-pedagogy would suggest otherwise. Despite the racial progress we have experienced through the Civil Rights Movement in the USA and the fight against apartheid in South Africa, white normativity remains central to the development of both Western and non-Western nations. Anti-hate groups, civil rights agendas, and racial dialogue maintain their marginal status in the inner workings of schools and society. Critical forms of multiculturalism have made significant progress in globalizing education (i.e., representing non-white cultures) but whiteness still remains at the center of many national curricula or culture. It is racialization which remains at the center, with deracialization staying at the margins.

In the Filipino diaspora, white or mestiza/o physical traits are considered beautiful (Root, 1997). In Brazil, color-blind discourse disables the nation's ability to locate white privilege in exchange for an imagined racial paradise of mixing, matching, and miscegenation (Warren, 2000). On European soil, the neo-Nazi Progress Party in Norway came in second during the presidential race, while Belgium, France, and Austria are witnessing an increase in white supremacist hopefuls in the government (Flecha, 1999). In the USA, whites feel minimized under the sign of multiculturalism, victimized by affirmative action, and perceive that they suffer from group discrimination despite the fact that white women are the largest beneficiaries of the above policies (Tatum, 1997; Marable, 1996) and the utter lack of empirical evidence for "imaginary white disadvantage" (Winant, 1997, p. 42; see also Kincheloe and Steinberg, 1997, pp. 14–16). Nevertheless, whites react with both intellectual and nationalist nativism, as evidenced by the reassertion of Euro-centric, humanist curricula and the Thatcherist brand of xenophobia to make Britain Great once more (Hall, 1996d; Hesse, 1997).[5]

Fragmentation of Consciousness and Global Racism

Such misconceptions fail to be explained at purely the empirical level. This state of affairs is nowhere more illuminated than white students who feel disadvantaged or victimized by civil rights legislation or racially motivated educational policies; they perceive themselves as institutionally "oppressed." Their understanding of the nature of racial advantage suffers from globalization's ability to fragment further our total understanding of race and racism. The appeal to white disadvantage is "real" to the extent that whites who believe in their perceived victimization act in a way that is consistent with such a world-view. Teachers may design lesson plans or respond to students' queries about such matters in a way that is empirically misinformed and appeals to the evidentiary state of affairs can only go so far. In other words, for whites who feel victimized, evidence of the utter lack of reality to white disadvantage fails to convince them. Students (of all ages) benefit from an ideological critique of whiteness so that they understand the total, global implications of whiteness, a sensibility that links the local with the global processes of racial privilege. But as long as white perspectives on racial matters drive the public discourse, students receive fragmented understandings of our global racial formation.

Ramon Flecha (1999) mobilizes the concept of "postmodern racism" to describe a condition wherein racial and ethnic differences become incommensurable and subjects fail to address the important issue of equality in the face of difference. As Flecha distinguishes, "Modern racism occurs when the rules of the dominant culture are imposed on diverse peoples in the name of integration. Postmodern racism occurs when people deny the possibility of living together in the same territory" (p. 154). Postmodern racism assumes the guise of tolerance only to be usurped by relativism, a proliferation of differences rather than a leveling of power relations. To be clear, Flecha is not putting the onus of racism on the shoulders of either postmodern thought or postmodern theorists. Rather, he indicts the *postmodern form* of racism, some of which may be logical consequences of postmodernism but is certainly not created by it. That is, according to Flecha, postmodern racism fragments educators and students' ability to discern the difference between democracy and dictatorship, the difference being a certain will to power rather than truth or virtuosity. In contrast, the dialogical methods of Habermas and Freire offer a viable alternative to postmodern excess because they recognize the value of rationality and critical consensus through criticism (see also Sirotnik and Oakes, 1986).

Dialogical approaches represent a counter-strategy to the fragmenting effects of white consciousness, perhaps most recently exhibited by postmodern theories that emphasize incommensurability of worldviews. The incommensurability argument that affects racial dialogue suggests that we are all different and should be valued as such. Without critical attention to the ways that asymmetrical relations of power inscribe difference, Flecha finds that ludic postmodernism degrades into a relativistic discourse and fails to integrate disparate peoples within a given territory. Or as McLaren *et al.* (2001) assert, ludic multiculturalism—which should not be confused with critical forms of multiculturalism—refers to the flattening out of difference, as if they were equal and transitive. This reasoning allows for the mistaken claim that whites suffer from discrimination (e.g., reverse affirmative action) just as blacks have suffered from it "in the past."

The fragmenting effects of the global economy work in tandem with the fragmenting tendencies of whiteness. As a perspective, whiteness is historically fractured in its apprehension of racial formations. In order to "see" the formation in full view, whites have to mobilize a perspective that begins with racial privilege as a central unit of analysis. Since starting from this point would mean whites engage in a thorough historical understanding of "how they came to be" in a position of power, most whites resist such an undertaking and instead focus on individual merit, exceptionalism, or hard work. The act of interpreting the totality of racial formations is an apostasy that white students and educators must undertake but one which does not come easy or without costs. The costs are real because it means whites would have to acknowledge their unearned privileges and disinvest in them, as suggested by abolitionism. This is a different tack than saying that whites benefit from renouncing their whiteness because it would increase their humanity. Whites would lose many of their perks and privileges. So, the realistic appraisal is that *whites do have a lot to lose* by committing race treason, not just something to gain by forsaking whiteness. This is the challenge.

In his discussion of gender and race, Terry Eagleton (1996) provokes a distinction between identity politics and class relations. He calls class position relational in a way that gender and race are not, because possessing a certain skin color or body configuration does not prevent another person from owning such traits. By contrast, a landless laborer occupies a material position because the gentleman farmer owns the land or property. Eagleton goes on to say that being black does not mean one is of a different species from a white person. Pigmentation is not definitive of a general human experience in the same way that freckle-faced people do not constitute an essentially different human category. In this, Eagleton exposes the racist and patriarchal imagination by highlighting its contradictions and illogics. However, his analysis leaves out a more powerful explanation of how racism actually works. No credible race scholar would disagree with Eagleton's contention that blacks do not constitute a different species from whites. Moreover, having a different skin tone does not make one more or less human than another. *But whites have orchestrated a racialized system that makes this so.* Like most oppressive systems, racism functions through an illogical rationalization process. For instance, the one-drop rule, or the Rule of Hypodescent, demarcates blacks from whites by drawing an artificial and arbitrary line between them in order both to create more slaves and limit people's power to achieve whiteness. Thus, the power of whiteness comes precisely from its ability to usurp reason and rational thought, and a purely rationalistic analysis limits our understanding of the way it functions. Race is not supposed to make sense outside of white supremacy. Despite its contradictions, the contours of racism can be mapped out and analyzed and this is what Cheryl Harris (1995) attempts when she compares whiteness to owning property.

First, whiteness becomes property through the objectification of African slaves, a process which set the pre-condition for "propertizing" human life in its modern sense (Harris, 1995, p. 279). Whiteness takes the form of ownership, the defining attribute of free individuals, which Africans did not own. Second, through the reification and subsequent hegemony of white people, whiteness is transformed into the common sense that becomes law. As a given right of the individual white person, whiteness can be enjoyed, like any property, by exercising and taking advantage of privileges co-extensive with whiteness. Third, like a house, whiteness can be demarcated and fenced off as a territory of white people which keeps Others out, unless whiteness deems it necessary to lend the key. Thus, calling a white person "black" was enough reason, as late as 1957, to sue for character defamation; the same could not be said of a black person being mistaken for "white." This was a certain violation of property rights much like breaking into someone's house. In all, whites became the subjects of property, with Others as its objects.

As Charles Mills (1997) explains, the Racial Contract is an agreement to misinterpret the world as it is. It is the implicit consensus that whites frequently enter into, which accounts for their fragmented understanding of the world as it is racially structured. When confronted with the reality of racial oppression, according to Hurtado, whites respond with:

> I will listen to you, sometimes for the first time, and will seem engaged. At critical points in your analysis I will claim I do not know what you are talking about and will ask you to elaborate *ad nauseam*. I will consistently subvert your efforts at dialogue by claiming "we do not speak the same language" (cited in McLaren *et al.*, 2001, pp. 211–212; italics in original).

The frequent detours, evasions, and detractions from the circuits of whiteness cripple our understanding of the racio-economic essence of schools and society. It is a distortion of perfect communication in Habermas' (1984) sense of I, which creates what I call an altogether "ideological speech situation." That is, communication is ideological to the extent that the "ideal speech situation" is *systematically* distorted, which is different from saying that it is always a bit distorted. As Hurtado plainly describes, radical communication about the Contract meets apathy and indifference, perhaps a bit predictably. Admitting the reality of white racism would force a river of centuries of pain, denial, and guilt that many people cannot assuage.

In several instances, both in colleagues' courses as well as mine, white students have expressed their emotions and frustrations through tears when white privilege is confronted. In fact, Rains (1997) has described the same event occurring in her courses. Although it might seem cynical or unfeeling to analyze critically such an occurrence, it is important to deploy such a critique in the name of political and pedagogical clarity. It is imperative to address the local moment and "be there" for all students but in slicing through the pathos,

one also benefits from reflection on the moment in its larger, global significance. The times when I have confronted this scenario can be described as the
honest interrogation of racial power engaged by both white and non-white
students. At certain moments, some anger has been expressed, sometimes frus-
tration. In general, the milieu is emotional and politically charged. How can it
not be? In one particular case, I witnessed a situation where a black student
interrogated the issue of racial privilege and questioned a white colleague's
comments for failing to do the same. By the end of the exchange, the white
student left the room crying and the discussion halted. In another case, an
earnest discussion took place about racism and ways to address it in schools. A
white student cried because she felt frustrated and a little helpless about how
she comes into the fold of becoming an anti-racist educator. After a minute of
pause, students of color returned to the discussion at hand, not breaking their
stride. In a third instance, in the midst of discussing the importance of building
solidarity between teachers against racism, a white student cries and asks her
colleagues to remember that they must stay cohesive and support each other as
comrades in struggle. A colleague reports a fourth instance where, during a
dialogue about the experiences of women of color, a white woman repeatedly
insisted that the real issue was class, not race, because her experiences as a
woman were similar to the women of color. When a faculty of color informed
her that she was monopolizing the discussion and in the process invalidated the
voices of women of color, the white woman cried and was unable to continue.
In all these cases, we observed the guilt of whiteness prompting the women to
cry in shame. Made to recognize their unearned privileges and confronted in
public, they unwittingly react with tears of admission.

Discussing (anti-)racism is never easy and is frequently suppressed in mainstream classroom conditions. The establishment of the right conditions is pre-
cious but often precarious. In the first case, we must keep in mind that it was
the black student who felt dehumanized and subsequently felt enough courage
to express her anger about comments she perceived to be problematic. The act
of crying by the white student immediately positioned the black student as the
perpetrator of a hurt and erased/de-raced the power of her charge. A reversal
of sorts had just occurred. The white student earned the other students' sym-
pathy and the professor followed her to the hallway to comfort her while the
black student nursed her anger by herself. Likewise, I could not help feel for the
white student. Upon reflection, an important difference needs to be discussed.
In the act of crying, the student attenuated the centuries of hurt and oppression that the black student was trying to relay. In the act of crying, the student
transformed racism into a local problem between two people. I couldn't help
feeling that other students in the class thought the black person was both
wrong and racist, erasing/de-racing again the institutional basis of what she
had to say. The room's energy suddenly felt funneled to the white student.

Clearly, there are more "harmonious" ways of teaching the topic of race and racism. However, they also often forsake radical critique for feelings. Feelings have to be respected and educators can establish the conditions for radical empathy. That said, anger is also a valid and legitimate feeling; when complemented by clear thought, anger is frighteningly lucid. Thus, a pedagogy of politeness only goes so far before it degrades into the paradox of liberal feel-good solidarity absent of dissent, without which any worthwhile pedagogy becomes a democracy of empty forms. White comfort zones are notorious for tolerating only small, incremental doses of racial confrontation (Hunter and Nettles, 1999). This does not suggest that educators procure a hostile environment, but a pedagogical situation that fails to address white racism is arguably already the conduit of hostility. It fragments students' holistic understanding of their identity development through the ability of whiteness to deform our complete picture of the racial formation. It practices violence on the racialized Other in the name of civility and as long as this is the case, racial progress will proceed at the snail's pace of white racial consciousness. White race traitors and race-conscious Others shall piece together a whole from the fragmentary pieces that whiteness has created out of this world.

The Contract challenges educators of the new millennium to explain the untruth of white perspectives on race, even a century after Du Bois's initial challenge. Obviously, this does not mean that whites cannot grasp the Contract; many do, but they cannot accomplish this from the white point of view, a worldview which, according to Gibson, projects a "delusional world," "a racial fantasyland," and "a consensual hallucination" (cited in Mills, 1997, p. 18). With the rise of globalization, education—which prides itself for inculcating into students knowledge about the real world—struggles to represent the world in the most real way possible. White epistemology can be characterized as fragmentary and fleeting because white livelihood depends on this double helix. It is fragmentary because in order for whiteness to maintain its invisibility, or its unmarked status, it must by necessity mistake the world as nonrelational or partitioned (Dwyer and Jones, III, 2000). This allows the white psyche to speak of slavery as "long ago," rather than as a legacy that lives today; it minimizes racism toward non-white immigrants today through a convenient and problematic comparison with white immigrants, like the Irish or Jews. It is also fleeting because it must deny the history of its own genesis and the creation of the Other. It can only be concerned with "how things are and not how they got to be that way."

As a socio-spatial epistemology, whiteness sees the world upside down. Mills (1997) and I agree when he says:

> *Thus on matters related to race, the Racial Contract prescribes for its signatories an inverted epistemology, an epistemology of ignorance, a particular pattern of localized and global cognitive dysfunctions (which are psychologically and socially functional), producing the ironic outcome that whites*

will in general be unable to understand the world they themselves have made (p. 18; italics in original).

According to Mills, whiteness concerns itself with racial details and misses the totality of the Racial Contract. Like the way it partitions the world according to its own image, whiteness constructs history as separate racial details without coherence. As a result, it fails to provide our students the language to link together California's Proposition 187 (anti-immigrant), 209 (anti-affirmative action), and 227 (anti-bilingualism) as related to white hegemony. With the exception of specific Asian ethnic groups (to which I will return below), all three legislations limit the rights of students of color, particularly Latinos. Fortunately, white and non-white activists have countered such measures with unrelenting protests and public organizing because as Hopson *et al.* (1998) remind us, "[R]ecognizing and valuing language varieties and multiple ways of speaking among students is a precondition to understanding how to teach them" (p. 5). As a racial epistemology, whiteness is necessarily idealist in order to construct the Other as abstract, rather than concrete. Enslavement, discrimination, and marginalization of the Other work most efficiently when they are constructed as an idea rather than a people. They can be more easily controlled, aggregated as the same, or marked as unchanging and constant when textbooks idealize them as inconsequential to the history and evolution of humankind. In effect, whiteness eggs us on to yoke together different peoples around the globe under the sign of sameness.

Flexible Whiteness and Accommodation of the Other

Clearly, whites can no longer hide behind the façade of a color-blind discourse. Not that this stops many whites from doing so. However, with the increasing interrogation of whiteness as a social construction, an unearned center, and its spurious claims to superiority, it becomes more difficult to assert its invisibility (Winant, 1997). Through certain social developments, whites are coming to see themselves as racialized whites, not merely as individuals. In fact, invisibility has been its historical double bind. As a sort of Foucauldian (Foucault, 1979) racial panopticon, whiteness remained cloaked in darkness while marking those with darker complexion for purposes of effective surveillance. As a marker of the Other, whiteness was able to dodge relative scrutiny as a positionality, a morally-conditioned, socially-informed perspective. Instead, whiteness has long reserved the privilege of making everyone but itself visible, lest it be exposed as a position within a constellation of positions. At the same time, whiteness becomes the ubiquitous marker of all that is right because it is associated with being white.

On the other hand, like finance capital whiteness becomes more abstract and harder to locate. Whiteness, as a discourse, and whites as the subjects of such discourse have had to respond to this *ongoing* crisis, much like late capitalism, with whiteness studies only its recent challenge. In order to maintain its racial hegemony, whiteness has always had to maintain some sense of flexibility. That is, like late capital, late whiteness must work with scope, not scales, of influence, especially in times of crisis. It must accommodate subjects previously marked as Other in order to preserve its *group power*. In other words, for it to remain dominant, whiteness has to seduce allies, convince them of the advantages of such an alliance, and sometimes be able to forsake immediate advantages for long-term goals of domination. Nowhere is this more pronounced than the literature on the induction of the Irish into the white race. To a lesser extent, one can trace some of the same tendencies in the recent incorporation of Asians into the American racial polity.

Whiteness has had to show signs of flexibility in its ongoing quest for global domination. In the 1800s white domination in the USA was introduced to a new problem: the Irish. As an oppressed group in Western Europe, Irish immigrated to the USA first to escape racial oppression and religious persecution on their homeland (Takaki, 1993). However, with the coming of the potato famine, Irish emigration from their beloved land became one of survival and simple existence. On U.S. soil, Irish were regarded as "black niggers" who were initially perceived as being closer with blacks than whites on the chain of being. Similar epithets and descriptions were leveled against Irish as those used against blacks. They were called "a race of savages" with a low "level of intelligence," "lacking self control," and sexually animalistic (Takaki, 1993, p. 149). Negroes referred to them as "a Negro turned inside out" (Takaki, 1993, p. 153).[6] The "great educator" of the nineteenth century, Horace Mann, was greatly concerned about education's ability to civilize the Catholic and lazy-perceived Irish. In his comparisons between Irish racial oppression in Ireland and African and Indian racial oppression in the USA, Theodore Allen (1994) finds many intersecting themes in the groups' treatment by their oppressors. For example, he writes:

> The essential elements of discrimination against the Irish in Ireland, and against the African-Americans, which gave these respective regimes the character of racial oppression, were those that destroyed the original forms of social identity, and then excluded the oppressed groups from admittance into the forms of social identity normal to the colonizing power (p. 82; italics in original).

Like North American Indians, the Irish became strangers in their own land through slow deculturalization campaigns by their oppressors. In Ireland, British rule outlawed the practice of Catholic holidays and the Irish language, beginning with the edict of King Henry the VIII in 1541 (Purdon, 1999). On U.S. soil, colonists "civilized" Indians through English instruction and Protestant conversion (Spring, 2000). Like African slaves, the Irish, though not enslaved *en masse* and considered as free labor, suffered extreme labor exploitation as indentured servants and wage laborers. With respect to education, Charter Schools for Irish kids in Ireland bear the imprints of colonial education, complete with paltry material conditions, neglect, and low levels of literacy.

However compelling the similarities may appear, Irish people eventually *became* white whereas blacks and Indians remain nonwhite. In addition, their racial oppression does not follow the modern sense of race as a form of skin color stratification. Moreover, the Irish embraced whiteness as a path to social mobility and economic independence. Takaki (1993) documents the shift from Irish abolitionism when in Ireland to acceptance of slavery upon arrival in the USA. This ironic twist highlights the contradiction in whiteness' ability to modify its own "purity" in order to retain group power. What it previously marked as subhuman, it later accepts as brethren. Irish ascendancy also shows the wicked flexibility of whiteness to offer broader membership for newcomers in exchange for allegiance to the white nation state. It marks the general transition of the Irish from green to white (Ignatiev, 1995), a process of both push and pull factors.

As competition for labor intensifies, the Irish are pushed away from working class solidarity with blacks in order for the (white) bourgeoisie to disrupt class cohesion. At the same time, the Irish are pulled into white identity in order to maintain their privileges as white inductees. A purely economistic analysis fails to ask why the Irish vehemently competed with blacks for labor, rather than with the Germans and Italians who outnumbered free black laborers. In fact, as Roediger (1991) puts it, competition with Irish people for unskilled jobs was most felt from other arriving Irish. Irish labor became increasingly regarded as white labor and as such would promote greater white solidarity and the naturalized expectations that came with this new found social position. Race and class make strange bedfellows when racial solidarity confounds class politics (see McLaren, Leonardo, and Allen, 2000). Were the Irish to align themselves with black labor, an intersectional coalition threatens both white supremacy and bourgeois power. Because we know whiteness is partner-in-crime with capital, it makes sense that the whitening of the Irish subverts both racial and class equality.

White flexibility works in tandem with capital's flexibility. They are the hour and minute hands of a clock so predictable, it should not surprise the critical educator that where you find one, the other lurks closely behind. A global pedagogy of neo-abolitionism understands that whiteness is a nodal point in the triumvirate with capitalist exploitation and patriarchy. Thus, it makes little rhetorical sense to pose the question of: For a people persecuted on their own land, how could the Irish choose to oppress another group? Such a question betrays a certain politics of surprise about the reality of racial power. Whiteness conjures up a fictive solidarity when this is deemed convenient. To explain the Irish question as an instance of the bourgeoisie duping an unsuspecting slice of the working class overlooks the racial analysis that is mobilized by the transitional white group. It is a bit like a white family choosing to enroll their children into a school that boasts a weak or mediocre academic curriculum over a superior school because the latter is populated by too many Others, be they black or otherwise (Holme, 2000). At first glance, the rationalist or economic analysis suggests that the family in question forsakes its own immediate interests through an irrational thinking process. Upon further reflection, the family advances the long-term and global imperatives of white supremacy by encouraging racial segregation and white racial solidarity.

In many parts of the USA, today's Asian American student is commonly touted as the "model minority." When discussing race relations, we must keep in mind that this favorable image is a commentary on the perception of African American and Latino students as less than ideal students. In a clever appropriation of Du Bois, Prashad (2000) asks Asian Americans, "How does it feel to be the solution?" Thus, it has been asserted that the apparently favorable status accorded Asian Americans is a ploy to discipline their non-white counterparts. Also it must be noted that although not all Asian American groups benefit from such status in the same way, such as Hmong or Cambodian refugees, there is a general perception of Asians as the "intelligent minority." Dubbed as "whiz kids," "probationary whites," "honorary whites," or "Asian whites," Asian Americans have prompted Hernnstein and Murray (1994) to revisit the eugenics debate to find proof of the genetic make-up of Asian intelligence. The authors also make claims on the African lag behind the Asian wonders. Citing a combination of hereditary and environmental factors, Hernnstein and Murray earned their controversy by raising the specters of de Gobineau and Binet. Neither their genetic nor environmental assertions are new. The main controversy surrounds their *reaffirmation* of the hereditary, essentialist argument about intelligence that many scholars have refuted, dating back to Boas' (2000) study of the problems in more or less biological explanations of race.

For this present study, the Asian American case is instructive because it exposes the educational construction of whiteness and its political consequences. Historically degraded as "brown monkeys," "heathen Chinee," or "pagan," Asian Americans and their educational ascendancy in the USA now signify their approach toward whiteness. This is not as impossible as it sounds when we keep in mind that certain south-east Asian groups have already claimed Aryan status based on geographical and linguistic roots (Mazumdar, 1989). This should not be confused with the position that Asian Americans *are* white, but rather, *approaching* whiteness within certain historical assumptions. Moreover, it is not necessarily the case that whites think Asian Americans are white or for that matter, that the latter consider themselves white. There are too many differences between whites and Asian Americans to suggest that this is happening, ranging from cultural practices to certain forms of ethnic nationalism, not to mention continuing racist denigration of Asian Americans.

However, this shows again the flexibility of whiteness to incorporate groups into its borders previously thought of as foreign to it. President George W. Bush's multiracial cabinet is a perfect example of the attempt to represent people of color within the confines of color-blind discourse.[7] Bush's cabinet selections are honorary members of the neo-conservative project's inability to confront the race question, let alone the white question. Black and brown masks do not necessarily translate into progressive minds when it comes to racial discourse.

The favored status of Asian Americans reminds us that whiteness mutates according to historical conditions. Amidst consistent criticisms of racial oppression in the USA, enter the bleaching of Asian Americans. White supremacist discourse presents their particular position in the USA as proof that immigrant children can succeed in schools and thrive in society. More insidiously, in the case of African immigrant achievement it suggests that the problem is traceable to African Americans. As latecomers after the 1965 Immigration Act, Asian Americans, as a racial group, provide more than enough evidence for the endorsement of USA opportunity structure. Anyone can succeed; moreover, apparently anyone can be white (Can blacks?). With much effort and heart, African Americans, Latinos, and Native Americans can also realize the American dream . . . of being white (or at least its pretenses). But as we have seen in the Irish case study, becoming white is a two-way process. Not only must the structure provide the space for a group to become white, the group in question must desire whiteness. It is questionable whether such a two-way process is happening for some non-white groups today. There are some key differences.

With British imposition of English in Ireland, indigenous languages, like Gaelic, remain secondary for many Irish. Thus, unlike the Irish, many Asian students speak a language other than English. Unlike the Irish, most blacks bear skin tones darker than most whites. And unlike the Irish, Native Americans have never considered themselves Euro-Americans. The incorporation of non-white students into the discourse of whiteness is tenuous at best. However, this does not suggest that it is impossible at worst. There are certain characteristics about Asian Americans, for example, that suggest at least a compatibility with whiteness. One, certain Asian American communities have developed a pattern of avoiding racial analysis of their lives (Sethi, 1995), opting instead for the discourse of hard work. Two, Portes and Rumbaut's (1990) research finds that Asian immigrants, by and large, arrive to the USA with a different class status and different material resources than their Latino counterparts. As a result, they comprise a selective group of immigrants and have a different contact experience with American class structure, which puts them closer to white experience. In schools, Asian American students are tracked with their white classmates and away from other racial groups, giving them an educational experience closer to whites. With respect to global expansion, China and

Japan's imperialist histories resemble European military occupations all over the world. Clearly, the whitening of Asian peoples in the USA is a struggle without a verdict. The prerequisites have been cited but they are insufficient to suggest that Asians are transitioning from yellow to white.

Future Directions in Pedagogy, Whiteness, and Globalization Studies

Within Marxist debates, the advent of western or neo-Marxism inaugurated the cultural arm of social analysis. Lukacs, Frankfurt critical theory, and Gramsci emphasized the role of consciousness, subjectivity, and consent to explain what the blind spot of orthodox Marxism neglected. Rejecting both the determinism and teleology of Leninist varieties of historical materialism, neo-Marxism opted for a more variegated and nuanced theory of the social formation. It even engaged bourgeois culture and thought, suggesting that revolutionary theory must come to grips with high culture and art in order to map out the general superstructural features of social life. Likewise, in race theory whiteness studies may be called a form of *neo-race theory*. More orthodox accounts of the racial formation traced white racism's effect on the lives of people of color through studies of slavery, discrimination, and school segregation. By contrast, neo-race theory finds it imperative to peer into the lives and consciousness of the white imaginary in attempts to produce a more complete portrait of global racism and ways to combat it. Recent themes of neo-race theory include white privilege, genesis of the white race, and white abolitionism (McIntosh, 1992; Allen, 1997, 1994; Roediger, 1994, 1991).

This new development in social and educational theory has been extremely productive and provides educators and students a critical vernacular with which to dismantle racist practices and chip away at white supremacist institutions. In our rush to consume such frameworks, bell hooks (1997) warns against neglecting the lessons learned from more orthodox explanations of racism's effect on people of color (see also, Morrison, 1970). As hooks explains, in the black imagination whiteness is a form of "terror" (p. 169) that haunts all black people, regardless of their class position or politics (p. 175). With much attention being devoted to deconstruction of the white center, experiences on the margin fade to black. Nonetheless, any problematization of the margin necessitates a similar assault on its supplementary center. Said (1979) says as much in his study of Orientalism whereby the Orient is written into history by the Occident. Simultaneously, the Occident invents itself by inventing its Other.

White students do not disinvest in whiteness by claiming "I'm not white," since this is how whiteness currently operates. By and large, whites already believe they are individuals and not a racial group. The abolition of whiteness would counter this process. Neo-abolitionism is not the process of denying one's whiteness because white power is efficiently maintained through strategies of invisibility. White students must first own their racialization by naming its source in whiteness and recognizing it as fundamental to their development as alienated human beings. For whiteness, as a global formation, is alienating to its subjects and objects. As such, the global formation of whiteness is the target of critique. Abolishing race is mutually dependent with abolishing whiteness (Ignatiev and Garvey, 1996a) because the "possessive investment in whiteness" (Lipsitz, 1998) is arguably the strongest form of racialization, contrary to popular beliefs about minority identity politics. The English-only movement, anti-immigrant nativism, and western-centric curricula represent white identity politics. It is responsible not only for the racialization of white subjects but also of non-white people. Moreover, a "critical race pedagogy" (Lynn, 1999) cannot be guided by a white perspective, which is not to say that it cannot include white experiences as points of departure. Although experiences do not speak for themselves, interpretation always begins with their lived dimensions (Sleeter, 1995a). Taking its cue from critical race theory, or CRT, critical race pedagogy does for education what CRT accomplishes for law: the interrogation of racially structured rules for social participation (Solorzano and Yosso, 2000). Global studies of whiteness work in partnership with critical race theories to arrive at the racialized core of knowledge production in schools.

A critical pedagogy of whiteness must be dialectical in order to avoid the reductive notion that white choices are reduced to the double bind of whites as either enemies or allies of students of color (Ellsworth, 1997). As Roediger has suggested, whiteness as a racial category seems nothing but false and oppressive. When whites have articulated their choices through whiteness, the results have been predictable. Taken strategically, critical pedagogy must forge a third space for neo-abolitionist whites as neither enemy nor ally but a concrete subject of struggle, an identity which is "always more than one thing, and never the same thing twice" (Ellsworth, 1997, p. 266). This new positionality will be guided by non-white discourses. Again and to reiterate, there is a difference between white people, white culture, and whiteness. Students would do well to recognize the point that as they work against whiteness, they are undoing the self they know and coming to terms with a reconstructed identity, even an abolished one. Like the abolitionists of the nineteenth century, white subjects of the twenty-first century commit one of the ultimate acts of humanity: race treason. This act of repudiation must be accompanied by a racial project of rearticulation whereby whites and students of color actively work to dismantle the material basis of white privilege (Winant, 1997). In other words, global pedagogy and neo-abolitionism are not only acts of free speech but of praxis.

Notes

Introduction

1. The Philippine archipelago became a nation under Spanish rule between 1565 and 1898. Spanish was imposed, became the official language of government and the academic system, but not the dominant language of everyday life. Tagalog, which is now the dominant language in the Philippines, includes many Spanish words, even tagalogization of certain Spanish words, such as *lamesa* for "table" rather than the Spanish *la mesa* and *kamusta* rather than *como esta* for common greetings. However, Spanish speakers are basically incomprehensible to Tagalog speakers and vice versa.

2. Critical Race Theory is a specifically U.S. innovation (Peters, 2005). As an intervention within legal studies, CRT responds with a particularly US-based analysis of law, racial stratification, and methodology. Although CRT has been imported to explain other national contexts, by and large it has maintained a USA-centered analysis (see for example, Gillborn's 2008 book-length use of the CRT framework to explain Great Britain's racial contestation in education).

3. This position is not necessarily in opposition to Bell's assertion of the "permanence of racism," which is an empirical or descriptive statement and not a prescriptive one. In other words, Bell is not suggesting that racism *should* be permanent. Rather, based on historical evidence there is more reason to suggest that it will not whither away, thus achieving a permanent status in U.S. society. Alternatively, Bell may be spurring readers to disrupt racism by recognizing this apparently simple truth and absurd state of racial affair. Here, he resembles Roediger's (1994) ironic appropriation of a problematic refrain from color-blind discourse: "Reverse racism!" Bell is not merely adopting a cynical position on racism, but a radical realism. Where Bell may be criticized is in his apparent lack of a utopian discourse that imagines an alternative state of affair, whether or not it may be realized.

Chapter 2

1. For a more extended analysis of the four moments in Althusser's theory of ideology, see Leonardo, Z. (2003c). Reality on Trial: notes on ideology, education, and utopia. *Policy Futures in Education, 1*(3), 504–525.

Chapter 4

1. Paul Taylor delivered a keynote at the conference, "New Perspectives on Race Theory." University of San Francisco, CA. April 26, 2008.

2. Again, white ethnics are termed "white" for convenience. Without race, they are merely ethnic groups involved in ethnic, not racial, contestation.

Chapter 7

1. The gift concept was offered by Marcel Mauss (1967) based on his ethnographic studies of the Melanesian islands where he found an economy based on gift-giving as a form of challenge. In *The Gift*, Mauss documented the process whereby Melanesian natives obligated each other through gifts, instituting power in favor of the giver. In order to cancel out the gift, the receiver must respond with a different and deferred gift, usually raising the stakes and obligating the original giver. This process goes on and on in order to balance power relations. The gift concept has since been appropriated by several theorists, among them George Bataille, Pierre Bourdieu, and Jean Baudrillard. In education, McLaren, Leonardo, and Allen (2000) applied the gift concept to the study of whiteness.

Chapter 8

1. Color-blindness is not actually the "inability to see race" and is therefore an imperfect term. In the USA, color-blind people cannot fail to see race, but they choose to see it in a *particular* way. In asserting that race should not matter in either social policy or transactions, color-blind people—especially Whites—experience what psychologists call cognitive dissonance. Color-blindness prevents them from dealing with the racial conditioning of their behavior, which is considered as incidental rather than causal. Racial consequences may then be dismissed as unintentional or the common refrain that actions or words have been "taken out of context." Be that as it may, color-blindness is useful as a term to describe people's attempts to avoid race as an explanatory framework. For this reason, I will use it for the remainder of the essay.
2. David Gillborn delivered a symposium, titled "It's Not a Conspiracy, It's Worse Than That," for the Center for Multicultural Education, University of Washington, November 9, 2005.

Chapter 9

1. We define the ghetto as a racially demarcated space actively constructed by whites, as a method for containing black community development and mobility. In this definition, we are not far off from Massey and Denton's study of the ghetto, in their book *American Apartheid*, as a social phenomenon that began at the turn of the twentieth century. Before this time, the "dissimilarity index" between whites and blacks in U.S. neighborhoods was not radical. It was not until whites enacted neighborhood policies as well as social behaviors during reconstruction that the ghetto was created. As such, the ghetto is not only a poor place, but rather a *racial* place where one finds heavy concentrations of African Americans. Unlike other groups, like Eastern European and Jewish immigrants, for whom the ghetto has a fleeting history, the black ghetto seems to have an enduring place in U.S. racial relations.
2. In 2005 several U.S. newspapers showcased a photo taken by the Associated Press on August 30 from the New Orleans tragedy, featuring a caption describing a black family holding food and drinks as "looting." In contrast, some newspapers featured a similar photo of white families taken by Getty Images describing its members as having "found" such items. Sometimes this contrast was featured on the very same page of a particular newspaper, making the racist juxtaposition even more glaring.

Chapter 10

1. In the USA, a slew of books have been designed for beginners in specific subjects, such as *Weddings for Dummies* and *Homebuying for Dummies*. They provide an introduction to such topics and are not designed to be critical. Unlike Anderson *et al.*'s (2000) introductory but critical book, *Field Guide to the Global Economy*, the fictive book, *Globalization for Dummies*, would offer uncritical analysis of global processes.
2. I use "Negroes" to observe Du Bois' terminology. African American or black will be used for more contemporary arguments.
3. *Color of Fear* has become a popular instructional video in the USA. It is a dialogue about race relations between nine men representing Latinos, blacks, Asians, and whites.
4. The Zapatistas of Chiapas, Mexico are a group of indigenous revolutionary guerillas who have banded together against the Mexican government in order to protect their land and human rights. Their symbolic leader is Subcomandante Insurgente Marcos whose assistance has allowed the group to use the internet for relaying their communiqués on a global scale (see Juana Ponce de León, 2001).
5. For nativism American style, see Hopson *et al.*, 1998, pp. 6–10.
6. Again, I use Negroes to observe terminology of the time.
7. U.S. President George W. Bush's cabinet is a multicultural group, comprised of representatives from different ethnic and racial groups but each bringing a right-wing agenda to government: e.g., Secretary of State Colin Powell (African American), Secretary of Education Rod Paige (African American), National Security Adviser Condoleezza Rice (African American), Transportation Secretary Norman Mineta (Japanese American), Labor Secretary Elaine Chao (Chinese American), Energy Secretary Spencer Abraham (Lebanese American), White House Counsel Alberto Gonzales (Latino American).

References

Aanerud, R. (1997). Fictions of whiteness: Speaking the names of whiteness in U.S. literature. In R. Frankenberg (Ed.), *Displacing whiteness* (pp. 35–59). Durham: Duke University Press.

Adams, H. (Ed.) (1970). *Critical theory since Plato*. New York: Harcourt Brace Jovanovich, Publishers.

Adorno, T. (1973). *Negative dialectics*. E. B. Ashton (Trans.). New York: Continuum.

Agger, B. (1992). *The discourse of domination*. Chicago: Northwestern University Press.

Alcoff, L. (1998). What should White people do? *Hypatia, 13*(3). Available online at http://iupress.indiana.edu/journals/hypatia/hyp13-3.html (accessed 5 January 2009).

Alcoff, L. (2000). Mestizo identity. In R. Bernasconi and T. Lott (Eds.), *The idea of race* (pp. 139–160). Indianapolis: Hackett Publishing Company, Inc.

Allen, R. (2005). Whiteness and critical pedagogy. In Z. Leonardo (Ed.), *Critical pedagogy and race* (pp. 53–68). Malden, MA: Blackwell.

Allen, R. L. (2002). The globalization of white supremacy: Toward a critical discourse on the racialization of the world. *Educational Theory, 51*(4), 467–485.

Allen, T. (1994). *The invention of the white race*. Vol. 1. London: Verso.

Allen, T. (1997). *The invention of the white race*. Vol. 2. London: Verso.

Allen, W. and Farley, R. (1989). *The color line and the quality of life in America*. Oxford, UK: Oxford University Press.

Althusser, A. (2003). *The humanist controversy and other writings*. F. Matheron (Ed. and Trans.) and G.M. Goshgarian (Trans.). London: Verso.

Althusser, L. (1969). *For Marx*. B. Brewster (Trans.). New York: Verso.

Althusser, L. (1971). *Lenin and philosophy*. B. Brewster (Trans.). New York: Monthly Review Press.

Althusser, L. (1976). *Essays in self-criticism*. G. Lock (Trans.). London: Humanities Press.

Anderson, E. (1990). *Streetwise*. Chicago: University of Chicago Press.

Anderson, E. (2000). *Code of the street*. New York: W.W Norton & Co.

Anderson, S., Cavanagh, J., Lee, T., and Ehrenreich, B. (Eds.), (2000). *Field guide to the global economy*. New York: The New Press.

Anyon, J. (1997). *Ghetto schooling: A political economy of urban educational reform*. New York: Teachers College Press.

Anzaldua, G. (Ed.) (1999). *La Frontera/Borderlands* (2nd ed.). San Francisco: Aunt Lute Books.

Aoki, D. (2000). The thing never speaks for itself: Lacan and the pedagogical politics of clarity. *Harvard Educational Review, 70*(3), 345–369.

Apple, M. (1990). *Ideology and curriculum*. New York: Routledge. First published in 1979.

Apple, M. (1998). Foreword. In J. Kincheloe, S. Steinberg, N. Rodriguez, and R. Chennault (Eds.), *White reign* (pp. ix–xiii). New York: St. Martin's Griffin.

Apple, M. (2000). *Official knowledge: Democratic education in a conservative age* (2nd ed.). New York: Routledge and Kegan Paul. First published in 1979.

Apple, M. (2003). Freire and the politics of race in education. *International Journal of Leadership in Education, 6*(2), 107–118.

Appleman, D. (2000). *Critical encounters in high school English: Teaching literary theory to adolescents*. New York: Teachers College Press.

Aronowitz, S. and Giroux, H. (1987). *Education under siege*. Westport, CT: Bergin and Garvey.

Bakhtin, M. (1981). *The dialogic imagination*. C. Emerson and M. Holquist (Trans.). Austin: University of Texas Press.

Balibar, E. (1990). Paradoxes of universality. In D.T. Goldberg (Ed.), *Anatomy of racism* (pp. 283–294). Minneapolis: University of Minnesota Press.

Banks, J. (1993). Multicultural literacy and curriculum reform. In J. Noll (Ed.), *Taking sides* (pp. 219–226) (7th ed.). Guilford: The Dushkin Publishing Group.

Banks, J. (2002). *An introduction to multicultural education* (3rd ed.). Boston: Allyn and Bacon.

Banks, J. (2005). Multicultural education: Characteristics and goals. In J. Banks and C. Banks (Eds.), *Multicultural education: Issues and perspectives* (pp. 3–30) (5th ed.). New York: Wiley.

Banks, J. (2006). *Race, culture, and education.* New York: Routledge.

Barrera, M. (1979). *Race and class in the Southwest.* Notre Dame, IN: Notre Dame University Press.

Bartolome, L. and Macedo, D. (2001). *Dancing with bigotry.* New York: Palgrave MacMillan.

Barton, A., Drake, C., Perez, J. G., St. Louis, K., and George, M. (2004). Ecologies of parental engagement in urban education. *Educational Researcher, 33*(4), 3–12.

Beilke, J., Brooks, N., and Welsh, B. (2004). The consequences of getting it white. *Academic Exchange Quarterly, 8*(4), 38–44.

Bell, D. (1992). *Faces at the bottom of the well: The permanence of racism.* New York: Basic Books.

Benhabib, S. (1987). The generalized and the concrete other. In S. Benhabib and D. Cornell (Eds.), *Feminism as critique* (pp. 77–95). Minneapolis: University of Minnesota Press.

Bennett deMarrais, K. and LeCompte, M. (1999). *The way schools work: A sociological analysis of education* (3rd ed.). New York: Longman.

Benshoff, H. and Griffin. S. (2003). *America on film.* New York: Blackwell.

Berger, P. and Luckmann, T. (1966). *The social construction of reality.* New York: Anchor Books.

Bernard-Donals, M. (1998). *The practice of theory: Rhetoric, knowledge, and pedagogy in the academy.* Cambridge, UK: Cambridge University Press.

Bernasconi, R. and T. Lott (Eds.). (2000). *The idea of race.* Indianapolis: Hackett Publishing Company, Inc.

Biesta, G. J.J. (2001). "Preparing for the incalculable:" Deconstruction, justice and the question of education. In G.J.J. Biesta and D. Egea-Kuehne (Eds.), *Derrida & education* (pp. 32–54). New York: Routledge.

Bishop, R. S. (2005). Working together for literacy: Faces of hope. In B. Hammond, M. Hoover, and I. Mcphail (Eds.), *Teaching African American learners to read: Perspectives and practices* (pp. 105–114). International Reading Association.

Blackmore, J. (2000) Warning signals or dangerous opportunities? Globalization, gender, and educational policy shifts, *Educational Theory, 50*(4), pp. 467–486.

Blanchard, J. (2006). Supreme Court to hear Seattle schools race case. *Seattle Post-Intelligencer*, June 6, A1 and A8.

Blauner, R. (1972). *Racial oppression in America.* New York: Harper and Row.

Boas, F. (2000). Instability of human types. In R. Bernasconi and T. Lott (Eds.). *The idea of race* (pp. 84–88). Indianapolis: Hackett Publishing Co. Inc.

Bobo, L. and Kluegel, J. (1993). Opposition to race-targeting: Self-interest, stratification ideology, or racial attitudes? *American Sociological Review, 58*(4), 443–464.

Bobo, L. and Smith, R. (1998). From Jim Crow racism to laissez-faire racism: The transformation of racial attitudes. In W. Katkin, N. Landsman, and A. Tyree (Eds.), *Beyond pluralism: The conception of groups and group identities in America* (pp. 182–220). Urbana: University of Illinois Press.

Bonilla-Silva, E. (1997). Rethinking racism: Toward a structural interpretation. *American Sociological Review, 62*(3), 465–480.

Bonilla-Silva, E. (2001). *White supremacy and racism in the post-civil rights era.* Boulder: Lynne Rienner Publishers.

Bonilla-Silva, E. (2003). *Racism without racists: Color-blind racism and the persistence of racial inequality in the United States.* Lanham, MD: Rowman & Littlefield.

Bonilla-Silva, E. (2004). From biracial to tri-racial: The emergence of a new racial stratification system in the United States. In C. Herring, V. Keith, and H. Horton (Eds.), *Skin/deep: How race and complexion matter in the "color-blind" era* (pp. 224–239). Urbana: University of Illinois Press.

Bonilla-Silva, E. (2005). Introduction – "Racism" and "new racism": The contours of racial dynamics in contemporary America. In Z. Leonardo (Ed.), *Critical pedagogy and race* (pp. 1–36). Malden, MA: Blackwell.

Bourdieu, P. (1977). Cultural reproduction and social reproduction. In J. Karabel and A.H. Halsey (Eds.), *Power and ideology in education* (pp. 487–511). Oxford, UK: Oxford University Press.

Bourdieu, P. (1984). *Distinction: A social critique of the judgment of taste.* R. Nice (Trans. and Ed.). Cambridge, MA: Harvard University Press.

Bourdieu, P. (1991). *Language and symbolic power.* J. B. Thompson (Ed.) and G. Raymond and M. Adamson (Trans.). Cambridge, MA: Harvard University Press.

Bowles, S. and Gintis, H. (1976). *Schooling in capitalist America.* New York: Basic Books.

Brodkin, K. (1999). *How Jews became White folks and what that says about race in America.* New Brunswick: Rutgers University Press.

Brown, M., Carnoy, M., Currie, E., Duster, T., Oppenheimer, D., Shultz, M., and Wellman, D. (2003). *White-washing race.* Berkeley: University of California Press.

Buras, K. (2008). *Rightist multiculturalism.* New York: Routledge.

Burawoy, M. (2000). Marxism after communism. *Theory and Society, 29*(2), 151–174.

Bush, M. (2005). *Breaking the code of good intentions: Everyday forms of whiteness.* Lanham, MD: Rowman & Littlefield.

Bush, R. (2000). *We are not what we seem: Black nationalism and class struggle in the American century.* New York: New York University Press.

Calhoun, C. (1995). *Critical social theory.* Cambridge, MA: Blackwell.

Callinicos, A. (1976). *Althusser's Marxism.* London: Pluto Press.

Carlton, D. (2006). School district pulls Web site after examples of racism spark controversy. *Seattle Post-Intelligencer,* June 2, B1.

Carnoy, M. and Levin, H. (1985). *Schooling and work in the democratic state.* Stanford: Stanford University Press.

Césaire, A. (2000). *Discourse on colonialism.* New York: Monthly Review Press. First published in 1955.

Cherryholmes, C. (1992). Knowledge, power, and discourse in social studies education. In K. Weiler and C. Mitchell (Eds.), *What schools can do* (pp. 95–115). Albany: State University of New York Press.

Cho, S. (2008). Politics of critical pedagogy and new social movements. *Educational Philosophy and Theory.* Abstract available online at http://www3.interscience.wiley.com/journal/120120240/abstract.

Chubbuck, S. (2004). Whiteness enacted, whiteness disrupted: The complexity of personal congruence. *American Educational Research Journal, 41*(2), 301–333.

Churchill, W. (1998). *A little matter called genocide: Holocaust and denial in the Americas 1492 to the present.* San Francisco: City Lights Publishers.

Churchill, W. (2005). *Since predator came.* Oakland: AK Press.

Cochran-Smith, M. (2005). No Child Left Behind: 3 years and counting. *Journal of Teacher Education, 56*(2), 99–103.

Cole, M. and Maisuria, A. (2007). "Shut the f*** up," "you have no rights here": Critical race theory and racialisation in post-7/7 racist Britain. *Journal for Critical Education Policy Studies, 5*(1). Available online at http://www.jceps.com/?pageID=article&articleID=85 (accessed on 2 September 2008).

Collins, P. (2004). *Black sexual politics.* New York: Routledge.

Collins, P. H. (1998). *Fighting words.* Minneapolis: University of Minnesota Press.

Collins, P. H. (2000). *Black feminist thought: Knowledge, consciousness, and the politics of empowerment* (2nd ed.). New York: Routledge. First published in 1990.

D'Souza, D. (1996). *The end of racism.* New York: The Free Press.

Da Silva, M. (2005) How is NCLB a mechanism of the American racial project? Available online at: http://www.educationnews.org/how-is-nclb-a-mechanism-of-the-a.htm (accessed 20 October 2005).

Dalton, H. (2002). Failing to see. In P. Rothenberg (Ed.), *White privilege* (pp. 15–18). New York: Worth Publishers.

Darder, A. (2002). *Reinventing Paulo Freire: A pedagogy of love.* Boulder: Westview Press.

Darder, A. and Torres, R. (2004). *After race.* New York: New York University Press.

Darling-Hammond, L. (2004). "Separate but equal" to "NCLB": The collision of new standards and old inequalities. In D. Meier and G. Wood (Eds.), *Many children left behind: How the No Child Left Behind Act is damaging our children and our schools* (pp. 3–32). Boston: Beacon Press.

Davis, A. (1981). *Women, race, and class.* New York: Random House.

Davis, A. (Producer) (1997). *The-prison-industrial-complex* [Audio-CD]. San Francisco: AK Press Audio.

Davis, A. (2003). *Are prisons obsolete?* New York: Open Media.

Davis, F. J. (2001). *Who is Black?: One nation's definition.* University Park, PA: Penn State University Press.

De Leon, J. P. (2001). Traveling back for tomorrow. In, J. P. De Leon (Ed.), *Our word is our weapon: Selected writings Subcomandante Insurgente Marcos* (pp. xxiii–xxxi). New York: Seven Stories Press.

Delgado, R. and Stefancic, J. (Eds.), (1997). *Critical white studies.* Philadelphia: Temple University Press.

Delpit, L. (1995). *Other people's children.* New York: The New Press.

Dewey, J. (1916). *Democracy and education.* New York: The Free Press.

Dewey, J. (1938). *Experience and education.* New York: Macmillan Co.

DiAngelo, R. (2006). The production of Whiteness in education: Asian international students in a college classroom. *Teachers College Record, 108*(10), 1983–2000.

Dilg, M. (2000). Response to Rosa Hernandez Sheets's review of *Race and culture. Educational Researcher, 29*(9), pp. 24–26.

Dillard, C. (2000). The substance of things hoped for, the evidence of things not seen: Examining an endarkened epistemology in educational research and leadership. *Qualitative Studies in Education, 13*(6), 661–681.

Dixson and Rousseau, C. (2005). And we are still not saved: Critical race theory ten years later. *Race Ethnicity & Education, 8*(1), 7–27.

Dog, M. and Erdoes, R. (1999). Civilize them with a stick. In S. Ferguson (Ed.), *Mapping the social landscape* (pp. 554–562). Mountain View, CA: Mayfield Publishing Company.

Douglass, F. (1982). *Narrative of the life of Frederick Douglass, an American slave.* New York: Penguin. First published in 1845.

Dreeben, R. (1968). *On what is learned in school.* Menlo Park, CA: Addison-Wesley.

Du Bois, W.E.B. (1984). *Dusk of dawn.* Edison, NJ: Transaction Publishers. First published in 1940.

Du Bois, W. E. B. (1989). *The souls of black folk.* New York: Penguin Books. First published in 1904.

Du Bois, W.E.B. (1998). *Black reconstruction in America, 1860–1880.* New York: The Free Press. First published in 1935.

Durkheim, E. (1956). *Education and sociology.* Glencoe: Free Press.

Durkheim, E. (1973). *Moral education.* New York: The Free Press.

Dutro, E., Kazemi, E., and Balf, R. (2005). The aftermath of "You're only half:" Multiracial identities in the literacy classroom. *Language Arts, 83*(2), 96–106.

Dwyer, O. and Jones, J. P. III (2000). White socio-spatial epistemology. *Social & Cultural Geography, 1*(2), 209–222.

Dyer, R. (1997). *White.* New York: Routledge.

Dyson, M. (2005). *Is Bill Cosby right? Or has the Black middle class lost its mind?* New York: Basic Civitas Books.

Eagleton, T. (1976). *Criticism and ideology.* London: Verso.

Eagleton, T. (1991). *Ideology.* London: Verso.

Eagleton, T. (1996). *Postmodernism and its illusions.* Oxford, UK: Blackwell.

Ebert, T. (1996). *Ludic feminism and after.* Ann Arbor: University of Michigan Press.

Ellsworth, E. (1989). Why doesn't this feel empowering? Working through the repressive myths of critical pedagogy. *Harvard Educational Review, 59*(3), 297–324.

Ellsworth, E. (1997). Double binds of whiteness. In M. Fine, L. Weis, L. Powell, L. Wong (Eds.), *Off white* (pp. 259–269). New York: Routledge.

Enciso, P. (2003). Reading discrimination. In S. Greene and D. Abt-Perkins (Eds.), *Making race visible: Literacy research for cultural understanding* (pp. 149–177). New York: Teachers College Press.

Enloe, C. (2001). *Bananas, bases, and beaches: Making feminist sense of international politics.* Berkeley: University of California Press.

Erickson, F. (2005). Culture in society and in educational practices. In J. Banks and C. Banks (Eds.), *Multicultural education: Issues and perspectives* (pp. 31–60). New York: John Wiley and Sons.

Essed, P. Goldberg, D. T. (2002). Introduction: From racial demarcations to multiple identifications. In P. Essed and D. T. Goldberg (Eds.), *Race critical theories* (pp. 1–11). Malden, MA: Blackwell.

Fanon, F. (1963). *The wretched of the earth.* C. Farrington (Trans.). New York: Grove Press.

Fanon, F. (1967). *Black skin White masks.* C. Markmann (Trans.). New York: Grove Press.

Feagin, J. (2001). *Racist America: Roots, current realities, and future reparations.* New York: Routledge.

Feagin, J. (2006). *Systemic racism.* New York: Routledge.

Feagin, J. and Vera, H. (1995). *White racism.* New York: Routledge.

Feagin, J., Vera, H., Batur, P. (2001). *White racism* (2nd ed.). New York: Routledge.

Fields, B. (1990). Slavery, race and ideology in the United States of America. *New Left Review*, I/181 (May–June), 95–118.

Fine, M., Weis, L., Powell, L., Wong, L. (Eds.), (1997). *Off white*. New York: Routledge.

Fishman, J. (1966). *Language loyalty in the United States*. The Hague: Mouton.

Flecha, R. (1999). Modern and postmodern racism in Europe: Dialogical approach and anti-racist pedagogies. *Harvard Educational Review*, 69(2), 150–171.

Fordham, S. (1988). Racelessness as a factor in Black students' school success: Pragmatic strategy or pyrrhic victory? *Harvard Educational Review*, 58(1), 54–84.

Fordham, S. (1996). *Blacked out*. Chicago: The University of Chicago Press.

Foster, M. (1993). *Savage Inequalities*: Where have we come from? Where are we going? *Educational Theory*, 43(1), 23–32.

Foucault, M. (1979). *Discipline and punish*. A. Sheridan (Trans.). New York: Vintage Books.

Foucault, M. (1986). *The care of the self*. R. Hurley (Trans.). New York: Vintage Books.

Foucault, M. (1991). What is an author? In C. Mukerji and M. Schudson (Eds.), *Rethinking popular culture* (pp. 446–464). Berkeley: University of California Press.

Frankenberg, R. (1993). *White women, race matters: the social construction of whiteness*. Minneapolis: University of Minnesota Press.

Frankenberg, R. (Ed.), (1997). *Displacing whiteness*. Durham: Duke University Press.

Fraser, J. (1997). *Reading, writing, and justice: School reform as if democracy matters*. Albany: State University of New York Press.

Freeman, J. (2005) No Child Left Behind and the denigration of race, *Equity & Excellence in Education*, 38, 190–199.

Freire, A. and Macedo, D. (1998). Introduction. In A. Freire and D. Macedo (Eds.), *The Paulo Freire reader* (pp. 1–44). New York: Continuum.

Freire, P. (1993/1970). *Pedagogy of the oppressed*. M. Ramos (Trans.). New York: Continuum. First published in 1970.

Freire, P. (1994). *Pedagogy of hope*. R. Barr (Trans.). New York: Continuum.

Freire, P. (1998). Pedagogy of the heart. In A. Freire and D. Macedo (Eds.), *The Paulo Freire reader* (pp. 265–282). New York: Continuum.

Fullan, M. (1991). *The new meaning of educational change* (2nd ed.). New York: Teachers College Press.

Funderberg, L. (1994). *Black, White, other*. New York: Quill.

Furumoto, R. (2005) No poor child left unrecruited: How NCLB codifies and perpetuates urban school militarism. *Equity & Excellence in Education*, 38, 200–210.

Gans, H. (1996). *The war against the poor*. New York: Basic Books.

Gay, G. (2000). *Culturally responsive teaching: Theory, research, & practice*. New York: Teachers College Press.

Geertz, C. (1994). Ideology as a cultural system. In T. Eagleton (Ed.), *Ideology* (pp. 279–294). London: Longman.

Geuss, R. (1981). *The idea of a critical theory*. Cambridge, UK: Cambridge University Press.

Gillborn, D. (2005). Education as an act of white supremacy: whiteness, critical race theory and education reform. *Journal of Education Policy*, 20(4), 485–505.

Gillborn, D. (2006). Public interest and the interests of White people are not the same: Assessment, education policy, and racism. In G. Ladson-Billings & W. F. Tate (Eds.), *Education research in the public interest: Social Justice, action, and policy* (pp. 173–195). New York: Teachers College Press.

Gillborn, D. (2008). *Racism and education: Coincidence or conspiracy?* London: Routledge.

Gilroy, P. (2000). *Against race*. Cambridge, MA: Belknap Press of Harvard University.

Giroux, H. (1983). *Theory and resistance: A pedagogy for the opposition*. Westport, CT: Bergin & Garvey.

Giroux, H. (1988). *Teachers as intellectuals*. Westport, CT: Bergin & Garvey.

Giroux, H. (1992). *Border crossings*. New York: Routledge.

Giroux, H. (1993). Paulo Freire and the politics of postcolonialism. In P. McLaren and P. Leonard (Eds.), *Paulo Freire: A critical encounter* (pp. 177–188). New York: Routledge.

Giroux, H. (1994). *Disturbing pleasures*. New York: Routledge.

Giroux, H. (1995). Language, difference, and curriculum theory: Beyond the politics of clarity. In P. McLaren and J. Giarelli (Eds.), *Critical theory and educational research* (pp. 22–38). Albany: SUNY Press.

Giroux, H. (1997a). Racial politics and the pedagogy of whiteness. In M. Hill (Ed.), *Whiteness: A critical reader* (pp. 294–315). New York: New York University Press.

Giroux, H. (1997b) *Channel surfing.* New York: St. Martin's Press.

Giroux, H. (1997c). Rewriting the discourse of racial identity: Towards a pedagogy and politics of whiteness. *Harvard Educational Review, 67*(2), 285–320.

Giroux, H. (1999). *The mouse that roared: Disney and the end of innocence.* Lanham, MD: Rowman & Littlefield.

Glazer, N. (1997). *We are all multiculturalists now.* Cambridge, MA: Harvard University Press.

Goldberg, D. T. (1990). The social formation of racist discourse. In D. T. Goldberg (Ed.), *Anatomy of racism* (pp. 295–318). Minneapolis: University of Minnesota Press.

Goldberg, D. T. (1993). *Racist culture.* Malden, MA: Blackwell.

Gonzalez, N. (2004). Disciplining the discipline: Anthropology and the pursuit of quality education. *Educational Researcher, 33*(5), 17–25.

Gore, J. (1993). *The struggle for pedagogies: Critical and feminist discourses as regimes of truth.* New York: Routledge.

Gotanda, N. (1995). A critique of "Our constitution is color-blind." In K. Crenshaw, N. Gotanda, G. Peller, and K. Thomas (Eds.), *Critical race theory* (pp. 257–275). New York: The New Press.

Gouldner, A. (1976). *The dialectic of ideology and technology.* New York: The Seabury Press.

Gramsci, A. (1971). *Selections from prison notebooks.* Q. Hoare and G. Smith (Eds. and Trans.). New York: International Publishers.

Grande, S. (2004). *Red pedagogy.* Lanham, MD: Rowman & Littlefield.

Greene, M. (1986). In search of a critical pedagogy. *Harvard Educational Review, 56*(4), 427–441.

Greene, M. (1988). *The dialectic of freedom.* New York: Teachers College Press.

Greene, S. and Abt-Perkins, D. (2003). How can literacy research contribute to racial understanding? In S. Greene and D. Abt-Perkins (Eds.), *Making race visible: Literacy research for cultural understanding* (pp. 1–31). New York: Teachers College Press.

Guerrero, E. (1993). *Framing blackness.* Philadelphia: Temple University Press.

Habermas, J. (1984). *The theory of communicative action.* Vol. 1. T. McCarthy (Trans.). Boston: Beacon Press.

Habermas, J. (1987). *The theory of communicative action.* Vol. 2. T. McCarthy (Trans.). Boston: Beacon Press.

Habermas, J. (1989). *The structural transformation of the public sphere.* T. Burger with F. Lawrence (Trans.). Cambridge, MA: The MIT Press.

Hall, S. (1996a). The problem of ideology: Marxism without guarantees. In D. Morley and K. Chen (Eds.), *Stuart Hall* (pp. 25–46). London: Routledge.

Hall, S. (1996b). New ethnicities. In D. Morley and K. Chen (Eds.), *Stuart Hall* (pp. 441–449). London: Routledge.

Hall, S. (1996c). Gramsci's relevance for the study of race and ethnicity. In D. Morley and K. Chen (Eds.), *Stuart Hall* (pp. 411–440). London: Routledge.

Hall, S. (1996d). What is this "black" in black popular culture? In D. Morley and K. Chen (Eds.), *Stuart Hall* (pp. 465–475). London: Routledge.

Hall, S. (1996e). On postmodernism and articulation: An interview with Stuart Hall. In D. Morley and K. Chen (Eds.), *Stuart Hall* (pp. 131–150). New York and London: Routledge.

Hargreaves, A., Lieberman, A., Fullan, M., and Hopkins, D. (Eds.) (1998). *International Handbook of Educational Change.* Dordrecht, the Netherlands: Kluwer.

Harris, C. (1995). Whiteness as property. In K. Crenshaw, N. Gotanda, G. Peller, and K. Thomas (Eds.), *Critical race theory* (pp. 276–291). New York: The New Press.

Harris, V. (1999). Applying critical theories to children's literature. *Theory into Practice, 38*(3), 147–154.

Hartmann, H. (1993). The unhappy marriage of Marxism and feminism: Towards a more progressive union. In A. Jaggar and P. Rothenberg (Eds.), *Feminist frameworks* (pp. 191–202) (3rd ed.). Boston: McGraw Hill.

Harvey, D. (1989). *The condition of postmodernity.* Cambridge, MA: Blackwell.

Henig, J., Hula, R., Orr, M., and Pedescleaux, D. (2001). *The color of school reform: Race, politics, and the challenge of urban education.* Princeton: Princeton University Press.

Hernnstein, R. and Murray, C. (1994). *The bell curve.* New York: The Free Press.

Hesse, B. (1997). White governmentality: Urbanism, nationalism, racism. In S. Westwood and J. Williams (Eds.), *Imagining cities: Scripts, signs, memory* (pp. 86–103). New York: Routledge.

Hirschman, C. (2004). The origins and demise of the concept of race. *Population and Development Review, 30*(3), 385–415.

Hirst, P. (1994). Problems and advances in the theory of ideology. In T. Eagleton (Ed.), *Ideology* (pp. 112–125). London: Longman.

Holme, J. J. (2000). The role of ideology and social networks in residentially-based school choices: a précis. Unpublished manuscript. Paper presented at Sociology of Education Association.

Holt, T. (1990). "Knowledge is power": The black struggle for literacy. In A. Lunsford, H. Moglen, and J. Slevin (Eds.), *The right to literacy* (pp. 91–102). New York: The Modern Language Association.

hooks, b. (1981). *Ain't I a Woman?: Black women and feminism.* Boston: South End Press.

hooks, b. (1984). *Feminist theory: From margin to center.* Boston: South End Press.

hooks, b. (1993). bell hooks speaking about Paulo Freire – the man, his work. In P. McLaren and P. Leonard (Eds.), *Paulo Freire: A critical encounter* (pp. 146–154). New York: Routledge.

hooks, b. (1994). *Teaching to transgress.* New York: Routledge.

hooks, b. (1997). Representing whiteness in the black imagination. In R. Frankenberg (Ed.), *Displacing whiteness* (pp. 165–179). Durham: Duke University Press.

Hopson, R. (2003). The problem of the language line: Cultural and social reproduction of hegemonic linguistic structures for learners of African descent in the USA. *Race Ethnicity & Education, 6*(3), 227–245.

Hopson, R., Green, P., Yeakey, C., Richardson, J., and Reed, T. (1998). Language and social policy: an analysis of forces that drive official language politics in the United States. *Chicago Policy Review, 2*(2), 1–24.

Horkheimer, M. and Adorno, T. (1976). *Dialectic of enlightenment.* J. Cumming (Trans.). New York: Continuum.

Horton, H. D. and Sykes, L. L. (2004). Toward a critical demography of neo-mulattoes: Structural change and diversity within the Black population. In C. Herring, V. Keith, and H. D. Horton (Eds.), *Skin/deep: How race and complexion matter in the "color-blind" era* (pp. 159–173). Urbana and Chicago: University of Illinois Press.

Houston, J. W. and Houston, J. (1973). *Farewell to Manzanar.* New York: Bantam Books.

Howard, G (2000). Reflections on the "white movement" in multicultural education, *Educational Researcher, 29*(9), 21–23.

Howard, G. (1999). *We can't teach what we don't know: White teachers, multiracial schools.* New York: Teachers College Press.

Huebner, D. (1981). Toward a political economy of curriculum and human development. In H. Giroux, A. Penna, and W. Pinar (Eds.), *Curriculum & instruction* (pp. 124–138). Berkeley: McCutchan Publishing Corporation.

Hunter, M. (1998). Colorstruck: Skin color stratification in the lives of African American women. *Sociological Perspectives, 68*(4), 517–535.

Hunter, M. (2002a). Rethinking epistemology, methodology, and racism: Or, is White sociology really dead? *Race & Society, 5*(2002), 119–138.

Hunter, M. (2002b). "If you're light you're alright:" Light skin color as social capital for women of color. *Gender & Society, 16*(2), 171–189.

Hunter, M. (2002c). Decentering the white and male standpoint in race and ethnicity courses. In A. Macdonald and S. Sanchez-Casal (Eds.), *Twenty-first century feminist classrooms: Pedagogies of identity and difference* (pp. 251–279). New York: Palgrave.

Hunter, M. (2005). *Race, gender, and the politics of skin tone.* New York: Routledge

Hunter, M. and Nettles, K. (1999). What about the white women?: Racial politics in a women's studies classroom. *Teaching Sociology, 27* (October), 385–397.

Hurtado, A. (1996). *The color of privilege.* Ann Arbor: University of Michigan Press.

Hurtado, A. (1999). The trickster's play: Whiteness in the subordination and liberation process. In R. Torres, L. Miron, and J. Inda (Eds.), *Race, identity, and citizenship* (pp. 225–243). Malden, MA: Blackwell.

Ignatiev, N. (1995). *How the Irish became White.* New York: Routledge.

Ignatiev, N. (1997). The point is not to interpret Whiteness but to abolish it. Talk given at the Conference on "The Making and Unmaking of Whiteness." University of California, Berkeley, CA, April 11–13, 2007. Available online at http://racetraitor.org/abolishthepoint.html (accessed 26 July 2007).

Ignatiev, N. and Garvey, J. (1996a). Editorial: When does the unreasonable act make sense? In N. Ignatiev and J. Garvey (Eds.), *Race traitor* (pp. 35–37). New York: Routledge.

Ignatiev, N. and Garvey, J. (1996b). Abolish the White race: By any means necessary. In N. Ignatiev and J. Garvey (Eds.), *Race traitor* (pp. 9–14). New York: Routledge.

Ignatiev, N. and Garvey, J. (Eds.), (1996c). *Race traitor*. New York: Routledge.

Ingram, D. (2005). Toward a cleaner white(ness): New racial identities. *The Philosophical Forum, XXXVI*(3), 243–277.

Jaggar, A. and Rothenberg, P. (Eds.), (1993). *Feminist frameworks* (3rd ed.). Boston: McGraw Hill.

James, C.E. (2005). *Race in play: Understanding the socio-cultural worlds of student athletes*. Toronto: Canadian Scholars' Press.

Johnson, D. (2001). Punitive attitudes on crime: Economic insecurity, racial injustice, or both? *Sociological Focus, 34*(1), 33–54.

Johnson, E. P. (2003). *Appropriating blackness*. Durham: Duke University Press.

Jordan, W. (1968). *White over Black*. Chapel Hill: The University of North Carolina Press.

Kanpol, B. (1991). Teacher group formation as emancipatory critique: Necessary conditions for teacher resistance. *The Journal of Educational Thought, 25*(2), 134–149.

Kant, I. (2000). *The critique of judgment*. J. H. Bernard (Trans.). New York: Prometheus Books.

Katz, M. (1990). *The undeserving poor*. New York: Pantheon.

Katz, M. (2002). *The price of citizenship*. New York: Owl Books.

Kelley, R. (1983). *Foreword to Black Marxism*. Chapel Hill: The University of North Carolina Press.

Kelley, R. (1998). *Yo' Mama's disfunktional!: Fighting the culture wars in urban America*. Boston: Beacon Press.

Kerdeman, D. (2003). Pulled up short: Challenging self-understanding as a focus of teaching and learning. *Journal of Philosophy of Education, 37*(2), 293–308.

Kidder, L. (1997). Colonial remnants: Assumptions of privilege. In M. Fine, L. Weis, L. Powell, L. Wong (Eds.), *Off white* (pp. 158–166). New York: Routledge.

Kincheloe, J. (1993). *Toward a critical politics of teacher training*. Westport, CT: Bergin & Garvey.

Kincheloe, J. and Steinberg, S. (1998). Addressing the crisis of whiteness: Reconfiguring white identity in a pedagogy of whiteness. In J. Kincheloe, S. Steinberg, N. Rodriguez, and R. Chennault (Eds.), *White reign* (pp. 3–29). New York: St. Martin's Griffin.

Kincheloe, J., Steinberg, S., Rodriguez, N., and Chennault, R. (Eds.), (1998). *White reign*. New York: St. Martin's Griffin.

Kinder, D. and Sears, D. (1981). Prejudice and politics: Symbolic racism versus racial threats to the good life. *Journal of Personality and Social Psychology, 40*, 414–431.

King, J. (2004a). Dysconscious racism: Ideology, identity, and the miseducation of teachers. In G. Ladson-Billings and D. Gillborn (Eds.), *The RoutledgeFalmer reader in multicultural education* (pp. 71–83). New York: RoutledgeFalmer.

King, J. (2004b). Culture-centered knowledge: Black Studies, curriculum transformation, and social action. In J. Banks and C. Banks (Eds.), *Handbook of research on multicultural education* (pp. 349–378). San Francisco: John Wiley & Sons.

Kohn, A. (2004). NCLB and the effort to privatize public education. In D. Meier and G. Wood (Eds.), *Many children left behind: How the No Child Left Behind Act is damaging our children and our schools* (pp. 79–97). Boston: Beacon Press.

Kozol, J. (1991). *Savage inequalities*. New York: Harper Perennial.

Ladson-Billings, G. (1998). From Soweto to the South Bronx: African Americans and colonial education in the United States. In C. Torres and T. Mitchell (Eds.), *Sociology of education: Emerging perspectives* (pp. 247–264). Albany: State University of New York Press.

Ladson-Billings, G. (2004). Just what is critical race theory and what's it doing in a *nice* field like education. In G. Ladson-Billings and D. Gillborn, (Eds.), *The RoutledgeFalmer reader in multicultural education* (pp. 49–67). New York: RoutledgeFalmer.

Ladson-Billings, G. and Gomez, M. L. (2001). Just showing up: Supporting early literacy through teachers' professional communities. *Phi Delta Kappan, 82*(9), 675–680.

Ladson-Billings, G. and Tate, W. F. I. V. (1995). Toward a critical race theory of education. *Teachers College Record, 97*(1), 47–68.

Lareau, A. (2000). *Home advantage*. Lanham, MD: Rowman & Littlefield.

Lareau, A. (2003). *Unequal Childhoods*. Berkeley: University of California Press.

Lather, P. (1996). Troubling clarity: The politics of accessible language. *Harvard Educational Review, 66*(3), 525–545.

Lee, S. (2005). *Up against whiteness*. New York: Teachers College Press.

Lemert, C. (Ed.), (1993). *Social theory: The multicultural and classic readings*. Boulder, CO: Westview Press.

Leonardo, Z. (2000a). Book review of Carlos Torres and Theodore Mitchell (Eds.), *Sociology of education: Emerging perspectives. Contemporary Sociology, 29*(1), 270–71.

Leonardo, Z. (2000b). Betwixt and between: Introduction to the politics of identity. In C. Tejeda, C. Martinez, and Z. Leonardo (Eds.), *Charting new terrains of Chicana(o)/Latina(o) education* (pp. 107–129). Cresskill, NJ: Hampton Press.

Leonardo, Z. (2003a). Interpretation and the problem of domination: Paul Ricoeur's hermeneutics. *Studies in Philosophy and Education, 22*(5), 329–350.

Leonardo, Z. (2003b). *Ideology, discourse, and school reform.* Westport, CT: Praeger.

Leonardo, Z. (2003c). Reality on trial: Notes on ideology, education, and utopia. *Policy Futures in Education, 1*(3), 504–525.

Leonardo, Z. (2003d). Resisting capital: Simulationist and socialist strategies. *Critical Sociology, 29*(2), 211–236.

Leonardo, Z. (2003e). The agony of school reform: Race, class, and the elusive search for social justice. *Educational Researcher, 32*(3), 37–43.

Leonardo, Z. (2003f). Race. In D. Weil and J. Kincheloe (Eds.), *Critical thinking and learning: An encyclopedia* (pp. 347–351). Westport, CT: Greenwood.

Leonardo, Z. (2003g). Institutionalized racism. In D. Weil and J. Kincheloe (Eds.), *Critical thinking and learning: An encyclopedia* (pp. 341–347). Westport, CT: Greenwood.

Leonardo, Z. (2009). Afterword to Wayne Au's *Unequal by Design: High-Stakes Testing and the Standardization of Inequality* (pp.147–153). New York: Routledge.

Lewis, O. (1968). The culture of poverty. In D. P. Moynihan (Ed.), *On understanding poverty: Perspectives from the social sciences* (pp. 187–220). New York: Basic Books.

Linn, R. (2003). Accountability: Responsibility and reasonable expectations. *Educational Researcher, 32*(7), 3–13.

Lipsitz, G. (1998). *The possessive investment in whiteness.* Philadelphia: Temple University Press.

Loewen, J. (1995). *Lies my teacher told me.* New York: The New Press.

Lopez, D. (1997). Language: Diversity and assimilation. In R. Waldinger and M. Bozorgmehr (Eds.), *Ethnic Los Angeles* (pp. 139–164). New York: Russell Sage.

Lopez, I. (2006). Colorblind to the reality of race in America. *The Chronicle Review, 53*(11), B6.

Lott, T. (1999). *The invention of race: Black culture and the politics of representation.* Malden, MA: Blackwell.

Lukacs, G. (1971). *History and class consciousness.* R. Livingstone (Trans.). Cambridge, MA: The MIT Press.

Luttrell, W. (2003). *Pregnant bodies, fertile minds.* New York: Routledge.

Lynn, M. (1999). Toward a critical race pedagogy: A research note. *Urban Education, 33*(5), pp. 606–626.

Lyotard, J. (1984). *The postmodern condition.* G. Bennington and B. Massumi (Trans.). Minneapolis: University of Minnesota Press.

Macdonell, D. (1986). *Theories of discourse.* London: Blackwell.

Macedo, D., Dendrinos, B., and Gounari, P. (2003). *The hegemony of English.* Boulder: Paradigm Publishers.

MacLeod, J. (1987). *Ain't no makin' it.* Boulder: Westview Press.

Mander, J. and Goldsmith, E. (Eds.), (1996), *The case against the global economy.* San Francisco: Sierra Club Books.

Mannheim, K. (1936). *Ideology and utopia.* New York: Harcourt, Brace & World.

Marable, M. (1983). *How capitalism underdeveloped Black America.* Boston: South End Press.

Marable, M. (1996). Staying on the path to racial equality. In G. Curry (Ed.), *The affirmative action debate* (pp. 3–15). New York: Addison-Wesley Publishing Company, Inc.

Marable, M. (2002). The souls of white folk. *Souls, 4*(4), 45–51.

Martin, E. (1992a). Body narratives, body boundaries. In L. Grossberg, C. Nelson, and P. Treichler (Eds.), *Cultural studies* (pp. 409–423). New York: Routledge.

Martin, E. (1992b). *The woman in the body.* Boston: Beacon Press.

Marx, K. (1988). Theses on Feuerbach. In A. Wood (Ed.), *Marx selections* (pp. 80–82). New York: Macmillan.

Marx, K. and Engels, F. (1970). *The German ideology.* New York: International Publishers.

Massey, D. and Denton, N. (1993). *American Apartheid.* Cambridge, MA: Harvard University Press.

Mauss, M. (1967). *The gift.* New York: W.W. Norton & Company.

Mazumdar, S. (1989). Race and racism: South Asians in the United States. In G. Nomura, R. Endo,

S. Sumida, and R. Long (Eds.), *Frontiers of Asian American studies: Writing, research, and commentary* (pp. 25–38). Pullman: Washington State University Press.

McCarthy, C. and Dimitriadis, G. (2004). Postcolonial literature and the curricular imagination: Wilson Harris and the pedagogical implications of the carnivalesque. *Educational Philosophy and Theory, 36*(2), 201–213.

McDade, L. (1992). Sex, pregnancy, and schooling: obstacles to a critical teaching of the body. In K. Weiler and C. Mitchell (Eds.), *What schools can do* (pp. 49–73). Albany: State University of New York Press.

McDonnell, K. and Robins, K. (1980). Marxist cultural theory: The Althusserian smokescreen. In S. Clarke, V. Seidler, K. McDonnell, K. Robins, and T. Lovell (Eds.), *One-dimensional Marxism* (pp. 157–231). London: Allison & Bushby.

McIntosh, P. (1992). White privilege and male privilege: A personal account of coming to see correspondences through work in women's studies. In M. Andersen and P. H. Collins (Eds.), *Race, class, and gender: An anthology* (pp. 70–81). Belmont, CA: Wadsworth Publishing.

McIntyre, A. (1997). *Making meaning of whiteness.* Albany: State University of New York Press.

McIntyre, A. (2000) A response to Rosa Hernandez Sheets. *Educational Researcher, 29*(9), 26–27.

McLaren, P. (1991). Critical pedagogy: Constructing an arch of social dreaming and a doorway to hope. *The Sociology of Education in Canada, 173*(1), 137–160.

McLaren, P. (1995). *Critical pedagogy and predatory culture: Oppositional politics in a postmodern era.* New York: Routledge.

McLaren, P. (1997). *Revolutionary multiculturalism: Pedagogies of dissent for a new millennium.* Boulder: Westview Press.

McLaren, P. (1999). A pedagogy of possibility: Reflecting upon Paulo Freire's politics of education. *Educational Researcher, 28*(2), 49–56.

McLaren, P. (2000). *Che Guevara, Paulo Freire, and the pedagogy of revolution.* Lanham, MD: Roman & Littlefield.

McLaren, P. and Leonardo, Z. (1996). Paulo Freire. In E. Cashmore (Ed.), *Dictionary of race and ethnic relations* (pp. 134–136) (4th ed.). New York: Routledge.

McLaren, P. and Scatamburlo-D'Annibale, V. (2005). Class dismissed: Historical materialism and the politics of difference. In Z. Leonardo (Ed.), *Critical pedagogy and race* (pp. 1241–157). Malden, MA: Blackwell.

McLaren, P., and Torres, R. (1999). Racism and multicultural education: Rethinking "race" and "whiteness" in late capitalism. In S. May (Ed.), *Critical multiculturalism: Rethinking multicultural and antiracist education* (pp. 42–76). Philadelphia: Falmer Press.

McLaren, P., Carrillo-Rowe, A., Clark, R., and Craft, P. (2001). Labeling whiteness: Decentering strategies of white racial domination. In G. Hudak and P. Kihn (Eds.), *Labeling: Pedagogy and politics* (pp. 203–224). New York: Falmer Press.

McLaren, P., Leonardo, Z., and Allen, R. L. (2000). Epistemologies of whiteness: Transforming and transgressing pedagogical knowledge. In R. Mahalingam and C. McCarthy (Eds.), *Multicultural curriculum: New directions for social theory, practice, and policy* (pp. 108–123). New York: Routledge.

McWhorter, J. (2001). Losing the race: Self-sabotage in Black America. New York: Harper Perennial.

Memmi, A. (1965). *The colonizer and the colonized.* Boston: Beacon Press.

Memmi, A. (2000). *Racism.* S. Martinot (Trans.). Minneapolis: University of Minnesota Press.

Miles, R. (1993). *Racism after "race relations".* London: Routledge.

Miles, R. (2000). Apropos the idea of "race" . . . again. In Back and Solomon (Eds.), *Theories of race and racism* (pp. 125–143). New York: Routledge.

Miles, R. and Torres, R. (1999). Does "race matter? Transatlantic perspectives on racism after "race relations." In R. Torres, L. Miron, and J. Inda (Eds.) *Race, identity, and citizenship* (pp. 19–38). Malden, MA: Blackwell.

Mills, C. (1997). *The racial contract.* Ithaca: Cornell University Press.

Mills, C. (2003) *From class to race: Essays in White Marxism and Black radicalism.* Lanham, MD: Rowman & Littlefield.

Mohanty, C. (1988). Under western eyes: Feminist scholarship and colonial discourses. *Feminist Review, 30*(Autumn), 61–88.

Moll, L. and Gonzalez, N. (2004). Engaging life: A funds-of-knowledge approach to multicultural education. In J. Banks and C. Banks (Eds.), *Handbook of research on multicultural education* (pp. 699–715) (2nd ed.). San Francisco: Josey-Bass.

Morris, A. (1984). *The origins of the civil rights movement.* New York: The Free Press.

Morrison, T. (1970). *The bluest eye.* New York: Plume Books.

Morrison, T. (1993). *Playing in the dark: Whiteness in the literary imagination.* New York: Vintage Books.

Morrow, R. and Torres, C. (1995). *Social theory and education: A critique of theories of social and cultural reproduction.* Albany: State University of New York Press.

Murray, C. (1995). *Losing ground.* New York: Basic Books.

Myers, L. and Williamson, P. (2001). Race talk: The perpetuation of racism through private discourse. *Race and Society, 4*(1), 3–26.

Nakanishi, D. and Nishida, T. (Eds.), (1995). *The Asian-American educational experience.* New York: Routledge.

Nayak, A. (2006). After race: Ethnography, race and post-race theory. *Ethnic and Racial Studies, 29*(3), 411–430.

Nelson, J. (2001). *Police brutality.* New York: W.W. Norton & Co.

Neubeck, K. and Cazenave, N. (2001). *Welfare racism: Playing the race card against America's poor.* New York: Routledge.

Newitz, A. and Wray, M. (1997). What is "White trash?": Stereotypes and economic conditions of poor Whites in the United States. In M. Hill (Ed.), *Whiteness: A critical reader.* New York: New York University Press.

Nieto, S. (2003a). *Affirming diversity* (4th ed.). New York: Longman.

Nieto, S. (2003b). Afterword. In S. Greene and D. Abt-Perkins (Eds.), *Making race visible: Literacy research for cultural understanding* (pp. 201–205). New York: Teachers College Press.

Noguera, P. (1996). Confronting the urban in urban school reform. *The Urban Review, 28*(1), 1–19.

Novak, J. and Fuller, B. (2003). *Penalizing diverse schools? Similar test scores but different students bring federal sanctions.* Berkeley: Policy Analysis for California Education.

Oakes, J. (2005). *Keeping track* (2nd ed.). New Haven. Yale University Press.

Oakes, J., Joseph, R. and Muir, K. (2004). Access and achievement in mathematics and science: Inequalities that endure and change. In J. Banks and C. Banks (Eds.), *Handbook of research on multicultural education* (pp. 69–90). San Francisco: John Wiley & Sons.

Ogbu, J. (1995). Understanding cultural diversity in the classroom. In A. Ornstein and L. Behar (Eds.), *Contemporary issues in curriculum* (pp. 349–367). Boston: Allyn and Bacon.

Oliver, M. and Shapiro, T. (1997). *Black wealth, white wealth: A new perspective on racial inequality.* New York: Routledge.

Omi, M. and Winant, H. (1986). *Racial formation in the United States: From the 1960s to the 1980s* (1st ed.). New York: Routledge.

Omi, M. and Winant, H. (1994). *Racial formation in the United States: From the 1960s to the 1990s* (2nd ed.). New York: Routledge.

Outlaw, L. (1990). Toward a critical theory of "race." In D. T. Goldberg (Ed.), *Anatomy of racism* (pp. 58–82). Minneapolis: University of Minnesota Press.

Parker, W. (2005). Teaching against idiocy. *Phi Delta Kappan, 86*(5), 344–351.

Parker, L. and Stovall, D. (2005). Actions following words: Critical race theory connects to critical pedagogy. In Z. Leonardo (Ed.), *Critical pedagogy and race* (pp. 159–174). Malden, MA: Blackwell.

Peters, M. (2005). Editorial: Critical race matters. In Z. Leonardo (Ed.), *Critical pedagogy and race* (pp. vii–ix). Malden, MA: Blackwell.

Pillow, W. (2003). "Bodies are dangerous:" Using feminist genealogy as policy studies methodology. *Journal of Education Policy, 18*(2), 145–159.

Piven, F. and Cloward, R. (1993). *Regulating the poor.* New York: Vintage Books.

Pollock, M. (2004). *Colormute.* Princeton: Princeton University Press.

Popkewitz, T. (1998). The sociology of knowledge and the sociology of education: Michel Foucault and critical traditions. In C. Torres and T. Mitchell (Eds.), *Sociology of education: Emerging perspectives* (pp. 47–89). Albany: State University of New York Press.

Porter, P. and Vidovich, L. (2000). Globalization and higher education policy. *Educational Theory, 50*(4), 449–465.

Portes, A. (2002). English-only triumphs, but the costs are high. *Contexts, 1*(1), 10.

Portes, A. and Rumbaut, R. (1990). *Immigrant America: A portrait.* Berkeley: University of California Press.

Prashad, V. (2000). *The Karma of brown folk.* Minneapolis: University of Minnesota Press.

Pruyn, M. (1999). *Discourse wars in Gotham-West.* Boulder: Westview Press.

Purdon, E. (1999). *The story of the Irish language.* Dublin, UK: Mercier Press.

Rains, F. (1997). Is the benign really harmless?: Deconstructing some "benign" manifestations of operationalized white privilege. In J. Kincheloe, S. Steinberg, N. Rodriguez, and R. Chennault (Eds.), *White reign* (pp. 77–101). New York: St. Martin's Griffin.

Ranciere, J. (1994). On the theory of ideology—Althusser's politics. In T. Eagleton (Ed.), *Ideology* (pp. 141–161). London: Longman.

Reese, E. (2005). *Backlash against welfare mothers.* Berkeley: University of California Press.

Richardson, T. and Villenas, S. (2000). "Other" encounters: Dances with whiteness in multicultural education. *Educational Theory, 50*(2), 255–273.

Ricoeur, P. (1981). *Hermeneutics and the human sciences.* J. B. Thompson (Ed. and Trans.). Cambridge, UK: Cambridge University Press.

Rimonte, N. (1997). Colonialism's legacy: The inferiorizing of the Filipino. In M. Root (Ed.), *Filipino Americans* (pp. 39–61). Thousand Oaks, CA: SAGE.

Roberts, D. (1999). *Killing the Black body: Race, reproduction, and the meaning of liberty.* New York: Vintage Books.

Robinson, C. (1983). *Black Marxism.* Chapel Hill: The University of North Carolina Press.

Roediger, D. (1991). *The wages of whiteness.* London and New York: Verso.

Roediger, D. (1994). *Toward the abolition of whiteness.* New York: Verso.

Root, M. (Ed.), (1997). *Filipino Americans.* Thousand Oaks, CA: Sage.

Rose, T. (1994). *Black noise: Rap music and Black culture in contemporary America.* Hanover: Wesleyan University Press.

Rothenberg, P. (Ed.), (2002). *White privilege: Essential readings on the other side of racism.* New York: Worth Publishers.

Rovell, D. (2005). Will brush with law raise Kobe's "street cred?" ESPN.com. Available online at http://espn.go.com/nba/s/2003/0707/1577650.html (accessed 2 September 2008).

Rumbaut, R. (1996). Prologue. In S. Pedraza and R. Rumbaut (Eds.), *Origins and destinies: Immigration, race, and ethnicity in America* (pp. xvi–xix). Belmont, CA: Wadsworth.

Sadker, M. and Sadker, D. (1994). *Failing at fairness: How America's schools cheat girls.* New York: Charles Scribner's Sons.

Said, E. (1979). *Orientalism.* New York: Random House.

Said, E. (1983). *The world, the text, and the critic.* Cambridge, MA: Harvard University Press.

Said, E. (1994). *Culture and Imperialism.* New York: Vintage Books.

Said, E. (2000). *Reflections on exile.* Cambridge, MA: Harvard University Press.

San Juan, Jr., E. (1992). *Racial formations/critical transformations.* London: Humanities Press.

San Juan, Jr., E. (1994). Problematizing multiculturalism and the "common culture." *MELUS, 19*(2), 59–84.

San Juan, Jr., E. (1999). *Beyond postcolonial theory.* Boulder: Westview Press.

Sandoval, C. (1997). Theorizing white consciousness for a post-empire world: Barthes, Fanon, and the rhetoric of love. In R. Frankenberg (Ed.), *Displacing whiteness* (pp. 86–107). Durham: Duke University Press.

Sartre, J-P. (1963). Preface to *Wretched of the earth.* New York: Grove Press.

Scheurich, J. and Young, M. (1997). Coloring epistemologies: Are our research epistemologies racially biased. *Educational Researcher, 26*(4), 4–16.

Schlesinger, J. (1998). *The disuniting of America: Reflections on a multicultural society* (2nd ed.). New York: W.W. & Norton.

Schofield, J. (2005). The colorblind perspective in school: Causes and consequences. In J. Banks and C. Banks (Eds.), *Multicultural education* (pp. 265–288). New York: John Wiley & Sons.

Sethi, R. (1995). Smells like racism. In P. Rothenberg (Ed.), *Race, class, and gender in the United States: An integrated study* (pp. 89–99). New York: St. Martin's Press.

Sheets, R. (2000). Advancing the field or taking center stage: The White movement in multicultural education. *Educational Researcher, 29*(9), 15–21.

Shelby, T. (2003). Ideology, racism, and critical social theory. *The Philosophical Forum, XXXIV*(2), 153–188.

Shilling, C. (1992). Reconceptualizing structure and agency in the sociology of education: Structuration theory and schooling. *British Journal of Sociology of Education, 13*(1), 69–87.

Shor, I. (1993). Education is politics: Paulo Freire's critical pedagogy. In P. McLaren and P. Leonard (Eds.), *Paulo Freire: A critical encounter* (pp. 25–35). New York: Routledge.

Sirotnik, K. and Oakes, J. (1986). Critical inquiry for school renewal: Liberating theory and practice. In K. Sirotnik and J. Oakes (Eds.), *Critical perspectives on the organization and improvement of schooling* (pp. 3–93). Boston: Kluwer-Nijhoff Publishing.

Sleeter, C. (1995a). Reflections on my use of multicultural and critical pedagogy when students are white. In C. Sleeter and P. McLaren (Eds.), *Multicultural education, critical pedagogy, and the politics of difference* (pp. 415–437). Albany: State University of New York Press.

Sleeter, C. (1995b). An analysis of the critiques of multicultural education. In J. Banks and C. Banks (Eds.), *Handbook of research on multicultural education* (pp. 81–94). New York: Simon & Schuster Macmillan.

Sleeter, C. (1996). White silence, White solidarity. In N. Ignatiev and J. Garvey (Eds.), *Race traitor* (pp. 257–265). New York: Routledge.

Small, S. (1999). The contours of racialization: Structures, representations and resistance in the United States. In R. Torres, L. Miron, and X. Inda (Eds.), *Race, identity, and citizenship* (pp. 47–64). Malden, MA: Blackwell.

Snipp, C. M. (1996). The first Americans: American Indians. In S. Pedraza and R. Rumbaut (Eds.), *Origins and destinies: Immigration, race, and ethnicity in America* (pp. 390–403). Belmont, CA: Wadsworth.

Solorzano, D. and Yosso, T. (2000). Toward a critical race theory of Chicana and Chicano education. In C. Tejeda, C. Martinez, and Z. Leonardo (Eds.), *Charting new terrains of Chicana(o)/Latina(o) education* (pp. 35–65). Cresskill, NJ: Hampton Press.

Sowell, T. (1995). *Race and culture*. New York: Basic Books.

Spickard, P. (1992). The illogic of American racial categories. In M. Root (Ed.), *The multiracial experience: Racial borders as the new frontier* (pp. 13–23). Thousand Oaks, CA: Sage.

Spina, S. (2000). The psychology of violence and the violence of psychology. In S. Spina (Ed.), *Smoke & mirrors: The hidden context of violence in schools and society* (pp. 177–209). Lanham, MD: Rowman & Littlefield.

Spivak, G. (1988). Can the subaltern speak? In C. Nelson and L. Grossberg (Eds.), *Marxism and the interpretation of culture* (pp. 271–313). Urbana: University of Illinois Press.

Spring, J. (2000). *Deculturalization and the struggle for equality* (3rd ed.). Boston: McGraw-Hill.

Stanley, W. (1992). *Curriculum for utopia*. New York: State University of New York Press.

Steele, C. (2004). A threat in the air: How stereotypes shape intellectual identity and performance. In J. Banks and C. Banks (Eds.), *Handbook of research on multicultural education* (pp. 682–698). San Francisco: John Wiley & Sons.

Steinberg, S. (1998). The liberal retreat from race during the post-civil rights era. In W. Lubiano (Ed.), *The house that race built* (pp. 13–47). New York: Vintage Books.

Stepan, N. (1990). Race and gender: The role of analogy in science. In D. Goldberg (Ed.), *Anatomy of racism* (pp. 38–57). Minneapolis: University of Minnesota Press.

Suarez-Orozco, M., Suarez-Orozco, C., and Doucet, F. (2004). The academic engagement and achievement of Latino youth. In J. Banks and C. Banks (Eds.), *Handbook of research on multicultural education* (pp. 420–437) (2nd ed.). San Francisco: Josey-Bass.

Sunderman, G. and Kim, J. (2005). The expansion of federal power and the politics of implementing the No Child Left Behind Act. *Teachers College Record, 109*(5), 1057–1085.

Symcox, L. (2002). *Whose history?: The struggle for national standards in American classrooms*. New York: Teachers College Press.

Takaki, R. (1993). *A different mirror*. Boston: Little, Brown, and Co.

Tate, W. (1997). Critical race theory and education: history, theory and implications. *Review of Research in Education, 22*, 191–243.

Tatum, B. D. (1997). *Why are all the Black kids sitting together in the cafeteria?* New York: Basic Books.

Taylor, E. (1998). A primer on critical race theory: Who are the critical race theorists and what are they saying? *Journal of Blacks in Higher Education, 19*, 122–124.

Telles, E. (2006). *Race in another America: The significance of skin color in Brazil*. Princeton: Princeton University Press.

Thernstrom, S. and Thernstrom, A. (1999). *America in Black and White: One nation, indivisible*. New York: Simon and Schuster.

Thompson, A. (2003). Tiffany, friend of people of color: White investments in antiracism. *Qualitative Studies in Education, 16*(1), 7–29.

Thompson, B. (2001). *A promise and a way of life: White antiracist activism*. Minneapolis: University of Minnesota Press.

Trask, H. (1999). Lovely hula hands: Corporate tourism and the prostitution of Hawaiian culture.

In S. Ferguson (Ed.), *Mapping the social landscape* (pp. 90–98). Mountain View, CA: Mayfield Publishing Company.

Valdes, G. (2001). *Learning and not learning English.* New York: Teachers College Press.

Valenzuela, A. (1999). *Subtractive schooling: U.S.–Mexican youth and the politics of caring.* Albany: State University of New York Press.

Valenzuela, A. (2002). Reflections on the subtractive underpinnings of education research and policy. *Journal of Teacher Education, 53*(3), 235–241.

Van Ausdale, D. and Feagin, J. (2001). *The first R: How children learn race and racism.* Lanham, MD: Rowman & Littlefield.

Wacquant, L. (1997). For an analytic of racial domination. *Political Power and Social Theory, 11,* 21–234.

Wacquant, L. (2002). From slavery to mass incarceration: Rethinking the "race question" in the United States. *New Left Review, 13,* 41–60.

Wah, L. M. (Producer/Director) (1994). *The color of fear* [Video]. Oakland, CA: Stir-fry Productions.

Walberg, M. (Producer) and Neale, L. (Director) (2004). *Juvies* [video]. Pacific Palisades, CA: Chance Films.

Walfish, D. (2001). Tracing the echoes of the Bataan Death March. *The Chronicle of Higher Education,* May 11 2001.

Warren, J. (2000). Masters in the field: White talk, white privilege, white biases. In F. Winddance Twine and J. Warren (Eds.), *Racing research, researching race: Methodological dilemmas in critical race studies* (pp. 135–164). New York: New York University Press.

Warren, J. (2002). Critical race studies in Latin America: Recent advances, recurrent weaknesses. In D. T. Goldberg and J. Solomos (Eds.), *A companion to racial and ethnic studies* (pp. 538–560). Malden, MA: Blackwell.

Warren, M. (2005). Communities and schools: A new view of urban education reform. *Harvard Educational Review, 75*(2), 133–173.

Washington, B. T. (1986). *Up from slavery.* New York: Penguin Books.

Watkins, W. (2001). *The White architects of Black education: Ideology and power in America, 1865–1954.* New York: Teachers College Press.

Weber, M. (1978). The three pure types of authority. In G. Roth and C. Wittich (Eds.), *Economy and society* (Vol. 1, pp. 215–216). Berkeley: University of California Press.

Weedon, C. (1997). *Feminist practice & poststructuralist theory* (2nd ed.). Cambridge, MA: Blackwell.

Weiler, K. (1994a). Freire and a feminist pedagogy of difference. In P. McLaren and C. Lankshear (Eds.), *Politics of liberation* (pp. 12–40). New York: Routledge.

Weiler. K. (1994b). *Women teaching for change.* Westport, CT: Bergin & Garvey.

Wells, A., Carnochan, S., Slayton, J., Allen, R.L., and Vasudeva, A. (1998). Globalization and educational change. In A. Hargreaves, A. Lieberman, M. Fullan, and D. Hopkins (Eds.), *International handbook of educational change* (pp. 322–348). Dordrecht, the Netherlands: Kluwer.

Welner, K. and Weitzman, D. (2005) The soft bigotry of low expenditures, *Equity & Excellence in Education, 38,* 242–248.

West, C. (1988). Marxist theory and the specificity of Afro-American oppression. In C. Nelson and L. Grossberg (Eds.), *Marxism and the interpretation of culture* (pp. 17–33). Urbana: University of Illinois Press.

West, C. (1994). *Race matters.* New York: Vintage Books.

West, C. (1999a). The indispensability yet insufficiency of Marxist theory. In C. West (Ed.), *The Cornel West reader* (pp. 213–230). New York: Basic Books.

West, C. (1999b). Race and social theory. In C. West (Ed.), *The Cornel West reader* (pp. 251–265). New York: Basic Books.

Williams, R. (1977). *Marxism and literature.* Oxford: Oxford University Press.

Willis, A. and Harris, V. (2000). Political acts: Literacy learning and teaching. *Reading Research Quarterly, 35*(1), 72–88.

Willis, P. (1977). *Learning to Labor: How working class kids get working class jobs.* New York: Columbia University Press.

Wilson, W. J. (1978). *The declining significance of race.* Chicago: University of Chicago Press.

Wilson, W. J. (1987). *The truly disadvantaged.* Chicago: The University of Chicago Press.

Wilson, W. J. (1997). *When work disappears.* Chicago: University of Chicago Press.

Winant, H. (1997). Behind blue eyes. In M. Fine, L. Weis, L. Powell, and L. Wong (Eds.), *Off white* (pp. 40–53). New York: Routledge.

Wise, T. (2002). Membership has its privileges: Thoughts on acknowledging and challenging whiteness. In P. Rothenberg (Ed.), *White privilege* (pp. 107–110). New York: Worth Publishers.

Wise, T. (2007). *White like me: Reflections on race from a privileged son.* New York: Soft Skull Press.

Wittig, M. (1993). One is not born a woman. In A. Jaggar and P. Rothenberg (Eds.), *Feminist frameworks* (pp. 178–182) (3rd ed.). Boston: McGraw Hill.

Wright, H. (2003). An endarkened feminist epistemology? Identity, difference and the politics of representation in educational research. *Qualitative Studies in Education, 16*(2), 197–214.

Wu, F. (2002). *Yellow.* New York: Basic Books.

Yosso, T. (2006). *Critical race counterstories along the Chicana/Chicano educational pipeline.* New York: Routledge.

Index